DATE DUE

OCT 2 3 2008	
AUG 1 3 2009	
JUL 0 5 2012	
FEB 0 5 2013	

BRODART, CO.   Cat. No. 23-221-003

Under Pressure and Overwhelmed

Coping with Anxiety in College

Christopher Vye
Kathlene Scholljegerdes
I. David Welch

Westport, Connecticut
London

Library of Congress Cataloging-in-Publication Data

Vye, Christopher, 1960–
    Under pressure and overwhelmed : coping with anxiety in college /
Christopher Vye, Kathlene Scholljegerdes, and Ira David Welch.
        p. cm.
    Includes bibliographical references and index.
    ISBN 978–0–275–99089–3 (alk. paper)
    1. College students—United States—Psychology. 2. Stress
(Psychology) 3. College student orientation—United States.
I. Vye, Christopher II. Welch, I. David (Ira David), 1940–
III. Scholljegerdes, Kathlene, 1953– IV. Title
LA229.V94   2007
378.1'98—dc22   2007010222

British Library Cataloguing in Publication Data is available.

Library of Congress Catalog Card Number: 2007010222

ISBN-13: 978–0–275–99089–3
ISBN-10: 0–275–99089–3

First published in 2007

Praeger Publishers, 88 Post Road West, Westport, CT 06881
An imprint of Greenwood Publishing Group, Inc.
www.praeger.com

Printed in the United States of America

The paper used in this book complies with the
Permanent Paper Standard issued by the National
Information Standards Organization (Z39.48–1984).

10 9 8 7 6 5 4 3 2 1

To my mother, Beverly, for her love and support.
CSV

To my husband, Jim, who has faithfully supported and encouraged me each step of the way.
KAS

The stress and pressures of modern life are eased in the embrace of a loving family. To my family—my wife, Marie; our sons, David and Dan; and, the newest member of our family, Dan's partner, Alison.
IDW

Contents

List of Illustrations

FIGURES

BOXES

Preface

In the United States we have a paradoxical view of colleges and universities. While deemed valuable, necessary and even indispensable for many professions, they are at the same time seen as idealistic and impractical. The notion of the "Ivory Tower" suggests that protective walls surround campuses, insulating them from the stresses and strife of the larger world. While the first view promotes many of the anxieties associated with college and university life it is the second that prevents us from taking these concerns as seriously as we should. Many of our campuses are beautiful places in idyllic settings that contribute to an illusion of peace and tranquility.

Yet, increasingly, and perhaps somewhat grudgingly, we are coming to understand that the walls are porous and the world is not kept at bay. It is more and more evident that college students mirror the larger society with respect to the experience of psychological challenges and emotional difficulties. In this book, we speak to the specific and particularly prevalent matter of anxiety and its effects on the lives of students.

We have two major aims with this book. First, to enhance students' awareness of the expected and normal stresses of college life and the ways in which, like those in the larger society, they are affected by them. Evidence indicates that a significant number of college students carry serious psychological and emotional issues with them to campus, and that these are exacerbated by the additional strains of college life. In the United States we tend to value youth and associate it with resiliency and invulnerability. And, it is true, for many, the years between the ages of 18–24 are a time of vibrant physical strength and wellbeing. But we often don't soon enough or carefully enough acknowledge the various factors that impact the adjustment of a young person in college. Many students experience embarrassment or shame when suffering emotionally and may not reach out to family, friends, and to professionals. While it is not the intention of this book to provide a substitute for treatment for critical psychological issues or concerns, we do hope to help readers identify the nature of their struggles with anxiety and determine when to seek professional help. We also wish to provide a resource that may serve to augment the treatment of anxiety provided by a professional.

Second, it is the intention of the book to describe the nature of anxiety, its common manifestations, and provide methods for effectively coping with it. Students who possess strategies for managing their anxieties will be better able to make the most of what college and university life has to offer. We will describe the nature of anxiety, discuss anxiety-related mental health disorders, and review the many stresses that contribute to fears and worries throughout college. The knowledge, strategies, and skills in this book have been found to be empowering and effective. College is a rich and exciting time of life, but one that can overwhelm the unprepared. We hope this book will help prepare students to explore the reaches of their possibilities, accomplish many of their dreams, and meet life's challenges with better chances of success.

Acknowledgments

We are indebted to the pioneering researchers and practitioners who have developed and refined psychological treatment methods for anxiety, and to the many clients that have inspired us with their stories of courage and personal growth. Special thanks also goes to Dr. Rebecca Swan, who generously gave her time to thoroughly and critically review the manuscript. We would also like to acknowledge the help of Ms. Maura Smyth, the Social Sciences Librarian at the Charles Keffer Library at the University of Saint Thomas. We appreciate the interpretive expertise that is reflected in the artisitic contributions of Jonathan Kwok. We appreciate the efforts of our editor at Greenwood Publishing, Elizabeth Potenza, and our copyeditor, John Clement. We offer our gratitude to the many colleagues on college campuses who have influenced our professional lives with their wisdom, instruction, and dedication as they invest in the lives of college students.

PART ONE

Introduction to the Problem

CHAPTER 1

The Anxious Campus

Turning and turning in the widening gyre[1]
The falcon cannot hear the falconer;
Things fall apart, the center cannot hold.

—W.B. Yeats

Angelina is an outwardly confident young woman who had always done well in school. No one knew that she faced her college placement tests with the fear that she wasn't as smart as her teachers thought. She spent sleepless nights agonizing that she would do poorly, and could already anticipate the shame and humiliation of having no real college prospects. But even though she received high scores, she carried her fear of performance into her first year at Middle States University.[2] Now she spends uncounted hours each week studying, no longer participates in cocurricular activities she enjoyed in high school, and struggles to make friends at the U.

Jason was eager to escape the constraints placed on him by his parents and couldn't wait to get to college. It felt like he was trapped in an endless summer before it came time to leave for college. He purposefully picked a school far from home because he so desperately wanted to get away. Now, he finds himself separated by half a continent from his parents and roomed with a guy who thinks dust is a sign of alien life. His telephone bill is starting to rival his tuition and his parents have started to suggest he *shouldn't call so often. He never thought he'd miss his family and friends so much. The Thanksgiving break is too short to travel home and he'll be alone for the holiday for the first time in his life. He is sleeping badly and finds that he is unusually nervous and shaky around others. He wonders what could be wrong with him. He is procrastinating on his assignments and has skipped some classes—he thinks he might drop out after the first semester and maybe go to a college nearer home.*

Heather wasn't sure she wanted to go to college. She wasn't sure what she wanted to do. Her parents were divorced when she was nine and she grew up in a single parent home in which her mother worked a full time job outside the home. She wasn't much involved in her high school, as making friends seemed so hard for her. She always felt shy and awkward around the others who seemed to find things so easy. She always felt a little overwhelmed by the pressures of life in high school. She had hoped that college would be different, but it hasn't. Now in her second year, she goes to class, spends the rest of the time in the library or in her dorm room playing computer games or searching the Net. Her second semester was much the same as the first and things seem to be getting worse. Just today she skipped the class where she was supposed to give a presentation to the group. She is a little more outgoing in Chat Rooms but never reveals too much or pushes for intimate relationships, even anonymously.

These are the stories of three college students struggling with college life; anxious, at loose ends, and without much hope that things are going to get better. But, let's not leap to a conclusion that they are just three unusual students with abnormal problems. As we will see, the facts tell a different story. Angelina, Jason, and Heather aren't alone. They are examples of a rising trend on college campuses. How did these students get that way? Let's look at some possibilities.

THE ANXIOUS SOCIETY

First, college students aren't alone in their feelings of anxiety and stress. These are stressful times. There are, of course, particular anxieties that are associated with college and university life and that is the focus of this book. Colleges and universities, contrary to popular belief, aren't isolated from the larger society and reflect the times as much as any other institution in the United States. These are anxious times and the anxiety that permeates the United States is felt on college campuses. Here is a second point before moving on. Angelina, Jason, and Heather's experiences aren't unusual. They are normal college students dealing with anxiety and stress within the context of our society's many fears and dilemmas. Like all students, they have varying levels of experience with anxiety and may or may not have addressed problems with worry in the past. With the move to campus they are entering another culture, the culture of higher education, and its unique blend of demands and pressures.

These worried and anxious students are not only representative of an incoming college class; they are representative of our population at large. The National Institute of Mental Health reports that research indicates 40 million adult Americans (18.1%) currently suffer from an Anxiety Disorder.[3] And these

18% of Americans with an Anxiety Disorder may be just the tip of a growing iceberg of individuals experiencing problematic worry. If we label Middle States University as a mid-sized institution with approximately 12,000 students, then we have the possibility of over 800 students anxious enough to visit the counseling center—an overwhelming number.

The United States has not always been such an anxious place. The anxiety our society experiences tends to wax and wane depending upon the national and international crises that threaten our physical safety or economic well being. The Great Depression and the Second World War were such catastrophic events in the lives of U.S. citizens that these represented times of near unanimous national anxiety. Those times are long passed, of course, and not within the memory of a majority of Americans except as historical events. In the last decade there has been a noticeable trend toward greater levels of anxiety among Americans.[4] This decade has been marked with a number of tragic events: the terrorist attacks of 9/11, hurricane Katrina in 2005, and the shootings at Virginia Tech that occurred just as this book was going to press.

These certainly created feelings of fear among those directly affected and a general sense of insecurity and vulnerability across the nation. These appalling and calamitous events may touch some of you directly or personally. You may have seen your hopes for attending your local college dissolve, may be grieving the loss of a loved one, or may now find yourself in the grip of anxiety when attempting to board a plane. For most of us, however, these and the other more chronic stresses in our society provide a backdrop of vulnerability, an environment of insecurity within which our individual dispositions to anxiety run riot. Feelings of anxiety do not have to be tied directly to an actual event. Anxiety is, in fact, a normal reaction to either a real *or* perceived danger. It is in this arena of "perceived" danger that the shift toward increased anxiety seems to have occurred.

Even beyond the tragic and frightening events that have occurred, people in America are more concerned, in general, about job security, personal safety, personal appearance, social status and, financial concerns (like how to pay for college!). Americans now face a shifting economic climate where one cannot count on finding a life-time job, planting roots, raising a family, and sending children to a safe school. Business scandals and deadly violence in our schools such as shootings threaten any citizen's sense of security. We are caught in a national loss of confidence in our government, as our elected representatives seem to be controlled by "spin doctors" who manipulate any event to conform to ideological positions. The foundations of religion are under attack; the foundations of science are under attack. It may well be that the increasing complexity of life has left us without adequate ways of coping with our times.

Another important component of anxiety is a sense of uncontrollability— a feeling that one cannot control outcomes in one's life or environment. We know that many of us are biologically "wired" to be more sensitive to perceived threats to our well-being and more readily experience this emotional unrest. As we have discussed, the events that have occurred, the complexity of the world in which we live, and the pace of change in our current environment—all of these contribute to a sense of uncontrollability. The shift has been so substantial, so noticeable that our times have been labeled "The Age of Anxiety."[5,6] It isn't so important, perhaps, what we label it as it is to acknowledge that these are anxious times and they seem to be getting more stressful. As institutions, colleges, and university campuses move in tandem with the pressures, forces, and stresses of our complex society, so do, unfortunately, the students who attend them.

THE ANXIOUS CAMPUS

Anxiety is a growing problem on college campuses. In a recent study of students from 15 campuses, students listed anxiety as one of their top six concerns.[7] In another study, the counseling center at Kansas State University examined changes in client problems across 13 years. The study demonstrated a continued increase in severity of anxiety symptoms from 1989 to 2001.[8] While anxiety has increased for both men and women, there is evidence to suggest that female college students report greater levels of anxiety.[9] In addition, more students are presenting to counseling centers; they are bringing more complex problems; and the amount of distress they are reporting is increasing.[10] Anxiety and stress have replaced relationship issues as the number one cause of counseling center contacts.[11] By the mid-nineties, anxiety accounted for about 63% of counseling center contacts, levels that continued into 2001. College students report that they have less confidence in their physical health and sense of emotional self-confidence, as well

Box 1.1   Anxiety Disorders

The most common anxiety disorders are:

Panic Disorder—Recurrent, unexpected panic or anxiety attacks combined with ongoing fear of having additional attacks.

Social Anxiety Disorder/Social Phobia—Fear and discomfort in social or performance situations. Can range from specific fears of public speaking to an avoidance of all social contact.

Obsessive-Compulsive Disorder—Intrusive thoughts, impulses, or images that provoke anxiety. This anxiety typically triggers compulsive rituals or time-consuming repetitive behaviors.

Post-Traumatic Stress Disorder—Anxious thoughts and painful memories or reminders of a traumatic event.

Generalized Anxiety Disorder—Excessive worrying about a variety of topics that the individual feels unable to control.

Specific Phobia—Fear and avoidance of particular objects, places, or situations. Common phobias include fears of heights, insects, storms, and medical procedures.

as an increased sense of being overwhelmed.[12] Overall, these findings point to the conclusion that a higher and higher percentage of students do not believe they possess sufficient coping skills for managing their anxiety difficulties.

The increasing numbers of students approaching college and university counseling centers for help report a range of psychological disorders including panic, obsessive-compulsive disorders, and phobias. Take a look at box 1.1 for a list of Anxiety Disorders. These disorders will be more fully described in Chapter 2.

What are the stresses college students face that are different than those of other young adults in American society? Notably, the college experience is in and of itself a transformative time in a person's life. This seems to be true whether one enters the college experience at what is called the traditional age—17 or 18—or at a period of life identified for college students as nontraditional—say 24 or 25. What is true for traditional age college student (18–24) is that this is a time of life in which the issue of identity is a foremost developmental stage. Erik Erikson, the famous developmental psychologist, labeled this as a time when young people struggle with Identity versus Role Confusion evolving into a stage of young adulthood labeled Intimacy versus Isolation.[13] (See Chapter 3 for a more thorough discussion of developmental stages). Others have described it as a time when college students progress through a series of developmental stages including competence, management of emotions, autonomy, mature interpersonal relationships, identify, life purpose, and personal integrity.[14]

While these developmental issues certainly affect those young adults who do not attend college, there are some particular challenges that impact individuals who are attending school. Take a look at the top ten stresses identified by undergraduates at a Midwestern university (box 1.2). These stresses reflect a wide range of concerns, including adjustment to new living arrangements, the demands of academic life, holiday transitions, as well as more mundane difficulties like long lines at the bookstore and computer breakdowns.

Box 1.2   Top 10 Student Stresses

Change in Sleeping Habits	89%
Vacations/Breaks	82%
Change in Eating Habits	74%
New Responsibilities	74%
Increased Class Workload	73%
Change in Social Activities	71%
Financial Difficulties	71%
Waited in Long Lines	69%
Computer Problems	69%
Lower Grade Than Expected	68%

Source: Ross, S.E., Niebling, B.C., and Heckert, T.M. "Sources of Stress among College Students," *College Student Journal*, 33:2 (1999, June), 312–317.

The fears of not being smart enough, and corresponding worries about failure or letting down one's parent(s) plague students throughout college. For first year students these are often coupled with interpersonal concerns such as finding friends, fitting in and finding a social niche, which make for a particularly tough time in their college experience.[15,16,17] Ethnic minority students face the added burden of prejudices that compound the concerns listed above. Minority students may face unique challenges related to fitting in, fulfilling family expectations, and barriers related to stereotypes and attitudes in the campus environment. And while every student entering college is aware of these concerns, it is extremely difficult to predict—given the tremendous number of changes that occur—how the specific stressors associated with college life will impact you. Facing the daunting tasks of paying for college, developing a new social life, and coming to live or work in an unknown place at a relatively young age are anxious tasks. You are not alone if you feel that you were unprepared.

LEARNING TO COPE

So how do we learn to cope with worry, our anxious symptoms, and the stressors that cause or exacerbate them? Whether your anxiety symptoms are longstanding and have worsened or are new to your experience, a good starting place is the recognition that you're not a helpless being. You have a great deal of influence over your life and have more resources than you probably realize. We may not have control over the Age in which we live and we may not be able to manipulate all the stresses within the college environment. However, there are some things over which we do have control. We can learn to manage our anxiety in the midst of difficult times. As a college student, you have already demonstrated that you are intelligent, that you have a good capacity for learning, and can apply what you know to move you forward in your life. This book is one resource for helping you continue that process.

WHAT CAN YOU DO?

We hope that you now recognize that anxiety among college students like yourself is common. Knowing that others have had similar struggles can make a difference in understanding and working on your own concerns. People read a book like this or seek professional assistance because they want to change. They are hurting in some way and are dissatisfied with the course of their life. Yet, as much as people may want to change, change is challenging and often frightening. You have undoubtedly developed your own set of "coping tools" for dealing with life's challenges. Sometimes the tool set contains a limited assortment of tools. Getting better and changing has a lot to do with expanding the set of tools you have available for coping. We hope this book will provide you with some new tools and resources.

THE CHANGE PROCESS: MANAGING ANXIETY

We have good news and bad news about learning to manage anxiety. If you are like most of us, you want to hear the bad news first. The bad news is that making significant changes in the way you think and behave takes time and patience. The good news is that these changes can have a significant impact on your anxiety. Many anxiety symptoms and problems can be overcome. In fact, anxiety may be the most treatable of all mental health difficulties. Whether or not your experience of anxiety constitutes a mental health problem, decades of research have provided a wealth of valuable information about what is helpful to people who wish to conquer fears and anxieties. Throughout the book we will describe some of the most helpful strategies and techniques as they apply to you as a college student struggling with anxiety.

The process of change depends upon three important factors. The first is *awareness*. In order to change we have to become aware of what we are doing. We have ingrained patterns of feeling, thinking, and behaving of which we may not be aware. A big part of the change process involves cultivating awareness of your ways of operating; in this case the ways that tend to promote your anxiety. The second important factor is to become aware of *other options* for operating. In other words, changing involves coming to understand that there is another way of feeling, thinking, or behaving. This involves using tools for more effective coping. Finally, another important factor is *application*. You can become aware of what you are doing and what might be a better way of operating, but change does not occur until you actually apply or execute what you have learned. To a large extent, you get out what you put in.

Here's a key point: Any successful change process occurs in *small steps*. Let us just say, for illustrative purposes, that you are 5% improved by just beginning to read this book. Let's say you would gain another 5% with each of the strategies and techniques covered. Just think of where you could be by the end of the book!

It would be great if progress was linear, that every ounce of effort you put in would yield you an ounce of improvement. Unfortunately, the process of overcoming any problem does not work that way. Progress is typically irregular. At first you may make small, even frustratingly small, steps. You may then experience a quantum leap forward, only to fall back several steps within a short time. The "line of progress" is actually a jagged one, as depicted in figure 1.1.

Figure 1.1   The Line of Progress

Everyone's progress occurs differently. Don't be dismayed by small improvements in the beginning. Over time, there will be a cumulative effect that is well worth the struggle. Remember to celebrate the small victories over your anxiety. This is critical in helping you to stay with the program of overcoming and managing anxiety.

The process of change with respect to any problem is easier if you have understanding and supportive people to help you. They can help remind you of your goals, the progress you have made toward them, and encourage you through the process of learning to manage anxiety. Friends and loved ones can be very helpful, and remember that professional help is available as well (this is discussed in depth in Chapter 14).

THE CHANGE STRATEGIES: THOUGHT AND ACTION

Throughout this book we will focus on two sets of strategies that help in learning to manage anxiety. *The first set involves changing the way you think.* Feelings and thoughts go hand in hand. We need to take note of our feelings in order to cope effectively with the demands of life. However, as we will discuss at length throughout this book, your feelings are in large measure determined by how you view situations. In the case of anxiety, it is often fueled by evaluation of situations as threatening. Overcoming anxiety is largely about becoming aware of ways in which your thoughts and perspectives on situations contribute to your anxiety.

Changing thoughts and beliefs will be a great start. However, changing your thoughts alone is not the only way to overcome anxiety. *The second set of strategies involve taking action.* Maintaining your mental gains over anxiety is most

effective when it is strengthened with supporting evidence from your actual experience and with newer and more adaptive behaviors.

Thinking and action strategies form the basis for the *cognitive-behavioral approach* to addressing anxiety. The cognitive-behavioral approach has evolved from decades of research on the nature and treatment of anxiety.[18] In the late 1960's and the 1970's, Aaron T. Beck, an American psychiatrist, pioneered a theory and treatment of depression that emphasized the importance of particular styles of thinking in depression.[19,20] Beck's highly successful and influential approach to depression was later applied to anxiety.[21] Over the past 25 years, the cognitive techniques introduced by Beck have become merged with action strategies to form the cognitive-behavioral approach. The effectiveness of cognitive-behavioral strategies is well established with a number of different manifestations of anxiety.[22] We'll utilize this approach and these methods in a number of chapters to discuss their application with some of the specific challenges and anxieties you face. A more thorough review of thought and action strategies is contained in Chapter 11.

Thinking Strategies

We address steps in changing your thinking. They are:

1. Identify—This strategy involves a process of identifying thoughts that contribute to anxiety. These types of thoughts have errors, are negative, or are self-defeating. Thoughts such as this are typically called *cognitive errors*. Cognitive errors are often difficult to recognize because they become so routine and a natural part of the way we think. They include such patterns as *catastrophizing* which involves thinking the worst about situations, *polarized thinking* that involves viewing situations in all-or-none terms, and *mind-reading* where we erroneously assume we know what others are thinking. Throughout this book we will help you to learn to identify these patterns as the first step toward overcoming anxiety.

2. Challenge—The next step in this process is to learn to challenge cognitive errors. Since this way of thinking has become ingrained for most people struggling with anxiety, we need strategies to face and confront erroneous thinking. These strategies involve activities such as examining and testing thoughts, as well as finding new ways to change how we routinely look at things.

3. Transform—The third step is to transform the way we think. This involves learning to exchange patterns that fuel anxiety with new and more productive ways of thinking. In addition, it involves going deeper to uncover more fundamental beliefs that shape our thinking. These core beliefs can be adjusted—allowing for a change in thinking processes that will reflect more accurate and balanced perspectives.

Action Strategies

In order to change the way you think, you need to change your actions. You will only be confident in new ways of thinking in situations if you "try on" these new perspectives in actual situations in your life. Furthermore, it is important to face fears, not avoid them. Research has revealed that gradually facing your fears, armed with new ways of thinking, is the best way to overcome fear and anxiety. Changing your actions involves strategies that include: discovering anxiety triggers, facing your fears, practicing new skills, rewarding yourself, and making healthy lifestyle choices.

To better manage anxiety, it is also important to consider making broader changes in the way you live; in essence, to change your lifestyle. With a hectic and ever-changing schedule and consistent temptations that can compromise health, college life is a significant maze to negotiate in a low-stress manner. Yet, we also know that taking time to relax, managing time efficiently, and eating and sleeping well can be key factors in managing anxiety. In Parts 2 and 3 of this book we'll address a number of these topics.

THE FOCUS OF THIS BOOK

We have aimed this book at those of you who are struggling with the challenges that college life presents and those of you experiencing a level of anxiety that has you (and perhaps others) concerned. Some of you may be suffering from one of the anxiety disorders discussed in the following chapter. In initial chapters we examine some of the personal and developmental challenges faced by young adults and how they contribute to anxiety, and review some of the stresses inherent in the college experience. Some of you may struggle with anxiety that is specific to certain situations, like taking tests or interacting with others. Separate chapters address many of the contexts in which anxiety often arises, such as taking exams, planning for the future, and social interactions. Some of you may benefit from counseling or psychological treatment for your anxiety and at the end of the book we offer information and suggestions to help you seek help. Even if your anxiety is mild and you are unclear if it is a problem for you, this book will serve as a resource for understanding the demands of college life and how they contribute to stress and anxiety and coping more effectively with them. Finally, for those of you who are already involved in counseling, perhaps within your university or college counseling center, this book may help facilitate discussions about anxiety between you and your counselor.

EXPANDING YOUR LEARNING ENVIRONMENT

Hopefully, your primary motivation for attending college is to receive an education. College is a place for learning. Learning in college occurs on many levels. There is, of course, classroom learning. On top of that, though, is developmental learning. You learn how to be away from home and live on your own; how to interact with peers, staff, and faculty, among others. College can be a place of stress, but it is also a place to learn how to deal with stress and become more effective in the world. In doing so, you will worry less or be better able to moderate the effects of anxiety on your life. So college is a place to learn, to practice our learning, and a place where we can find the support we need as we practice life skills that will lead us on into the larger society better prepared for careers, relationships, and life.

SUMMARY

These are anxious times and college isn't a sheltered haven from the anxieties of the larger society. We know some people believe just the opposite, but it isn't true. University life isn't a sheltered eye of a storm where peace reigns for a temporary space of time until reality comes charging in again. The anxieties of the larger world do not stop at the door of a college dorm. In addition to the anxieties of the greater society, college can be a stressful place in and of itself. It has special tasks and events that can contribute to or exacerbate anxiety. Each of us can learn the strategies and skills that permit us to deal effectively with worries and fears. You can help yourself. And what you learn will assist you in dealing effectively with many of life's challenges. The good news for college and university students is that a campus provides the people, resources, skills, knowledge, events, and situations that promote that learning.

The terrible and tragic shootings at Virginia Tech occurred just days before this book went to press. This book does not broadly address concerns about personal safety; however, this is an important topic. We hope that in the wake of this tragedy resources will emerge to help students cope with this additional source of fear and anxiety. We recognize that students live in anxious times and we appreciate the courage that it takes to face anxiety and to look to the future with hope.

CHAPTER 2

The Many Faces of Anxiety: Anxiety and the Anxiety Disorders

Worry is interest paid on trouble before it falls due.
—W.R. (William Ralph) Inge

Mike feels his heart race as the instructor hands out the examination in his history class. He feels nervous and panicky and cannot get his mind off of how he is feeling. He wonders how he will be able to complete the exam feeling as he is. He has the urge to rush out of the classroom.

Janet cannot stop worrying about how she is going to make ends meet. She just returned from the bookstore where she found out she has to buy another expensive textbook for her chemistry class. She gets ready to go to her job, but is thinking about her big exam tomorrow. Janet worries that she will be too tired after staying up late studying again. She wonders whether she can handle college. She feels out of control.

For the third time this week, Selena awakens suddenly in her dorm room, just a couple of hours after going to sleep. She feels tightness in her throat, a racing heart, and strange sensations, as if her heart is missing beats. She feels dizzy. This has happened for several nights now. She fears that something terrible is happening to her or that something is wrong with her heart. She wonders whether to awaken her roommate to take her to the hospital.

Mike, Janet, and Selena are confronted by anxiety. All are experiencing a level of anxiety that is distressing and challenging. Mike is confronted with urges to leave the classroom while at the same time worried about his performance. Janet feels that her circumstances are out of control. Selena's sleep is disrupted and she fears she may be having a health crisis.

Anxiety has many forms. Some are natural and even helpful. Some interfere with a person's ability to meet his/her goals, relax, or have fun, while others are so debilitating that it feels as though one's whole life revolves around the experience of anxiety. In this chapter we will explore these many faces of anxiety. We will help you understand what anxiety is. We will address the continuum of anxiety reactions, from normal anxiety to what we call "anxiety disorders." Finally, we will discuss when and how to seek professional help for anxiety.

ANXIETY: WHAT IS IT?

Anxiety is very much a part of all of our lives. The experience of anxiety itself is universal. At its most basic level, anxiety is the apprehension, uneasiness, or worry we experience when we perceive a threat to our security. It doesn't matter whether the threat or danger is real or perceived, or whether it comes from outside of us or from within us. What matters is that we are sensing that something is dangerous, challenging, or not in line with our expectations.

THREE COMPONENTS

Anxiety expresses itself in three levels of experience; the cognitive or thinking level, the physical level, and the behavioral level. These three components are related to one another but their expression can vary from person to person. Later in this book when we discuss various ways of coping with anxiety, we will offer suggestions that address each of these levels of experience.

The *cognitive* component reflects the ways in which we *interpret* our circumstances. If our thoughts become focused on bad and threatening possibilities or outcomes, then we may experience trepidation, worry, and dread. People who experience high levels of anxiety perceive danger and threat more readily and in more situations than nonanxious people. They tend to expect the worst, magnifying the probability of harm and catastrophic consequences. If you are one of these people, you are also likely to underestimate your ability to cope with situations. So not only are you more likely to interpret a situation as dangerous, difficult, or threatening, you may also view yourself as less capable of coping with it.

The *physical* component refers to various physiological sensations or symptoms of anxiety. These can include experiences like shortness of breath, a racing heart, an upset stomach, tense muscles, and dizziness or unsteadiness. All of these symptoms are related to a natural biological mechanism that prepares us to respond to threat or danger. We will discuss this mechanism at some length in the next section. Sometimes, people can become bewildered or afraid of some of the physiological sensations or symptoms of anxiety. They may interpret their own physical arousal and reactivity as a further sign of danger and threat. For example, they may interpret their shakiness or dizziness as a sign that they might not be able to stand throughout their class presentation. They literally have developed a fear of their own fear response. We will discuss this later when we address the experience of a panic attack.

The *behavioral* component involves the person's behaviors or actions when they are experiencing anxiety. Some of the reactions we have in the face of anxiety are adaptive and help us cope with a situation, like being prepared or compensating in order to minimize the chances of a negative outcome (for example, studying well for a difficult exam one is worried about). However, it is often the case that behavioral reactions to anxiety are unhelpful and even add to the problem. Examples of problematic reactions can include procrastination, avoidance or refusing to participate (like missing the exam or not completing the paper). Of course, medicating the feelings with drugs, alcohol, or engaging in other risky activities are also unhelpful ways of responding to the fears. Yet another way some people respond to anxiety is by *overcompensating or overcontrolling* situations. For example, someone who is anxious about a test might overprepare, staying up late for several nights before an exam, only to discover that their efforts could have been much more efficient. Or a person concerned about a date might try to arrange the "perfect" situation, only to be disappointed when things do not turn out our precisely as planned.

What we can call *escape or avoidance behaviors* provide "fuel" for anxiety. It is a natural human response when experiencing high levels of anxiety, to look to exit a situation as soon as possible. If we have felt vulnerable in situations in the past, it is natural to consider avoiding them in the future.

COGNITIVE: ANXIETY INVOLVES NEGATIVE APPRAISAL

We are sure you have made the everyday observation that different people will react in very different ways to virtually the same stressful situation. All of us know of people who seem not to experience much worry no matter what is happening and others who worry constantly about seemingly everything. What makes one person anxious may not cause another to be troubled at all. This is because stress and anxiety cause us to perceive or *appraise* aspects of a situation from a different, often more negative, lens.[1] For example, turbulence experienced on an airplane flight may result in apprehension and even terror for some while others may experience the same turbulence as merely annoying. Hosting a holiday party will elicit calm and task-focused behavior in one person, worry and tension in another, and cause a third person to experience feelings of panic so strong that they feel compelled to cancel the gathering. In social situations, the anxious person selectively attends to the periods of silence in conversation as the evening begins and interprets them as awkward and uncomfortable, while the calm person notices looks of interest, anticipation, and reflection. In both cases, how the situation is perceived exerts substantial influence on how one feels about the situation. Anxiety is the direct result of a person's judgment, or appraisal, of the risk or danger inherent in a situation. This is a theme that we will return to often throughout this book: That how one thinks about or appraises situations plays a big part in their experience of anxiety. We will be discussing many of the ways in which anxiety affects you as a college student. You will build awareness about your own reactions and perceptions and the ways in which they impact your experiences.

In Chapter 11, we will take a closer look at the notion of appraisal and its relationship to anxiety. We will discuss how our thoughts are expressed in how we "talk to" ourselves (self-talk) and some of the common cognitive errors associated with anxious appraisals. We will discuss how anxious interpretations often involve several problematic characteristics, including faulty cause-effect chains and distortion of the probabilities of negative events.

PHYSICAL

Anxiety is Protective

We do not perceive anxiety to be pleasant, but it is both a necessary and valuable experience. Anxiety is associated with preparation and protection. It helps us "gear up" to react to danger and affords us protection from threat. It is associated with what the famous American physiologist, Walter Cannon, called the "fight or flight" response.[2] That is, in the face of anxiety, we are primed to tackle danger head-on (the fight) or to escape from it in order to protect ourselves (the flight). When primitive humans were confronted with such dangers as intruding predators, their autonomic nervous systems prepared them to respond to the threat with speedy retreat or aggressive attack. Anxiety enables this vital survival response to occur. It is necessary for our continued existence. So, as strange as it may seem, anxiety serves a useful purpose when it occurs in situations when we *need* to be activated very quickly to respond to threat. It is essentially a useful "alarm" when there is real danger, but a "false alarm" in most circumstances we confront daily.

Neurobiological Underpinnings of Anxiety

In addition to involving natural physical mechanisms, research has indicated that some people are temperamentally prone to experience higher levels of anxiety.[3] It appears that their nervous systems may be more reactive and easily aroused. In a sense, their fight or flight response engages more quickly and intensely than it does for others that are not as predisposed towards anxiety.

Anxiety is also associated with the functioning of certain areas of the brain. An area of the brain called the limbic system acts as a mediator between the "primitive" brain (the brainstem) and the part of the brain associated with "higher" thought processes (the cortex). The brainstem essentially monitors and senses threat and relays potential danger signals to the cortex through the limbic system.[4] There are a number of neural circuits at work in the brain's "anxiety and fear system."

As we have noted, perceptions of threat or danger activate the anxiety and fear system in the brain. Our thought processes play a vital role in whether and to what extent the fear and anxiety system is activated. In addition to appraisals of threat, however, the anxiety and fear system is influenced by a number of other physical factors.

While it is beyond the scope of this book to discuss all of these factors, some important ones will be noted. Box 2.1 indicates the many factors affecting anxiety. Our natural rhythms, including our sleep-wake cycles and hormonal variations, may have an affect. When a person lacks good sleep or when one

Box 2.1   Factors Affecting Anxiety

Source: Adapted from Spiegel, D.A. *Beating Anxiety and Fear: Workbook for the Treatment of Panic and Agoraphobia* (Boston University, 2001).

is menstruating, the anxiety and fear system may be more easily activated. Illness as well as medications or substances are also influences. Antianxiety medications have a general inhibiting effect on the nervous system while substances like caffeine and tobacco have the opposite effect making the system more sensitive to activation. Even our diet and whether we exert ourselves physically can be important. Fortunately, many of the things that can affect the anxiety and fear system are under our control or can at least be modified. These will be given special attention in Chapter 12 where we will address various lifestyle factors in relation to anxiety. Research into the neurobiology of anxiety is new and exciting and will undoubtedly enhance our understanding of anxiety and our ability to reduce it in the years to come.

BEHAVIOR: ESCAPE, AVOIDANCE, AND OVER-CONTROL

Avoidance and escape are perhaps the most powerful factors that perpetuate anxiety. We can avoid in obvious ways (procrastinating on a paper in that we are worried about), or in far more subtle ways. An example of a subtle, yet typical, form is avoiding eye contact with others in the classroom when fearful of how one will fit in. One of the major themes of this book is that fears can be (and must be) faced and can be overcome. How we exhibit avoidance in the face of fear and anxiety must be understood and then this avoidance must be challenged. Why is this important? Avoidance fuels anxiety through a process of what is called *negative reinforcement*. The concept of reinforcement comes out of behavioral psychology and is associated with the work of the psychologist, B.F. Skinner.[5] Negative reinforcement is actually a reward but it is often confused with punishment (because of the word "negative"). It is called negative reinforcement because the behavior (escape or avoidance) is rewarded with relief from anxiety. If someone is afraid of elevators and as a result looks for the stairs immediately upon entering a tall building, finding the stairs is likely to be associated with relief. The behavior of looking for the stairs rather than trying to determine whether the elevator indeed may be dangerous is negatively reinforced (rewarded with a sense of relief). This idea arose from the two-factor theory of avoidance learning.[6] According to the theory, a situation like riding in an elevator comes to be associated with frightening thoughts or experiences. Once the association is made, the person discovers that avoiding or escaping the elevator results in a reduction of anxiety.

This reinforces the belief that avoidance or escape are the only ways out. The person is less likely to use other coping mechanisms in order to ride the elevator. The problem with escape or avoidance is that when the threat resurfaces again, the person has no other way to cope. In addition, by not actually riding the elevator, the person fails to learn that there is no reason to be afraid. Thus, the

Figure 2.1   The Worry Process

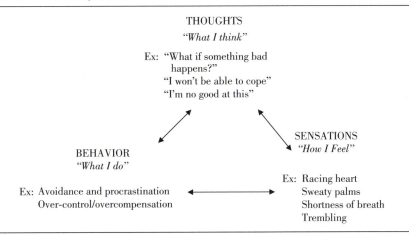

THOUGHTS
"What I think"

Ex: "What if something bad
happens?"
"I won't be able to cope"
"I'm no good at this"

SENSATIONS
"How I Feel"

BEHAVIOR
"What I do"

Ex: Avoidance and procrastination
Over-control/overcompensation

Ex: Racing heart
Sweaty palms
Shortness of breath
Trembling

cycle continues as the person, in the absence of other ways of reducing anxiety and in the absence of new experiences that indicate that the elevator is not dangerous, resorts to escape or avoidance again and persists in their view of the situation as threatening.

Another way that people attempt to cope is by compensating for their fears and worries by engaging in what we can term *over-control*. Over-control is intimately related to the concept of *perfectionism*. For example, if one is worried about failing in a given situation, such as when they are performing some task, they can attempt to control as many aspects of the situation as possible to avoid a negative outcome. On the face of it this might seem like a good coping strategy. However, in many cases with highly anxious people, their over-control goes too far and becomes a problem in its own right. Putting in a great deal of time trying to study perfectly for a test or practicing repeatedly for a performance in order to cope with worries can detract from other useful activities and when extreme, an ability to enjoy one's life.

How the Three Components Fuel Anxiety—Putting it Together

The three components work together to strengthen and fuel anxiety. Typically, there is a trigger; this can be something in your environment (sitting down for an exam) or something internal (such as an intrusive memory of a difficult test). The process begins with a particular sensation, thought, or behavior, which in turn is followed rapidly by the other components. Here's how it works. Anxiety primes us for danger making us vigilant for signs of threat. When anxious, we are highly sensitive to physical symptoms and are ready for avoidance, escape, or over-control if necessary. Anxious thoughts may lead to increased arousal and physical reactions. In turn, these may be interpreted as dangerous or unmanageable. Figure 2.1 depicts the relationship of the three components. Over time, an accumulation of experiences may lead to avoidance or to attempts to over-control. For example,

Juan is afraid of failing an exam and thinks, "it is too hard, I'm not prepared. I'm going to fail (anxious thoughts). In the classroom, he feels tense, has an upset stomach, and feels his heart pound (physical reactions). His mind is occupied with his upset stomach, he has difficulties focusing, and rushes through the test, making mistakes he ordinarily would not (behaviors). He gets a C- on the test, and this confirms his belief that it was too hard and that he wouldn't do well. He begins to lose confidence in his ability to take tests. He notices a surge in anxiety as he contemplates taking the next exam, and thinks about dropping the class.

Paula fears that she will not live up to the high standards she and others, such as her family, has for her. Her anxious thoughts are characterized by fears of disapproval and criticism. In response to these fears, she vows that she will study the material over and over again in order to make sure that she understands every single idea and concept. She feels exhausted after several nights of intensive study. But every time she stops, she tries to review the material in her head and then is anxious when she isn't able to focus and remember it all. Paula fears that she really isn't mastering the material and that she'll do very poorly. She has repeatedly turned down social invitations and her friends are beginning to wonder whether she wants to spend time with them. She is torn between feeling exhausted and alone and dreading the possibility that she will let her family down and be revealed as a poor scholar.

THE CONTINUUM OF ANXIETY

When anxiety is experienced as a normal reaction, it is protective and manageable. It does not tend to last a long time and it occurs in response to a limited number of situations. As a normal reaction, it helps us remain alert to potential hazards and threats. It can even motivate us to take steps or work harder. A good example is how we face the prospect of public speaking. In most performance situations, some anxiety is expected and can motivate us to work hard and prepare for potential challenges during the situation. Research relating stress and performance, known in psychology as the Yerkes-Dodson Law[7] suggests that there is an optimal level of emotional arousal for successful performance. If one experiences no anxiety whatsoever, we may be vulnerable to put ourselves in harm's way (by being unprepared for our speech or presentation). We might take undue risks or fail to attend to the risk inherent in situations. On the other hand, if we experience too much anxiety, our reactions may interfere with our ability to solve problems and function most effectively. Figure 2.2 depicts the relationship of anxiety and performance.

Figure 2.2   Anxiety and Performance

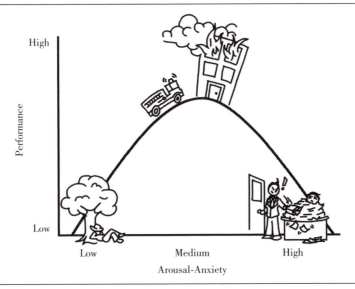

Anxiety becomes of significant concern when it begins to interfere with performance, or our ability to relate to others, or to gain satisfaction from our lives. We can think of anxiety as extending on a continuum from normal, to levels that interfere in some way with our lives, to having what we call an "anxiety disorder." An example of normal anxiety is the sense of apprehension a student may experience prior to an important exam. An anxiety disorder may involve the experience of intense levels of anxiety or worry that are experienced throughout the day, to the point where a student can think of little else. In between are experiences where anxiety might be expected (for example prior to speaking in front of the class) but is at a level of intensity that makes it difficult to concentrate on the presentation. Box 2.2 contrasts normal anxiety with the severe levels of anxiety associated with anxiety disorders. Keep in mind, though, as you look at the box that there is, in fact, a continuum of anxiety that ranges from normal to disorder. There are no clear dividing points along this line. It is important for you to consider the extent to which your anxiety is hindering you or affecting your degree of satisfaction with your life.

It is important to emphasize that anxiety that hinders performance or inter-feres with well-being is extremely common, especially in college students like yourself. Some of you reading this book may be experiencing a "clinical level of anxiety" that warrants a diagnosis of an anxiety disorder. However, for many of you, this book is of interest because you are struggling with your anxiety, but your anxiety is not at the level of severity for a diagnosis of an anxiety disorder. In this book, we offer ideas that can help you manage anxiety at any point along the continuum we are discussing. We also want to emphasize that there are resources

Box 2.2   Normative Anxiety vs. Anxiety Disorder

Normal Anxiety	Anxiety Disorder
Occasional worry about circumstantial events, such as an exam or break up that may leave you upset.	Constant, chronic, and unsubstantiated worry that causes significant distress, disturbs your social life, and interferes with classes and work.
Embarrassment or self-consciousness in the face of an uncomfortable social situation.	Avoidance of common social situations for fear of being judged, embarrassed, or humiliated.
Random case of nerves or jitters, dizziness, and or sweating over an important event like an exam or oral presentation.	Repeated, random panic attacks or persistent worry/anticipation of another panic attack and feelings of terror or impending doom.
Realistic fear of a threatening object, place, or situation.	Irrational fear or avoidance of an object, place, or situation that poses little or no threat of danger.
Wanting to be sure that you are healthy and living in a safe, hazard-free environment.	Performing uncontrollable, repetitive actions, such as washing your hands repeatedly or checking things over and over.
Anxiety, sadness, or difficulty sleeping immediately following a traumatic event.	Ongoing and recurring nightmares, flashbacks, or emotional numbing relating to a traumatic event in your life that occurred several months or years ago.

Source: Anxiety Disorders Association of America "What is an Anxiety Disorder?" http://www.adaa.org/stressoutweek/what_is_an_anxiety_disorder.asp (accessed on October 5, 2006).

and services that may be helpful whether or not your experience of anxiety is severe and debilitating. Seeking counseling is an option. We see counseling as a growth-enhancing activity, not just as treatment for a psychological disorder such as an anxiety disorder.

ANXIETY DISORDER

An anxiety disorder lies at the severe end of the continuum of anxiety. As we have emphasized, often it is a matter of degree rather than a more fundamental difference from normal anxiety. If there is a question in your mind about where you land on the continuum of anxiety, the descriptions on the following pages may help you determine whether you may wish to investigate this further. In addition, a qualified mental health professional (and we will discuss how to seek help at the end of the book) can assist you in determining whether you have an anxiety disorder. If you are experiencing an anxiety disorder, it is very important that you seek help from a qualified mental health professional, preferably one that has specialized experience in treating anxiety disorders. It is important for you to know that anxiety disorders are common, and very treatable with appropriate professional help.

See if your experience matches any of the descriptions below. Even if you are only occasionally troubled with worry, you may find these descriptions informative.

COMMON ANXIETY DISORDERS

Over 40 million American adults and one out of every eight children suffer from an anxiety disorder.[8] While we tend to associate anxiety with our busy, achievement-oriented culture, anxiety disorders are not limited to the United States and many studies around the world suggest that they commonly occur in many cultural contexts.[9] There are six general categories of anxiety disorders. As we will see, anxiety disorders include panic disorder, social anxiety disorder, obsessive-compulsive disorder (OCD), post-traumatic stress disorder (PTSD), generalized anxiety disorder, and phobias. Women outnumber men in each category except for OCD and social phobia, in which both sexes have a nearly equal likelihood of being affected. Results of a National Institute of Mental Health (NIMH) survey showed that female risk of developing PTSD following trauma is twice that of males.[10,11]

PANIC DISORDER

Lately, Jill has been bothered by "spells" of intense fear in which she is short of breath, her heart races, and she feels dizzy and strange. While they initially came on suddenly and seemingly from nowhere, she now worries that they will occur in class. She worries that she may pass out and embarrass herself during these times. She wonders if people will help her, and at the same time is concerned that she will draw attention to herself. She thinks about skipping her morning class, but decides to go as long as she can sit in the back by the door.

Jill's situation typifies the experience of the panic attack. Individuals who have panic disorder experience recurrent and severe attacks that arise suddenly and without obvious reason. The symptoms of a panic attack can make people feel as if they are having a heart attack or losing control of themselves. A wide variety of symptoms can occur including a racing heart, chest pain or discomfort, heart palpitations, shortness of breath, sweating, trembling, tingling sensations, and feelings of dizziness or unreality. The occurrence of these symptoms is associated with a number of fears including fear of a health crisis (e.g. a heart attack), fear of losing control, fear of embarrassment, fear of being incapacitated or dying, or a fear of losing one's mind. According to the National Co-morbidity Study funded by the NIMH[12] as many as 3–5% of the population may struggle with Panic Disorder at some point in the lifespan, making it a very common problem indeed.

PANIC DISORDER AND AGORAPHOBIA

In the face of panic attacks, some people begin to associate the situations in which they have panic symptoms with the occurrence of the panic. In Jill's case described above, she feared going to class as she might have an attack there. When a person comes to avoid situations due to fears of a panic attack, we call this agoraphobia. Unfortunately, avoiding situations rarely solves the problem but rather causes other problems, and a person can begin to feel as if they are "trapped" with the anxiety. Fortunately, like the other anxiety disorders described here, panic disorder can be treated with specific psychological therapy. Medication can also be helpful in many cases.

SOCIAL ANXIETY DISORDER

Ever since the first day on campus, John has found himself feeling anxious when meeting new people. He worries that he will not be accepted by others and will end up without friends. When around others, he feels intense anxiety and focuses on what he is saying and how he is coming across. He worries that he is saying things that will be seen as inane or boring. He worries that he is looking anxious and will do something to humiliate himself. John finds himself worrying about this to such an extent that he cannot focus very well on what others are saying. He has urges to just stick to himself or to give up on meeting friends. He finds that things are better if beer is available, which "takes the edge off."

John may be struggling with Social Anxiety Disorder. This problem involves a fear of social situations where you might anticipate being humiliated, ridiculed, or embarrassed. Physical symptoms such as blushing, sweating, or shaking may occur and can cause concern. People with social anxiety often have urges to avoid situations. This avoidance can further undermine their confidence and result in social isolation. Social gatherings, meeting new people, dating, or group situations in class may be avoided. It is important to differentiate Social Anxiety Disorder from a fear of test-taking or public speaking. Some fear of these situations, in which one feels under great scrutiny, is quite normal. However, if you find yourself paralyzed by worry in these situations to the point where you feel that your performance is significantly affected, you may have Social Anxiety Disorder.

Social Anxiety Disorder appears to be the most common of the anxiety disorders, according to the National Co-morbidity Study mentioned earlier, with as many as 11% of the population of the United States affected at some point in the lifespan. According to a 1995 study by Canadian researcher Michael Van Ameringen,[13] half of adults with social anxiety dropped out of school prematurely due to fears such as attending class and participating in social activities. Work by University of Minnesota psychologist Matt Kushner[14] has found a particularly strong link between social anxiety and excessive drinking. It seems that it is quite common for socially anxious college students to use alcohol to calm their nerves at parties and gatherings. Fortunately, as with Panic Disorder, there is help available for social anxiety that involves specific psychotherapies as well as medication.

OBSESSIVE-COMPULSIVE DISORDER

Devon sits in tears trying to determine what clothes to wear. For some time, though worse now since beginning school, she has been concerned that certain of her clothes have become contaminated. She carefully lifts her clothes out of the dresser, being careful that they do not touch the outside of the dresser. If they do, she will have to wash them despite knowing that they are clean. Her dorm room presents other challenges. There are many things she cannot touch due to her fears, such as the TV remote, her room-mate's keys, and the doorknob. Some things are unavoidable, and when she touches them she then feels compelled to spend a good deal of time in the bathroom washing her hands. She tries to hide it from her friends. She is embarrassed and ashamed as she knows that it doesn't make sense. Yet she feels like a prisoner to the feelings of disgust that she feels when she has to touch things.

Obsessive-compulsive disorder (OCD) is characterized by repetitive and distressing thoughts coupled with repetitive behavioral and/or mental compulsions. The compulsions represent an attempt to reduce anxiety, yet become time consuming and distressing to the sufferer. The repetitive and distressing thoughts, called obsessions, may be about contamination (often associated with washing compulsions), fears of catastrophes (often associated with checking compulsions), or many other areas. In fact, the fears can vary a great deal in OCD. The person with OCD is often crippled by doubt, and compulsions represent an attempt to reduce this uncertainly about whether situations are safe or dangerous.

OCD is much more common than previously thought, affecting as many as 3% of the U.S. population.[15] OCD often begins in childhood and if you feel you may have OCD, this may have been an issue in your life for some time. However, OCD frequently begins during the adolescent and college years.[16] OCD can interfere with academic performance and social activities. Obsessions and compulsions are often distracting and can prolong academic tasks like writing or taking tests. Compulsions are often embarrassing and many with OCD try to conceal them. In fact, the shame associated with OCD can interfere with seeking help.

POST-TRAUMATIC STRESS DISORDER

It had been 5 years since a burglar broke into Reema's family's home in the middle of the night. Reema vividly recalls being awakened by the broken glass and fearing the two men, who were rummaging through the house looking for money, jewelry, and other items of value that they could steal quickly, would come upstairs and find her awake and harm her. She thought she had dealt with it. After all, she had talked about it on many occasions and the memories of it seemed to fade with time as she moved through the stresses and strains of high school. Yet now she lays awake in the middle of the night in her new apartment near campus, vigilant for any sound that might indicate a prowler. She can't get the memories out of her mind and has started to have nightmares.

Traumatic events are, unfortunately, all too common. There are few who are not haunted, to some extent, by things that have happened to us in the past. When we have repeated difficulty putting painful events out of our minds, dream about the events, or seek to avoid painful reminders, we may be suffering from a post-traumatic stress reaction or Post-Traumatic Stress Disorder (PTSD). These feelings can occur immediately after the trauma or begin months, years, or even decades after the event. In Reema's case above, her fears were intensified when she moved out of the dorm and into an apartment for the first time.

In addition to distressing recollections of the event there is often a sense of vigilance or preparedness for danger, as if the same event may be lurking around the next corner. The experience of "flashbacks" involves feeling or acting as if the event is occurring all over again. You may have feelings of guilt or shame about the event or have difficulty making sense of why it happened or happened to you. Finally, a number of other experiences can occur including feelings of emotional numbness or detachment, difficulty concentrating, or a loss of interest in activities that used to give you pleasure.

Those experiencing post-traumatic stress reactions may not seek treatment as they fear having to face the memories of the event in order to recover. Yet, it is possible to feel better, and a wide variety of resources are available to help with post-traumatic reactions.

GENERALIZED ANXIETY DISORDER

Juan cannot stop worrying. When he began school, he felt overwhelmed by all of the changes, such as moving away from home, large amounts of homework, tests, and the challenge of fitting in on campus. Now he is experiencing a constant feeling of dread, and is having trouble concentrating on the simplest things, instead feeling preoccupied with his worries. He finds himself even worried about his worry, concerned about his inability to turn his mind off. He wonders whether he will be able to continue with school.

Juan may be experiencing Generalized Anxiety Disorder (GAD). While it is not unusual for students to feel overwhelmed at times and worried about various aspects of their lives, this is often short-lived. The worry passes with the events that provoked the worry. If you have GAD, you may be experiencing your worry as out of control. Your worry may seemingly shift from one area of your life to another. When one stress passes, another one takes its place. Your thoughts turn to the worst case scenario with each experience. You are unable to get perspective and people may tell you that your worries are out of proportion to the circumstances. While worry is a frequent experience when we are anxious, GAD involves very frequent and intense worry. Often, difficulty in sleeping and concentrating accompany GAD.

SPECIFIC PHOBIAS

Sarah received a call that her grandfather has died, and her parents want her to fly home for the funeral. She has been afraid to fly since she was in junior high school, and her fear began after she and her family returned from a trip to Florida. The flight they were on experienced considerable turbulence, although they arrived safely. It seemed dangerous to her and she noticed that others on the flight seemed frightened as well. While everyone was assured by the flight crew that the rough flight, while uncommon, did not represent a significant risk to their safety, she nevertheless began to dread flying and even turned down some opportunities for trips in high school due to her fear. Now, she must return home and there is no time to drive.

When people are afraid of specific situations like flying, heights, driving, or being in enclosed spaces, or objects like bugs, dogs, or needles, they are said to be suffering from specific phobias. While many people have some fear of these situations or objects, people who are phobic either have intense fear reactions or avoidance to the extent that their well-being is affected or their life is impaired. Specific phobias may or may not relate to a difficult or traumatic experience with the feared object or situation, though often there is a link as in the above example. Like all of the anxiety disorders described thus far, specific phobias are very amenable to treatment.

OTHER COMMON PROBLEMS AMONG COLLEGE STUDENTS

While this book is concerned with anxiety, there are other common mental health issues among college students that often relate to or occur along with anxiety problems. Depression deserves particular attention as recent research indicates that nearly half of the individuals struggling with anxiety disorders also experienced clinical depression at some point in their lifetime.[17] Conversely, most individuals experiencing depression also report some difficulties with anxiety. The two tend to go hand-in hand despite the fact that they often manifest in very different ways. Other problems include eating disorders and alcohol and drug abuse. When reading this book it is important for you to reflect on whether you struggle with these problems as well. Each is given attention in Chapter 13 and resources providing information about these problems appear at the end of the book.

SEEKING HELP FOR ANXIETY

Whether you are struggling with more normal anxiety and stress associated with college or with one of the anxiety disorders described above, you may benefit from professional assistance. Your college counseling center is a good place to start. College counseling centers are staffed with highly qualified mental health professionals who can provide a range of confidential services. Professionals in college counseling centers are well acquainted with the unique challenges you are facing with college. We'll talk more about this in Chapter 14.

A valuable resource for learning about the various anxiety disorders and helping you to determine whether you may suffer from one or more is the Anxiety Disorders Association of America (adaa.org). The ADAA website describes treatments for the various anxiety disorders and offers links to qualified therapists around the country and many outside of the United States. Inside the ADAA website is a special section pertaining to college students (gotanxiety.org) that serves as a terrific resource.

SUMMARY

Anxiety is a natural and expected reaction that has cognitive, physical, and behavioral components. When anxiety becomes a problem, it is fueled by all three components. There is a continuum from normal experiences of anxiety to severe and debilitating anxiety disorders. The fears associated with the various anxiety disorders differ greatly from one another but all of the anxiety disorders can be associated with significant emotional distress and effects on a student's ability to function in the college setting. At any level along the continuum, professional assistance such as counseling may be helpful.

CHAPTER 3

Anxiety and the College Student

A musician must make music, an artist must paint, a poet must write, if he is to be ultimately at peace with himself. What a man can be, he must be.

—Abraham Maslow

Integrity simply means not violating one's own identity.

—Erich Fromm

We began this book with a discussion about the problem of anxiety in our society and on college and university campuses. Chapter 2 provided an overview of what anxiety is and how it is experienced on a continuum of normal anxiety to severe anxiety disorders. As has been established, anxiety is a problem for many in our society. However, anxiety can be particularly difficult for college students. One reason for this difficulty is that young adults are dealing with significant changes and growth during the college years.

WHAT'S GOING ON?—DEVELOPMENT

Entering college can bring an exhilarating and sometimes frightening mix of contradictory emotions. From the moment you step on campus you are presented with a world of exciting new opportunities, and yet at the same time barraged with multiple challenges. So what's going on? Why does this new adventure seem like navigating a stormy sea? For almost all human beings the college-age years bring significant milestones of development. Theorists specializing in the field of development explain what takes place during these years. They view this process as stages that involve a series of tasks and a deepening maturity in several areas. See box 3.1 for a more detailed description of these stages. The first important stage involves the development of competence.[1] Young adults are developing competencies in a number of areas including intellectual, physical, interpersonal, social, and spiritual. Important tasks are involved in the development of competence. Let's focus on three areas—intellectual, physical, and interpersonal. Intellectual growth involves being able to master content of material as well as gaining new thinking skills such as comprehension, analysis, and integration of information. College students gain physical competence by growing in strength and self-discipline, as well as learning to master a variety of physical tasks. Interpersonal competence involves the development and fine-tuning of important people skills such as listening, communicating thoughts and emotions effectively, becoming more perceptive, and learning to respond appropriately.

There are a number of other stages involved in this important time of maturation. Along with developing competence, college students are becoming more adept at managing their emotions. They are learning to understand their emotions, express them, and use self-control to direct them in positive ways. They are moving toward autonomy, which means they are becoming self-sufficient and actively involved in setting and pursuing their own goals. A key growth area during these years is learning to build mature interpersonal relationships including tasks such as making good relationship choices, knowing how to experience intimacy, and creating appropriate commitments in significant relationships. Learning to become an independent adult also involves the formation of a strong, positive sense of identity. We will talk more about this in the "Who am I" section later in this chapter. Two other developmental stages include the college student's growth toward being an individual that has purpose as well as integrity. Having purpose is important as one seeks to make decisions and move toward a goal. Purpose provides direction in life and it leads to a sense of meaning. Developing integrity means that a person is beginning to adopt core values and beliefs. This helps to strengthen one's identity and means that a person will initiate actions that are based on an internal compass.

As you can see, a great deal is happening during these years! It's easy to see how the college experience can seem overwhelming at times. Along with all the developmental processes that are occurring, there are some other important issues that each college student faces. We will focus on two important areas that are a part of the transitional years of young adulthood that include leaving behind the familiar and answering the question "Who am I?"

Box 3.1   Developmental Stages

Stage	Description

1. Develop Competence	1. Intellectual
	  • Master content
	  • Thinking skills—comprehension, analysis, and integration of information
	2. Physical
	  • Grow in strength
	  • Self-discipline
	  • Master new physical tasks
	3. Interpersonal
	  • Develop and fine-tune skills
	  • Learn to listen, communicate, become more perceptive, and respond appropriately

2. Manage Emotions	1. Develop awareness of emotions 2. Learn to express emotions appropriately 3. Learn how to release emotions before they explode 4. Deal with fears so they won't paralyze 5. Heal emotional difficulties so they don't hurt new relationships
3. Move Toward Autonomy	1. Become more self-sufficient 2. Actively involved in setting and pursuing personal goals 3. Autonomy leads to healthy interdependence
4. Build Mature Interpersonal Relationships	1. Make good relationship choices 2. Learn to experience intimacy 3. Create appropriate commitments
5. Gain a Strong, Positive Sense of Identity	1. Comfort with appearance, gender, and sexual identity 2. Sense of self historically, socially, culturally 3. Clarify self-concept, self-acceptance, and self-esteem

6. Develop a Sense of Purpose	1. Be intentional
	2. Assess interests and options
	3. Clarify goals and make plans
	4. Persist in your course despite obstacles
7. Develop Integrity	1. Identify core values and beliefs
	2. Allow values and beliefs to guide behavior
	3. Link values and beliefs to self-respect

Source: Chickering, A.W., and Reisser, L. *Education and Identity* (2nd ed.) (San Francisco, CA: Jossey-Bass, 1993).

LEAVING THE FAMILIAR

Heading off to college usually involves a sense of excitement and a number of positive emotions associated with experiencing something new—dreams, hopes, and possibilities for the future. But for many students, this is only part of the picture. So many emotions are involved with this process. Sometimes students are eager to escape frustrating circumstances at home and others may feel anticipation for new adventures, yet these emotions may become confusing when feelings of indifference or uncertainty enter the picture. Leaving behind familiar people and places can be an extraordinarily difficult process. Most college students come from a more structured environment where they have been surrounded by friends and family. Going to college often means leaving behind these important relationships and exchanging this safe environment for a world of uncertainty. These enormous changes can trigger feelings of helplessness, being out of control, and a very real process of grief for what is left behind.

When you were younger did you ever think about getting out on your own and becoming independent from your parents? It probably sounded terrific at the time, but the reality of separating from parents can be quite distressing. There is a lot to think about as you look ahead to being responsible for and taking care of all the details of life, and what about saying good-bye to your family? For many, it's difficult to let go. Things will never quite be the same. Relationships tend to change as a result of this process and sometimes moving into adulthood involves conflicts with parents and siblings as one becomes more self-sufficient.

Friends are another important group of people that are impacted by the experience of entering college. Many students become preoccupied and concerned about the loss of friends they had before college or the changes in those friendships that occur as a result of being in college. Feelings related to the loss of friends at home can include insecurity and a fear of being unable to build new

friendships. Leaving behind important friendships brings with it a sense of grief and sometimes this grieving gets in the way of connecting socially in college and feeling comfortable with one's social environment.[2]

For some students, particularly minority and international students, entering college involves not only the adjustment to leaving friends and family, but to leaving one's familiar culture. Differences in cultural norms and expectations can be confusing and cause considerable worry during this time when establishing new friendships is so important. You may encounter dissimilarities in dress, greetings and social communication, schedules, and even the ways in which you may be expected to interact with your professors. All of these can contribute to a sense of isolation and insecurity.[3]

There is an old saying, "You can't go home again." Unfortunately there's some truth to this statement when it comes to leaving friends, and even family, back home. Think about all that is happening to you on the university campus. You are being stretched intellectually by the academic environment, the knowledge you are gaining, and the exposure to people who think differently. You are developing new critical thinking skills and new ways of looking at life. You have been exposed to a new and diverse group of people. Perhaps you are learning to view life through these new perspectives and you are seeing things in a completely different way. Your world has opened up, and to a certain extent you are becoming a new person. But what about the people back home? Things may have stayed the same for them. Friends who have decided not to attend college are not experiencing the same kinds of developmental challenges. Perhaps your family does not understand the changes occurring in your life as result of all that you are encountering. This can be a difficult situation for some students. Going home can sometimes be uncomfortable and you can feel like you really don't know the people who used to know you best. Perhaps you sometimes feel that you don't even know yourself.

ANSWERING THE QUESTION—WHO AM I?

Exploration

At the beginning of this chapter we mentioned an important concept that is a part of these significant years of young adulthood—identity. Identity development is a key task during the college years. Over the centuries, philosophers and psychologists have thought, written, and debated about the concept of personal identity. Although the issue is complex, the work of these thinkers has given us some basic ideas for forming an understanding of the definition of personal identity. We have come to understand that each individual is a conscious being made up of patterns of thought, memories, feelings, and behavior that characterize that person. These patterns distinguish us and make each person unique.

Perhaps you have wondered about your own identity and how you might be able to understand these patterns and essential characteristics that define who you are. It is extremely important to develop an understanding of your personal identity. This knowledge will give you insight into future decisions and life direction. Making these personal discoveries is foundational for effective decisionmaking, self-confidence, fulfillment, and the ability to take on responsibilities that will be challenging and rewarding.

Developing your identity means answering a central question, "Who Am I"? It means grappling with other questions such as: How am I different from other people; what makes me unique; what combination of abilities, talents, interests, and values characterize the real me? These discoveries and many others are a part of the transitions taking place as you move through late adolescence and into adulthood.

Understanding your identity involves the work of exploration. Exploration is a process in which you learn information about yourself, conceptualize new identities, try on these new identities, and then organize these new understandings into a clearer picture of who you are.[4] Individuals working through the process of exploration may find themselves in certain stages along the way.[5] You can see a summary of these stages in box 3.2. Young adults who are in the process of evaluating their goals and beliefs but have not firmly committed to them are in a stage called *identity moratorium*. This may sound negative but it's actually a good thing. It's healthy to stay open, take enough time to explore, and come to a solid understanding of yourself. We'll talk more about this later in this chapter.

Box 3.2   Identity Stages

Identity Stage	Description
1. Identity Diffusion	• Vague and meandering exploration of identity • No clear idea of identity • Not attempting to discover identity
2. Foreclosure	• Avoid exploration of identity • Adopt goals, values, and beliefs of others • Committed to identity without knowing what true identity is • Can be goal directed and inflexible
3. Moratorium	• In the process of exploration of identity • Starting to make commitments to identity • Still developing identity and in a state of ambivalence
4. Identity Achievement	• Worked through a period of exploration • Develop well-defined values • Have a solid self-concept • Know the basics of identity yet still expanding the understanding of it

Source: Marcia, J.E. "Development and Validation of Ego Identity Status," *Journal of Personality and Social Psychology*, 3 (1966), 551–558.

But there's another side to this. Let's take a look at Kim's situation.

Kim is in her first semester as a sophomore at Middle States University. Ever since she can remember Kim has been told that she would be a good teacher. Many of her middle school and high school teachers have encouraged her to become a teacher and her parents, both teachers, continually express pride in the fact that she is following in their footsteps. Kim planned out her four years of college with her admissions advisor even before coming to the university. Kim has some friends who are taking political science classes that sound interesting, but education is a difficult major and she has no room in her schedule to take electives. The past few weeks have been very difficult for Kim. She feels incredibly bored in her education classes. She likes the idea of being up in front of people but the thought of teaching subjects like math or social studies seems dull and uninteresting. Two weeks ago she began her first field assignment in a third grade classroom. Sitting in the classroom she suddenly began to wonder, "Is this what it's like?" "Day after day being trapped with all these kids and having to work on the same math skills over and over . . ." Kim started feeling panicky and could feel her heart beating wildly. For the first time ever, doubts about her career choice flooded her mind. What should she do? She had all these plans and every one was counting on her to carry on the teaching tradition in her family. She knew she had to put these thoughts aside and push forward. Perhaps things will feel better once she learns more about teaching. Maybe she'll like things better in another field assignment. "That's it," she told herself, "I have a great plan and I'm sticking to it." "Most of my friends don't even know for sure what to major in and I have my career all planned out." "I'll get over this if I just stay focused on what I need to do."

Kim, like many others, is in a stage called *identity foreclosure*. Individuals like this choose to take on an identity without doing the work of exploration, but this may be a premature decision. Some students feel a great deal of pressure from family or peers to choose a certain major that will lead to a corresponding career. Foreclosure means jumping right in to this career path without testing it out to see if it really fits. Students like Kim often come to a crisis point in their senior year or even after they graduate and begin working in a job that doesn't seem to fit.

Another difficult stage that some students find themselves in is called *identity diffusion*. This means they are not involved in either exploration of themselves or commitment to an identity. This can sometimes feel like drifting—attending school but not connected at all to what is ahead or focusing on the discovery of true self. Unfortunately, this can be a very frustrating phase in which a student lacks purposeful direction and it can create a number of difficulties in making decisions and moving forward in college.

And finally, students who complete the work of exploration reach a point of being *identity achieved*. Exploration takes time and it can lead to feelings of instability and insecurity. However, taking the time to examine yourself, trying on new identities, receiving feedback from others, and then reformulating this identity is an essential part of the process of moving into adulthood. Finding the "real you" will open up doors of opportunity for the future. Sounds exciting doesn't it! And yet this wonderful adventure can contribute to the anxiety that is experienced at college.

Trying on Identities

We've talked about the idea of staying open and exploring identity. Exploration is important as we begin to make sense of identity and move toward understanding ourselves better. But how do we begin to develop a sense of identity—a sense of self? One way to begin this process is to try on new identities. We do this by testing areas of interest, thinking about our values and belief systems, and learning to recognize the aspects about us that make us unique. The next sections will focus on these areas.

Interests. Exploring areas of interest can be a great adventure. It can be prompted by developing a list of all the areas of interest you know that you have. It can sometimes be helpful to take an interest inventory—an objective test that assesses your interests—in your college counseling or career center. Another way to tap into your interests is to look at your college catalogue. What courses sound interesting? What clubs or activities look like they might be fun?

Once you've developed a good list of interest areas, step out and try something new. Take a class that sounds interesting. Visit a club that you think you might like. Go to an activity that sounds fun or volunteer in an area that makes you feel passionate. Don't stop with the things that sound safe and interesting, try something you thought you'd never do! Go to an activity you wouldn't normally attend or take a class that you've never thought about taking. Using this method of testing interest areas will help you to get a better picture of the real you.

Values and Beliefs. College is a terrific time to explore your values and belief systems. Reviewing your values begins with self-reflection and a focus on what is most important to you. This again is a place in which your college counseling or career center can be helpful. They often have values inventories that can assist you in recognizing your current values as well as exploring areas in which you may be developing new values.

Belief systems are often challenged in a variety of ways on the college campus. Take opportunities to talk about your beliefs in the classroom as you discuss topics of interest. Get involved in formal and informal forums for discussing a variety of belief systems—those that are familiar and those that you have never explored. Talk with international students and friends from a variety of cultural backgrounds. Or connect with groups of students that share your cultural background, faith, or traditions. Talk with friends—both from school and those back home. Talk about emerging ideas with parents or other family members. Write about your ideas in papers and in a personal journal. As you talk and write about your beliefs, they will become more comfortable and more a part of who you are.

Aspects of You. This is a good process and you may be beginning to see an emerging picture of you—a self-concept. But there is more. Exploration involves coming to understand your unique personality and the gifts and abilities you possess. Both of these areas can be explored with the help of a good counselor or career counselor.

There are many assessments that can help you to understand your personality. An assessment such as this can help you to recognize your strengths, growth areas, and ways in which you best relate to others and to the world around you. Taking an assessment can also assist you in understanding your gifts and abilities. Or in an informal way you can develop a list of the things you do well. What abilities have you demonstrated since you were very young? What kind of things have others noticed that you do well? As you learn about your personality and unique abilities, it is helpful to write about this and reflect on your growing sense of self.

BUILDING A SELF-CONCEPT

If you have engaged in this exploration process, you have a good sense of the emerging picture of who you are. This picture is your self-concept. The formulation of your self-concept is an important part of the formation of identity and a critical task at this stage of development. You can strengthen your self-concept by developing a profile of what you have learned about yourself. The worksheet in box 3.3 can assist you in summarizing what you have learned.

Box 3.3   My Profile

Elements of My Identity	What I Have Learned
Interests	
Values	
Beliefs	
Personality	
Abilities	

As you develop this profile of your self-concept, others can be a source of information and encouragement. You can discuss what you have learned about your personality with close friends or with your parents. They can reflect what they see in you and you can add this to your profile. As you learn about your gifts or beliefs, you may want to discuss them with trusted professors and see what new insights they can add. Some people find that seeking out a mentor is a positive way to learn about their gifts, abilities, areas of strength, and areas that may need growth. The profile that you develop can help you make great strides in the process of understanding your identity and having a strong self-concept.

WHY IS ANXIETY A PROBLEM?

We have discussed a great deal in this chapter about what is going on during the college years. Most students are experiencing development, personal growth, and progress toward a stronger sense of identity. Growing into mature, healthy adulthood is a challenging process. Identity development involves the ability to deal with ambiguity. We described this previously as a stage called identity moratorium. This stage involves the work of exploring one's identity. Students can sometimes experience conflict between elements of identity that seem to fit and at the same time a feeling of uncertainty about whether any identity fits at all. Consider the struggles experienced by Samuel.

Samuel is a sophomore at a large university. He distinguished himself in high school as a high achiever and an entrepreneur. He created his own web development business that earned him a scholarship for minority entrepreneurs at the university. Samuel had always thought he would become a successful businessman. However, he misses the close connection with his family and the support of his tightly-knit community. He often feels unable to identify with others in his major. Many of them seem materialistic and overly competitive.

Samuel has begun to struggle with his life direction and the decisions made previously. He recently began volunteering as a tutor with inner-city children. Samuel has been amazed at the enjoyment he finds when teaching concepts and working with children. He feels confused and uncertain. Should he explore his newfound interests? Should he continue in his business major? What will happen to his scholarship if he considers other options? What will his family think?

Samuel is experiencing the ambiguity, uncertainty, and discomfort often associated with identity exploration. Identity exploration can be exciting but it can also create stress, pressure, and anxiety. In addition, today's college students experience this exploration process, as we discussed, in an Age of Anxiety. But there is more. The college campus presents unique challenges. The next chapter will discuss the elements of the college environment that contribute to anxiety for college students.

SUMMARY

Before we leave this chapter let's reflect on some of what we have covered. We talked about the developmental stages that occur during this time of life and the important tasks associated with this development such as developing competence, learning to manage emotions, moving toward autonomy, building mature interpersonal relationships, gaining a strong and positive sense of identity, developing a sense of purpose, and developing identity based on core values and beliefs. We discussed the issues related to leaving family and friends and becoming more independent. We reviewed the process of identity formation through exploration, trying on identities, and learning about interests, values, beliefs, and the unique aspects of personality, gifts, and abilities. As you can see there is certainly a great deal to consider during the college years. The next chapter will focus on the sources of anxiety that are specific to the college environment.

PART TWO

Addressing the Sources of Anxiety
in College Life

CHAPTER 4

Adapting to Campus Life

Every tomorrow has two handles.
We can take hold of it with the handle of anxiety or the handle of faith.
We should live for the future, and yet should find our life in the fidelities of the present; the last is only the method of the first.

—Henry Ward Beecher

INTRODUCTION

The adaptation to life at college involves a number of unique challenges and stresses. This chapter will offer a summary of some of the sources of anxiety associated with the college campus and will focus on two areas: *times of the year* and *seasons of the college career*. The section on *times of the year* will review the varying stressors across the academic calendar. The section on *seasons of the college career* will offer an overview of the various tasks involved during each year in college and the stressors associated with these tasks.

TIMES OF THE YEAR

By now, you are very familiar with the details of the college calendar specific to your school. You probably know the dates of your break times and during which weeks you'll be taking your finals. Heading off to college does bring with it some predictable anxieties related to the college calendar. The sections that follow are a review of some of the predictable anxieties that new and returning students face. Many of these may be a review for you. However, by enhancing your awareness of the timing of these particular stresses, you'll be better able to prepare for these aspects of your college experience.

August/September—Checking In

August and September are the start up months for colleges and universities. New students, freshmen, and transfers are arriving at a relatively unknown place. Returning students are reestablishing contacts and revisiting old haunts. It's the beginning. It's probable, that some anxious feelings begin even before you get to campus. We call this anticipatory anxiety. Before you "check in" you have to "leave home" and that carries with it some sense of loss and saying goodbye, not an easy task for many. Sure, the first days and weeks of the college experience are crowded with activities, events, and structured experiences carefully planned and orchestrated by the Student Affairs office of your college. Yet, for some students, going back to the dorm room at the end of the day brings the reality of loss and an awkward sense of newness mixed with loneliness. In a survey of entering freshmen at a large state university, 45% reported feeling lonely or homesick even though most described having daily contact with new friends. Most of these freshmen (92%) reported feeling at least somewhat successful at making friends yet as many as 8% indicated a complete lack of success in this regard.[1]

While facing the prospect of making new friends, many freshmen struggle with the realization that their previous relationships are likely to change, possibly irrevocably. This concern regarding the losses or changes in precollege relationships has been termed "friendsickness" by researchers examining this phenomenon.[2] Friendsickness can contribute to difficulties in forming new relationships, lowered self-confidence, and loneliness. This can be an overwhelming time that can cause difficulty with academics as well as personal distress. For most students the loneliness and homesickness tend to dissipate after the first couple of months of college and are replaced by other stresses of college life.

Those who are living at home or attending school close to home do not face the potentially painful challenge of separation, but may experience their own complicated set of concerns. In their case, establishing some "separateness" and individuation from parents and friends can be difficult when it's easy to succumb to others' desires to keep you close and your own desires for their company and care giving. Some students, of course, don't experience loneliness and home-sickness but are exhilarated by their newly found freedom. They explode into the vacuum of restraints without the structure of home rules and expectations. New freedoms without structure can naturally lead to excesses and the college experi-ence can be one of experimenting with alcohol, drugs, sex, and other previously unexplored experiences. In the midst of this new found freedom, anxiety can surface when the demands of attending class, reading texts, preparing projects, writing papers, taking tests, and the other academic demands become intense. Some find it hard to replace the structured life style of home with a self-developed life style that balances newly found social freedoms with academic requirements and responsibilities. Most students find that the academic challenges of college are intense but many are also stretched to fit in with the social aspects of this busy environment. Finding a balance can be difficult.

In addition to the academic and social challenges of college life, there are values issues confronting new college students that can create anxiety. Values can be challenged in social contexts such as living with roommates, joining clubs, and hanging out at parties. One's values can be confronted when finding new friends and social groups present choices for activities and experimentation that have not been previously experienced. Individuals in college often find they are faced with decisions about what to be involved in and what activities they may need to avoid. This is often more complicated than it seems. Take the situation at one large Midwestern university, where an annual fall celebration is essentially a giant party, attracting as many 75,000 students from area colleges and other schools in neighboring states, leading to hundreds of arrests for drunken or disorderly behavior.[3] It can be particularly difficult to maintain one's personal boundaries and values when the culture at large seems to demonstrate certain behaviors. Adult responsibilities as well as opportunities can all pose threats to values and as a consequence create stress and anxiety for many.

College is purposefully designed to present students with new information, new knowledge, new experiences, and new people. Experiences like this that might come as a gradual part of anyone's maturation but they come in rapid succession for the college student. Students are meeting people whose values, religious beliefs, cultural background, ethnicity, sexual orientation, and even native language are different from their own. Often this means that students are forced to examine their own beliefs and values.

Some college students may face discrimination for the first time in their lives. This may be the discrimination of class, region, background, speech, or merely exclusive snobbishness. It can be frightening, bewildering, and painful. It may be encountered in rejection by some social groups such as fraternities or sororities. For incoming freshmen and some transfer students, this may come from a changing status where one is now a first year, inexperienced newcomer rather than a member of the school paper, a part of the drama program, a member of an athletic team, a participant in student government, and known throughout the entire school. All the work that went into becoming an active member of one's previous school now has to be repeated on a different stage with new people. Starting fresh means building this social network all over again and this can create anxiety. Many in our society are familiar with discrimination. Students of color, females, individuals with disabilities, and people from other nations with different customs, religions, and languages have already faced prejudices and may have some coping skills in place. Many, however, face new injustices and discriminatory behaviors that they could not have been prepared for.

Now add the stresses associated with registering for classes, meeting your advisor, and many of the cold realizations of dorm life, and you see the recipe for an intensely stressful life transition. At this point in time, it is not uncommon for students to doubt their decisions and feel somewhat panicked about their commitment.

October/November—Settling in

Whew! You made it through the first couple of months. October and November bring a new set of challenges. It might seem odd after the list of possible stressors that come with just showing up at college, but that is only the beginning.

Roommate stress often emerges in the first few weeks of settling in at college. This can occur even for juniors and seniors. Perhaps you chose to room with someone who seemed so easy to relate to in class but living with that person is a different matter. Or perhaps you find that you simply can't study in your new apartment due to the seemingly unending flow of your roommates' friends. It may be that loneliness is a continuing issue. Students who have not been able to form new friendships and find a new social group may tend to seek the refuge of their dorm room and feel isolated and lonely.

October and November bring the stresses of academic pressure. Some students find that balancing social and academic demands are simply too difficult and they may go to one extreme or the other. Some withdraw from social contacts in order to keep up with studying and writing papers. Others find that mid-term exams loom and realize that they are completely unprepared. This can be a wake up call for poor planning, procrastination, and a vibrant social life.

One of the difficult times of this middle period of the first semester comes in November—the Thanksgiving break. The Thanksgiving holiday may not be an important family occasion for all college students but for many, it is a relaxing, welcome break from classes and an opportunity to go back home and reconnect with family, friends, and boy or girl friends. For others, it can be a time of sadness because distance, time, and expense of travel may prevent going home. It may be the first time in the lives of many that they have spent Thanksgiving away from home. Finding a place to spend the Thanksgiving break can create anxieties—especially for those who have not made any significant new friends or contacts that could make it possible to spend the holiday with a local family. Still others may dread going home because of the fear of family conflicts. Stresses like these may involve long simmering family tensions but others may be the result of poor performance and having to face a parent or parents about academic difficulties.

December—Hump Month

December at most colleges means the semester is coming to an end and it's time to finish all assignments and papers, and to prepare for final examinations. Most students are familiar with this kind of stress but some do not anticipate the work involved due to carrying a high number of credits or the expectations of a particularly difficult professor. There may be regrets that one didn't put in as much work as needed which creates an internal source of anxiety and perhaps problems with self-esteem. Some students begin to wonder if they have the ability to compete at this level and be successful in an intellectually demanding world. Others may come face-to-face with the reality that they are not as independent as they thought they were and resent their dependency on their parent or parents.

Financial pressures may begin to surface toward the end of the first semester (some colleges use a quarter system but these typically end during December as well). Simply getting back home can pose financial challenges for some students. There are additional concerns for some if grades have not been high enough to maintain financial aid.

Meeting the demands of college course requirements represents only one side of the anxiety faced during the month of December. Just as the Thanksgiving break posed different stresses for different students because of finances and family relationships, the December holiday break is typically longer and holds the possibility of even greater stress. Some students might fear the loss of their newfound freedoms as they return for an extended holiday visit at home with its previous structure and restrictions. Others may fear the boredom of home and miss their new friends and new involvements. Some of those looking to the holiday break as a relief from their loneliness may experience disappointment at the difficulties of reconnecting with old friends who've established themselves elsewhere. Some students with stressful family relationships may fear what they feel will be the inevitable family conflicts of any extended visit home. The December break is, as you can see, a jumble of possible anxieties, hopes, wishes, and joys for college students.

January—Reengaging

Some colleges have a short term often labeled "J-Term" in which case reengagement starts much sooner for students who participate. Nevertheless, the beginning of the spring semester or winter quarter is a time for quickly reestablishing with the contacts and friends made during the fall term. For those coming back with new friends and new connections, it can be an eagerly awaited return. For those who were not successful at making new friends, coming back can easily create new anxieties about whether the coming term will be as lonely as the first one. It can be a time of loss for some, whose new friends have not returned.

Students who did not perform well academically in their first semester may face significant worry and anticipation about the demands of the new term.

There can certainly be heightened anxiety over the challenges the second semester poses if the first one was tough. It requires adjustments and adaptations that were not made in the first semester regarding the need to find a balance between new social freedoms and academic demands. There can be increased anxiety regarding one's ability to succeed and compete at this level.

February/March—Resettling

Sometimes this three-fourths stage is one of assessing the decisions and involvements that have happened up to this point. It may be a time when newly formed couples take stock of their new relationship and seek to deepen it or to pull back. Either can be a cause of anxiety. For those who have not formed either friendship ties or romantic relationships, this is a time of growing frustration over not being connected by now and seriously questioning whether this is the right college. Individuals struggling with social difficulties may question themselves and their abilities to make friends.

For many students, Spring Break is a wonderful and enjoyable time or an opportunity to pursue potential career options or community activities. Choices regarding involvement in service projects or short international study trips can be exciting. However, Spring Break brings many challenges for other students. Some face choices regarding participation in activities that involve exuberance, excess, and risky behavior. It is, as we all know from tragic news reports, a time not only of fun and harmless excess, but one of dangers as well. Other students may face frustration due to work schedules or a lack of funds that prohibit using the time for adventure, fun, or meaningful pursuits.

Spring Break is often a time of year when seniors may begin to feel a wake-up call. They may experience anxiety as they reflect on whether or not their major is a field in which they actually want to work. The need to move out into the larger world is rapidly approaching and job concerns are becoming more intense. We'll talk more about that in the next section.

April/May—Checking Out

Although the weather may be inviting, the academic calendar still demands attention. Final exams seem to produce anxiety for all students—freshmen through seniors. The end of the year brings closure on projects, final papers, and final exams—all in a short span of time. In addition, many students begin to review their grades and assess their grade point average. This can involve changes in classes for the next year or changes in strategy so that grades can be improved. This time of reflection and evaluation can add to the academic stressors at a very busy time of year.

All students face some form of transition at this time of year. Most returning students are arranging housing for the coming year. This can create enormous stress that often includes uncertainty, worries about finding roommates, and

Box 4.1   Stresses on Your Horizon

What challenges are you contending with at this point in your year? (loneliness, academic pressures, family expectations for holidays, etc.)

What stressful events are you anticipating over the next several months? (getting a job, writing a resume, dating, etc.)

Are you worried about your ability to manage any of these stresses? If so, what are these worries?

insecurities about one's relational skills. Summer brings relief from the intense academic pressure, but it often brings stresses such as competition for internships or summer jobs. In addition, decisions have to be made and plans implemented regarding summer plans, whether to stay in the area or go home, how to find housing, and who to live with in order to share expenses. Take a few moments to answer the questions in box 4.1. In Chapter 11, you can review and address these concerns.

SEASONS OF THE COLLEGE CAREER

As we have seen, the college campus presents unique stressors at different times of the year. In addition, most students are presented with a number of significant challenges throughout college—what we have identified as *seasons of the college career*. This section of the chapter will present the tasks associated with each year of college and discuss the associated anxieties that many face.

Freshman Year: Self-assessment

The freshman year is a particularly important time of self-discovery and reflection. A great deal of maturation and development occurs during this year and it is essential to take the time to learn about oneself as new learning and new experiences unfold. The following goals and action steps are associated with the freshman year and can be helpful in navigating the first year of college.

Goals:

- Discover important aspects of oneself such as abilities, skills, values, interests, and goals.
- Develop a good academic record
- Begin to narrow choices for a major
- Develop a social support network

Take action:

- Meet with a career counselor or counselor to take assessments and discuss abilities, skills, values, interests, and goals
- Get involved on campus and evaluate what skills and interests emerge

- Take introductory courses in majors in which you have an interest
- Talk with faculty, parents, and friends about different majors and career fields

Sophomore Year: Exploration

The sophomore year is a terrific time for students to do some exploration of themselves and of the world around them. This is a time for refining the self-assessment that began in the freshman year and to develop a good understanding of oneself. In addition, the sophomore year is a time when many students explore options on campus, off-campus, and around the world. Opportunities abound for involvement in specific interest groups, leadership positions on campus, study abroad, and volunteer positions off-campus. This is a time to try new things and discover inner strengths as well as lifework areas that seem most interesting to explore.

Goals:

- Solidify your understanding of important aspects of who you are
- Investigate lifework areas, needs within society, and parts of the world in which you have an interest
- Choose an academic major and plan your coursework for the years ahead

Take action:

- Investigate opportunities for leadership and involvement on campus, study abroad trips, and volunteer positions off-campus
- Talk with faculty members about what they see in you and what opportunities exist for development and exploration in your academic major
- Review your GPA and adjust study skills if necessary
- Begin the process of arranging an internship
- Learn all you can about careers in your major through attendance at career panels on your campus, career fairs, and informational interviews with individuals in careers that interest you

Junior Year: Making Decisions

The junior year is a key time to begin to solidify future goals and plans. Many students make the mistake of waiting until the senior year to make important decisions about the future. This intensifies anxiety that may already exist regarding these decisions and it makes an individual less competitive in approaching the job search in the senior year. This list of suggestions can help juniors to move forward and take action so that important decisions are made at the appropriate times in the college career.

Goals:

- Evaluate and make career decisions based on knowledge about yourself and the understanding you have gained about the world of work
- Solidify academic direction and consider options such as graduate school
- Gain added experience that will help to shape your career choices

Take action:

- Talk to faculty members, family, and your advisor about your plans to finish college and the next steps after college
- List tentative life and career goals and weigh options
- Meet with a career counselor to discuss your ideas, goals, and options
- Develop a resume and apply for an internship
- Complete an internship and evaluate career fields that seem interesting
- Conduct informational interviews, attend career fairs, and go to recruiting functions on campus
- Utilize the summer to work in your career area of interest or explore career options

Let's focus again for a moment on anxiety. Look back over the goals and action steps that we have listed. This is significant work and the steps taken at this time of life can have a huge impact on future direction in life. Many students find that they experience a great deal of anxiety related to this aspect of college life. It's difficult enough to adjust to campus living and the academic rigors on a university campus, but adding these types of decisions and necessary tasks can combine to produce a great deal of anxiety. For many, these challenges can seem overwhelming. The following chapters in this book will include suggestions and strategies for dealing with anxiety so that college students can move forward to accomplish the necessary tasks and make good decisions throughout college and beyond.

Senior Year: Moving Forward

We will end this section with a focus on the senior year. The senior year is filled with hard work, excitement, and a mix of emotions as students prepare to finish the college career and leave behind the people and surroundings that have become home. For most students, the workload is increased while pressures to make career decisions also intensify. The following list reviews the goals and action steps associated with the senior year.

Goals:

- Focus on a chosen career field and begin the job search or graduate school application
- Prepare for a successful transition from student to employee or graduate student

Take action:

- If attending graduate school, choose schools, take the Graduate Record Examination (GRE or other exam required by a graduate program), begin application process, and obtain reference letters from faculty members
- Meet with a career counselor to review career interests and make plans for the job search
- Revise resume for the senior year and for your career focus
- Obtain and complete a senior-year internship
- Reevaluate career choices based on what is learned in the internship, informational interviews, and discussions with faculty members and family

Box 4.2   Job Search Strategies for Seniors

Job Search Goals	Action Steps
1. Finalize career exploration	• Identify your abilities, interests, values, and requirements for a job • Search career fields to find areas in which you would want to work • Match your preferences to three or four career fields
2. Define goals	• Create a list of items that are most important to you (e.g. relationships, interests, financial responsibilities, etc.) • Develop short term goals for your career
3. Initiate the job search	• Return to the three or four career fields and look for specific jobs that interest you • Narrow the possibilities to a few jobs • Write a resume specific to these jobs • Write a cover letter that will get you an interview • Research organizations of interest • Network and begin to distribute your resume and cover letter • Prepare for interviews • Interview • Make decisions on offers
4. Launch your life plan	• Make a final decision and accept an offer • Begin your new job • Develop a plan for personal development in your job and in your career field

- Begin the job search (see box 4.2)
- Develop a budget, housing arrangements, and plans for your first year out of college

The senior year is a unique time of transition. This is a time to reflect on all that you have learned in college, learned about yourself, and come to understand about the world of work. The focus begins to change from finishing college to becoming a young professional. There is much to learn and many decisions ahead. As has been discussed, the job search is one of the critical tasks of the senior year and can also be one of the most anxiety-producing experiences in the college career. The information in box 4.2 lists the tasks associated with the job search. More information and strategies on finding a career will be outlined in Chapter 9.

SUMMARY

College is a unique time in an individual's life. You are changing. There is a lack of structure from home, encounters with newly found freedoms, times of struggle, challenges to values, the constant barrage of school work, and new and rigorous academic requirements. As the years pass, you gain new knowledge—not only academic knowledge, but new social knowledge, new emotional maturing, and new coping skills. You confront unknown and unexpected challenges and learn to adjust, adapt, and improvise. These are the skills you will need for the rest of your life. Managing the anxiety that can accompany times of transition, growth, and change is part of the process. The next chapters will focus in depth on some of the most anxiety-producing aspects of college life.

CHAPTER 5

Looking Good

Beauty's where you find it.

—Madonna

Love built on beauty, soon as beauty, dies.

—John Donne

Thus far we have discussed several stresses that are associated with college life. One significant stressor that almost all college students face is the pressure to "look good." Our society places great value and an inordinate amount of pressure on looking good, whether that is through personal appearance, personality characteristics, or how we present ourselves socially. Much of the pressure to have a positive "image" in this culture is related to physical attractiveness. We have created a billion-dollar industry selling products to make us attractive to one another. This image-making industry extends to name brand clothing, makeover television shows, and even cosmetic surgery. Most of us have a sense of how significant these cultural messages are on our lives; however, research gives us evidence that helps us to understand this powerful influence. This chapter will offer a summary of the research regarding social norms for attractiveness and provide strategies for building positive self-esteem in a culture that can have a destructive effect on a positive sense of self.

The pressure to be physically attractive is felt by many students and can add to the stresses experienced on the college campus. Research suggests that being physically attractive affects social acceptance at college.[1] Much of the research on attractiveness focuses on women; however, men are also affected by this societal pressure. One research study suggests that "attractive" males experience greater social acceptance than those who are not perceived to be attractive.[2] If there are expectations that a student needs to be attractive in order to be accepted, this certainly heightens the level of stress in the college experience. So, what is the standard for physical attractiveness and what does this mean for most college students?

While there may be many factors related to current standards of physical attractiveness, the media is definitely a significant influence in American culture. Every day in this country the average person is exposed to about 5,000 advertising messages.[3] In a study of over 4,000 network television commercials, 1 commercial out of every 3.8 contained some sort of "attractiveness message." Estimations from this research suggest that the average adolescent views more than 5,260 attractiveness messages per year.[4]

What are the attractiveness messages that fill the media? Researchers who have reviewed current magazines see an ongoing trend toward thinness in American culture. Women in these magazines are 13–19% thinner that what is considered healthy and normal.[5] This can be compared to descriptions of body weights below 15% of expected weight as part of the criteria for eating disorders such as anorexia nervosa. This cultural emphasis on thinness is seen as a significant contributor to the prevalence of eating disorders among college women. We will address the topic of eating disorders in Chapter 13.

Overall as a culture, we seem to be internalizing social norms for what is and what is not attractive, and these standards seem to have a direct link to media images.[6] These norms involve unrealistic images of thinness from air-brushed photographs of ultra-thin models and beauty standards for men and women that are narrowly defined and reflective of external criteria rather than the inward qualities of an individual.

The result of this media barrage is that it impacts a host of attitudes such as ideals for beauty, dating, sexual stereotypes, dieting, fashion, and so on. For many, these media images have a strong influence on body image. Much research has reported the influence of the media on the body image satisfaction of college women. College students, who compare themselves to others, indicate that they are very dissatisfied with their own body image.[7,8] In a study examining the influence of fashion magazines on body image, college women reported higher levels of dissatisfaction with body image and the desire to weigh less, compared to those reading news magazines. For young women who already experience body dissatisfaction, exposure to health and fitness magazines can result in even greater levels of dissatisfaction with one's body.[9,10] Research investigating these distorted images suggests that, undergraduate women who are concerned about their own body shape rate thin women in the media as being thinner than they actually are, while women less concerned rate them accurately.[11] The women in this study that felt poorly about their own body shape believed that the images of women in the media were much thinner than they actually are. This demonstrates the connection between standards in the media and the way people see themselves. These media standards can result in distorted images of the way we see ourselves and others.

The drive to be attractive and to look like media images is apparent throughout American culture. The college campus is a place in which students are together in large numbers, often scrutinizing one another and competing with one another. This environment can potentially contribute to the pressures and anxiety experienced by individuals at a time when, as was discussed previously, identity development and a deeper understanding of self and others is being formed.

For both men and women, the ongoing media images, the pressure to adhere to certain standards for physical attractiveness, and the comparisons between students on campus—all these may contribute to a view of oneself that is less than perfect. Many students find that the college campus only adds to negative feelings about themselves and feeds a sense of low self-esteem. Low self-esteem often goes hand in hand with anxiety. As we have seen, anxiety is often associated with negative self-appraisals. Low self-esteem is characterized by feelings of insecurity. When insecure, one is more vulnerable to social pressures, expectations, and challenges.

So how can a student struggling with a sense of low self-esteem respond to these pressures from without and feelings from within? A strategy that has been found to be helpful is to strengthen one's self-esteem. Building a positive sense of self can be compared to building a house. This "house," as we will refer to it, can be constructed with a solid foundation, a roof that is strong and storm-proof, and thick, protective walls. In the next few sections, we will use these construction terms to illustrate important concepts that can improve self-esteem and offer protection from the negative messages in the college environment and beyond.

IDEAS FOR CHANGE

Building Self-esteem

Building a healthy sense of self-esteem begins with understanding two concepts regarding a person's self: the self-concept and self-worth.[12] The self-concept was discussed in Chapter 3. Self-concept relates to the idea of identity and knowing who we are. In order to build self-esteem, we need to have a good understand of our self-concept—those characteristics that make us who we are. Some strategies for strengthening self-concept were discussed in Chapter 3.

The second area of focus regarding self is the idea of self-worth. Once we have established some ideas about who we are (self-concept), we can attach value to this identity or in other words, increase our self-worth. A positive sense of self can only be built when there is a willingness to view oneself as a good person worthy of good things. For some individuals this is a new way of seeing themselves. What about you? Perhaps it is difficult to look at yourself in this way. This section of the book will help you to begin constructing a positive self-esteem by focusing on three areas that include: taking care of your needs, learning to find value in you, and developing a positive inner voice.

Foundation: Taking Care of Your Needs

The construction of a self-esteem "house" begins with a good, solid foundation. People who experience low self-esteem often find it difficult to focus on their own needs and take care of themselves. There can be many reasons for this. Perhaps an individual was not well taken care of as a child. When a child's needs are not met, it is hard to know how to meet those needs as an adult. Maybe the individual had a number of siblings to care for, or a parent struggling with ill health or other problems, and this left little time or energy for learning to care for oneself. Other circumstances in life such as a lack of financial support, an unsupportive environment, or even cruel teasing by peers can create a situation in which a person's basic needs are not met.

Whatever the situation, the outcome may be that a person develops negative self-esteem. The good news is that this outcome can be changed. As emerging adults we need to learn to recognize our needs and meet them in appropriate ways. The first step is to identify our needs, and for the reasons already mentioned, this may seem like a huge hurdle. One way to begin this process is to review a list of basic human needs and reflect on what we may have lacked while growing up. This exercise is not intended to cast blame on anyone. None of us had a perfect childhood and we all have needs that were not met perfectly. This exercise is designed to make it possible to recognize basic needs that may have been unmet and may still be unmet in the present. The following list is a summary of some basic human needs and may be helpful in building an awareness of areas that may be lacking in a person's life. As you review it, notice any areas that seem to apply to you.

The second step in this process is to learn to meet these needs in appropriate ways. This may take some thought and planning. Here's an example. Perhaps, due to a very chaotic home environment, an individual never had a sense of making progress toward a goal. In this case, the individual may want to set some attainable goals in college that will provide a sense of accomplishment as these goals are met. One way to begin meeting this need is to set small goals that can be accomplished in a short amount of time, keeping track of progress along the way. As smaller goals are achieved, medium size goals can be established and the individual will have an ongoing sense of accomplishment. Perhaps you identified some unmet needs in the previous exercise. The next step is to learn to meet those needs in a positive fashion. Take a moment to review some of your own unmet needs (box 5.1). Based on the goal-setting example, think about how you

Box 5.1   Basic Human Needs

Need	Met or Unmet
Physical safety and security	
Financial security	
Friendship	
Attention of others	
Being listened to	
Guidance	
Respect	
Validation	
Expressing and sharing feelings	
Sense of belonging	
Nurturing	
Physically touching and being touched	
Intimacy	
Loyalty and trust	
A sense of accomplishment	
A sense of progress toward goals	
Feeling competent in some area	
Making a contribution	
Fun and play	
Sense of freedom, independence	
Creativity	
Spiritual awareness	
Unconditional love	

Source: Adapted from Bourne, E.J. *The Anxiety and Phobia Workbook* (CA: New Harbinger Publications, 2005).

might begin to meet those needs. Then write out your thoughts about meeting those needs.

The Walls: Find Value in You

The next area of focus in the construction of positive self-esteem is to learn to find value in ourselves. This helps to provide structure and to positively define who we are. We learn to value ourselves in three ways. First, learning to do good self-care is essential for this process of valuing ourselves. Second, we can more effectively attribute value and worth to ourselves when we learn to be a good friend to the inner self. This idea will be developed more fully in the chapter. It may be a bit difficult to grasp, but it is effective. And finally, we can learn to value the self-concept by giving ourselves positive feedback.

Self-care. Self-care is essential to building self-esteem. Individuals with low self-esteem are sometimes able to take care of others but they find it very difficult to do good self-care. Caring for ourselves is a fairly simple thing to do, but many of us don't take the time to do it. Self-care is about doing something nice for yourself or doing something which you enjoy. It involves little things like taking time to relax, taking a walk, watching a good movie, taking a nap when tired, listening to music, exercising, or reading a book (for relaxation—not for class).

Perhaps the following list (box 5.2) will get you started and you can add your own unique self-care items. It's good to keep a list like this close at hand and maybe even schedule self-care time into your week.

Be a friend to your inner self. We mentioned earlier that another way to value yourself is to be a friend to the inner you. What does it mean to be a friend to your inner self? This may seem strange but it's actually an important idea. Think about how we treat our friends. We usually invest in our friends by getting to know them. We focus on what we like about them and what makes them special. We enjoy spending time with them and focusing on the qualities that make them unique.

Being a friend to your inner self is similar to that. It means getting to know yourself by thinking about your dreams and your goals for the future. It means looking at yourself as you would look at a friend. What do you like about yourself? What things do you do well? What are your unique talents or abilities? What are some things about you that set you apart? These are excellent things on which to focus. Box 5.3 provides a worksheet that may be helpful.

Box 5.2   Self-care Activities

---

1. Listen to your favorite music
2. Take a long hot shower or bath
3. Read a novel
4. Take a nap
5. Go for a walk at a nearby zoo or botanical garden
6. Implement a regular exercise program
7. Do something fun with a friend
8. Create something (write a poem, sculpt, paint, finish a scrapbook)
9. Take pictures of beautiful scenery
10. Call or email someone you love
11. Play basketball, tennis, Frisbee, or a game with a friend

   Make your own list of self-care activities

Box 5.3   Being a Friend to Me

Categories	What I Know About Me
Goals and dreams for the future	
Things I like about me	
Things I do well	
My unique talents and abilities	
Things that set me apart	
Other	

Now that you've taken some time to think about what makes you valuable, review the list. Then, just like you would treat a friend, begin to focus on these things and develop an appreciation for yourself.

Give yourself positive feedback. The final step in learning to value yourself is to begin to give yourself positive feedback. Here's where the list comes in. We all need reminders about what makes us valuable. Positive self-esteem can be developed by taking time to review your list each week or more often if needed. One helpful technique is to read the list and make positive statements about yourself. For example, "I like my sense of humor." "I make others laugh and I think this provides encouragement to them." This positive feedback will become more a part of your identity if you practice this regularly.

There are other ways to increase positive feedback in your life. You can give yourself mental compliments when you do something that you are proud of, write about yourself in a journal, or jot a positive comment on a post-it-note and put it on your mirror. You can enlist the help of other people as you work on this. Ask friends about what positive things they see in you. Most of us receive compliments from friends, family, or professors. It's good to write down these compliments rather than dismissing them. This is valuable information that can be used to increase your sense of value and strengthen your self-esteem.

The Roof: Develop a Positive Inner Voice

Finally, self-esteem is enhanced as we construct a sense of protection from the forces around us that tear us down. This sense of protection is actually a positive inner voice that will shield us from influences around us such as cultural expectations and comparison with others. A positive inner voice can also help us cope with our own negative feelings and thoughts.

The place to start constructing this protective inner voice is to look first at any negative messages we are giving ourselves through negative self-talk and other negative patterns of thinking. At some point in time we all encounter a negative way of thinking about ourselves. This negative view of self can include thoughts such as:

- "I can't do this as well as she does."
- "I'm such a failure."
- "Oh, I messed up again."
- "I don't deserve to have good things happen to me."

When this negative self-talk is our primary source of information regarding who we are, it can lead to negative feelings, such as anxiety and low self-esteem.

So how does an individual overcome these negative self-thoughts and develop a positive inner voice? Chapter 11 describes ways in which we can identify our negative thoughts and begin to adopt new and more positive thoughts. However, here are a few ideas that may get you started.

- Identify—begin by identifying negative thoughts about yourself.
- Challenge—challenge those thoughts. Ask: "What is true about this negative thought?" "What is false about this negative thought?"
- Transform—exchange the negative thoughts with new, positive thoughts.

Example:
Identify—I can't do this as well as she can. *I should be able to.*
Challenge—Right! I can't. (true) I have to do as well as she does (false). No I don't!
Transform—I do a great job and I can be satisfied with my performance!

The worksheet at the end of this chapter (figure 5.1) summarizes the concepts we have discussed. The exercises in this chapter are designed to provide some practical tools to help individuals make positive steps forward in the way they feel about themselves. It may be helpful to work through each successive exercise and then summarize your learning in the worksheet at the end of the chapter.

SUMMARY

We began this chapter by reviewing the research about our society's norms for attractiveness. We learned, based on research, that feeling good about oneself on the college campus can be challenging. The remainder of this chapter focused on strategies for increasing an individual's value of self and positive self-esteem. So what's the point? How does this relate to looking good? Deep down, most of us realize that the standards for attractiveness in our culture are shallow and focus primarily on the outer characteristics of the person. Genuine attractiveness is found in the unique qualities within each person. The strategies in

Figure 5.1   The Self-esteem House

Positive Inner Voice

Identify Negative Thoughts	Challenge What's True/What's False	Transform

Value Me

Self Care How can I take care of me?	Friend to Self Things I like, do well, dreams, talents, abilities, etc.	Positive Feedback

Taking Care of My Needs

My Need	Plans to Meet that Need
Physical safety and security	
Financial security	
Friendship	
Attention of others	
Being listened to	
Guidance	
Respect	
Validation	
Expressing and sharing feelings	

this chapter are meant to help you recognize what's already in you—those things that others around you value and appreciate every day. Building positive self-esteem will help you in college and beyond and can certainly help you in overcoming your worries and anxieties. The bottom line is to learn to celebrate you. You are one of a kind and worth celebrating, so take some time to value who you are!

CHAPTER 6

Fitting In

A friend may well be reckoned the masterpiece of nature.
—Ralph Waldo Emerson

Hold a true friend with both your hands.

—Nigerian Proverb

When a group of 1586 college students were recruited from 15 colleges and asked about their top emotional/psychological issues, anxiety ranked in the top ten.[1] As has been discussed, anxiety can be caused by the many changes occurring during this time of life as well as the factors unique to the college campus. Anxiety has been shown to impact students' academic performance and to influence whether or not they will go on to graduate from college.[2,3] Anxiety and the difficulties it creates can affect success in a student's motivation to achieve, ability to develop and work toward academic goals, self-confidence in academic abilities, and an overall concept of self.

One factor that seems to be help students to deal with the stress experienced in college is a good social support network. In fact, research suggests that high levels of social support can provide protection from the experience of emotional distress.[4] Students who have higher levels of social support are more likely to have a buffer that will make them more resistant to stressors and the emotional difficulties that increased stress can cause. We experience this "protection" because supportive friendships provide opportunities to share positive emotions with others as well as offering a sense of stability during difficult times.[5]

So what is a social support network? This type of network involves being connected to supportive friendships with peers both on and off campus, involvement in campus activities, relationships with professors and college staff members, and the broader network of family and other off-campus attachments. A social support network involves levels of friendship that provide support in a variety of ways. As you know, life on campus isn't perfect and, at times, conflicts in relationships occur. When students have higher levels of social support they are better able to deal with difficulties that arise from discord in relationships. For example, supportive roommates may be a source of comfort when breaking up with a boyfriend or girlfriend. This kind of support leads to a greater sense of well-being and offers a safeguard against burnout in college.[6,7]

How can this concept be defined? Important elements of this concept include: 1) a sense of being supported in relationships—students actually feel that they have social support, 2) being involved socially on campus, and 3) feeling positive about the campus environment itself. How is your social support on campus? Below are some questions to help you evaluate your own social support.

COLLEGE SOCIAL SUPPORT

1. Feelings about social support: Do you feel you have groups of people around you who are encouraging and supportive (i.e. friends, roommates, family members)? Is it easy to meet new people? Do you have a few close friends with whom you can share personal thoughts and feelings? Do you feel there is a positive quality to your relationships with peers, professors, and others on campus?

2. Social involvement: Do you feel connected to the college campus? What campus activities are you involved in? Would you like to see more activities or different types of activities? Does your campus provide enough opportunities to get involved? How easy is it to get involved?

3. The college environment: How do you feel about the size of the institution? Do you have access to enough supportive resources for academic, social, emotional, spiritual, or financial needs? What do you like and dislike about the physical layout of the campus? How do you feel about facilities such as classrooms, dorms, dining area, study areas, and places for recreation?[8]

The social life of the college student is a topic that has received a great deal of attention, as young adulthood is a time of constructing intimate relationships and supportive friendships. In addition, an individual's ability to build social support networks is essential to a successful transition into college life. However, there can be both positive and negative elements to the college social environment.

We have discussed the positive aspects but let's focus for a moment on some of the negative aspects of the social sphere of the college experience.

Although the social aspects of college offer important benefits, college social life also carries the potential for difficulties that can increase anxiety and emotional distress. Not all social interactions are positive. Some students find that dorm life is difficult. Living in small spaces in crowded conditions can increase emotional distress. Even though social support is normally beneficial, extended periods of time in crowded living situations can actually erode the positive buffer of social support making it ineffective in protecting students from stress.[9]

The shared life of the college campus can lead to escalation of other difficulties. Environmental stressors such as increased noise levels acting together with social activity can sometimes increase anxiety in college students.[10] Shared life can also be problematic for students who live with individuals that have significant emotional or psychological difficulties. Even though a student has never had emotional or psychological difficulties prior to coming to college, living with someone with these types of problems may increase anxiety or lead to depression or other types of problems.[11]

Students who come to campus with personal difficulties may find it very challenging to adjust to the social aspects of the college environment. Students who have had problematic childhoods may have a great deal of difficulty in being able to build the necessary supportive social networks. Another important consideration is that emotional and psychological problems such as depression and a number of anxiety disorders can begin to emerge in the college years. Students who are encountering an emerging disorder such as social anxiety may experience social isolation, difficulties integrating into campus life, and discomfort in a variety of social interactions.[12] Students struggling with these symptoms may find that trying to adjust to an increasingly social environment can be an incredibly difficult challenge. In Chapter 7 we'll address shyness and social anxiety in more detail.

Some students adjust to their social surroundings naturally and comfortably. But many students find they need assistance in building skills and confidence for assimilating socially at college. Later in the chapter there is a section that offers a guide to making social connections. It covers topics which include taking the initiative in social settings, deepening connections, and dealing with fear related to initiating social interactions. But let's focus first on Jessica's story.

Jessica is in the first semester of her sophomore year. College has been a real struggle for Jessica. She was always labeled a "shy girl" as she grew up and found it difficult to make friends. Once she made friends, she developed deep relationships and enjoyed her small group of acquaintances very much. Jessica was very torn as she left her high school friends and came to Middle States University. Her parents really pushed her to follow her dream of becoming a teacher and this school definitely had the best teaching program around. This year as she began her education classes, Jessica had a sense of meaning and excitement as she began to realize her dream of teaching Kindergarten.

The classes are keeping her in school but the daily isolation she feels is almost too much to bear. Last year she was thrown into a large and crowded dorm and found it almost impossible to get to know anyone. This year she is in a smaller dorm but she feels that she is surrounded by cliques. She believes that everyone in her dorm and in her classes belongs to some sort of group and she is totally alone. Worse, she feels no one would want to get to know her and draw her into their group.

Although she loves her classes, Jessica is considering leaving Middle States University. However, she is afraid that even in a smaller college she won't fit in. She just doesn't believe that she can make friends and she longs to be back with her group of friends at home. Unfortunately, they have all gone off to different colleges.

If you find that you have trouble "fitting in," you may have the belief that those who do are funnier, smarter, or more attractive. This is not likely the case. One major difference is that people who seem to fit in *believe* that they belong. As we have discussed elsewhere in this book, feelings and behaviors are related to beliefs. If you believe you belong, then you will likely feel and behave as if you do, and others will accept that idea as well.

There are probably a number of thoughts and beliefs that you experience that contribute to feeling apart from others, or inferior to them. We will examine some of those in this chapter. Before doing so we need to make some distinctions between different kinds of thought processes and the impact that they have on you. These basic ideas stem from the pioneering work of Aaron Beck, M.D., the founder of cognitive therapy, one of the most frequently used and effective forms for psychological therapy today.

OUR THINKING ABOUT FITTING IN

Self-talk

While we are often unaware of it, we have a running commentary about moment to moment experiences. Self-talk can be positive or negative. We can encourage ourselves with self-statements like "you can do it" or hold ourselves back with self-talk like "you are going to make a mistake." Self-talk has a powerful effect on emotions. Fortunately, we are able to change this "inner dialogue."

Automatic Thoughts

Automatic thoughts are a form of self-talk that have a tendency to "pop into one's head" in specific situations. Automatic thoughts have a fleeting and, well, automatic nature. They have become recurring patterns of thinking. These are the well-worn put-downs and disparagement that so easily come to mind when we're anxious and insecure. They tend not to be noticed but have a powerful effect on feelings and behavior. Automatic thoughts can include images (e.g. of past difficult social experiences), or thoughts (no one will like me). Automatic thoughts can be changed but first they must be identified and examined.

Beliefs

Beliefs are ingrained ideas that have arisen over time. They are more fundamental than self-talk and automatic thoughts. They tend to persist across situations and influence the way we perceive the world. An example of a belief related to social life is "I am not good at talking to people." Beliefs are more difficult to change than the others, but they can be changed and greatly affect how one feels and perceives the world.

Jessica is experiencing difficulties in fitting in. Many students face what Jessica is dealing with but they move forward and begin to find relationships on campus. Jessica has not been able to make the adjustment to college and this may impact her plans for the future. She is most likely dealing with some specific and powerful automatic thoughts that hold her back. She has beliefs that keep her from taking the initiative that would help her to make friends.

IDEAS FOR CHANGE

Identifying Thoughts

Let's focus on Jessica's story and discuss some ways in which she can begin to address her problem. Remember that there is a more detailed discussion of coping strategies later in the book. First, Jessica needs to understand her thought processes and how they impact her in social environments. She needs to *identify* these thoughts. As noted earlier in the book, it may be useful for her to monitor and write down her thoughts.

Once Jessica understands some of her automatic thoughts and self-talk, it will be helpful for her to reflect on how these thoughts make her feel. In her case, these thoughts are associated with anxiety and perhaps thoughts of inadequacy in making social contacts. Unfortunately, these thoughts seem to prevent her from taking steps to build relationships.

Building on her understanding of automatic thoughts and self-talk, Jessica needs to go deeper to understand the underlying beliefs that she has about herself and the social world. Remember that Jessica was always *labeled* a "shy girl" and she has come to believe that she is shy and incapable of making new friends.

Challenge the Thoughts

Jessica can accept her thoughts as they are. She can believe that these are the facts about her and the people around her on campus. Or she can look at her thoughts more objectively and find some other ways to view them. She can *challenge the thoughts*—this is the next step in changing the situation. Our thinking is central to the experience of anxiety. The good news is that the way we think can be challenged and transformed. There are questions that Jessica can ask about her self-talk such as:

- What is the evidence for or against this thought or belief?
- Might there be other ways of looking at the thoughts?
- What if the thought is true; how can I cope and what does it mean?
- Are there skills that I can gain that can help me in social situations?

Let's begin by looking at Jessica's belief that she is shy and incapable of making new friends. Beliefs such as this tend to be focused only on our weaknesses. These beliefs do not take into account evidence that may support other conclusions. In this case, Jessica can reflect on past experiences such as her success in building a few close friendships in high school. Or, she can focus on the fact that while people may view her as shy, they are not likely to draw negative conclusions about her character or what she could bring to a relationship. Many people recognize that shy individuals typically are more open and comfortable with those with whom they've become familiar. While it may be difficult for Jessica to take the initiative and begin to make friends, she has done it before and she can do it again. She can focus on her success in the past and begin to change her beliefs about herself.

It is true that Jessica tends to be quieter than some of the other people she sees on campus. However, her friends in high school found her to be a warm and caring individual and they truly valued her friendship. It is important for her to recognize these qualities so that she can feel comfortable about reaching out to others.

Jessica's story shows how she can begin to *identify* and *challenge* negative thoughts regarding her ability to connect socially on the college campus. As we have discussed previously, it is also important to change behavior. In addition to dealing with her thoughts, it would be helpful for Jessica to begin to change her behavior by becoming more proficient with the nuts and bolts of social interactions. Perhaps she could work at developing some basic communication skills so that she will feel more comfortable.

Acquiring better social skills will provide confidence and practical steps for getting to know others and can open the door to building significant friendships at college. This next section offers some suggestions.

MAKING SOCIAL CONNECTIONS

You are certainly not alone if you find it difficult to take the first step and initiate connections with people in social settings. Taking the initiative to make social connections involves some basic skills that, with practice, can improve and even feel natural. Basic communication involves the following fundamental concepts:

1. Prepare—Before taking the initiative it helps to make some basic preparations. This is similar to taking an exam and one of the ways to perform well on a test is to prepare—to study. Preparation for social situations is much the same. If you've struggled in the past, you may not want to remember those experiences. However, if you work at taking perspective you are likely to learn some important information that can help you prepare for the present. Another preparation strategy is to review a list of conversation topics and a list of conversation starters so that you will know what to say when you encounter the individual or group with which you want to connect. We'll talk about this in more detail in a later section. And finally, it may be helpful to rehearse in your mind what you plan to do. Athletes do this in order to have a successful performance, so this is a proven strategy. Just think about how you will approach the group or individual, what you will say, and how you will present yourself, and then imagine a positive outcome.

2. Present yourself confidently—Feeling good about taking the initiative socially involves a sense of confidence. This can be challenging for many individuals. Presenting yourself confidently involves demonstrating body language that puts others at ease. This body language includes maintaining good eye contact, having good posture, and demonstrating an open and inviting stance and expression. Sometimes it is helpful to practice this by looking in the mirror. Ask yourself—What do I look like when I present myself confidently? Then pose that way and practice so that it feels more natural. Another way to improve confidence is to focus less on oneself and more on the other person. Become an active listener and tune in to the needs of the other person. Think about how to be helpful to the person with whom you are interacting. This can be a very effective strategy for presenting yourself confidently.

3. Practice—Another fundamental concept to remember is that social interaction, just like any other skill, can improve with practice. Think about this as you would about learning to play the piano. When learning to play the piano an individual will learn simple melodies and practice until they become fairly comfortable to play. Then new and more complex pieces will be added so that skills are developed over time. In the same way, practicing social skills should begin with small encounters and then practiced until there is a level of comfort. So if talking with one person is fairly easy, it would be best to practice this and gradually add conversations with two or three people and so on until interacting with large groups becomes comfortable. Whatever is most challenging for you can be practiced in small steps until it becomes a natural part of the way you relate to people.

The next section outlines the steps that are involved in taking the initiative to reach out socially. Taking the initiative begins with observation. Observation of your surroundings is important when you encounter a social setting such as time in the dorm or the student union. Look around to see if there is an individual or small group of students that seems open to a newcomer. The second section offers practical suggestions that are helpful as you begin to step out and initiate. And finally, the last section provides a list of recommendations for taking initial steps in making conversation.

Take the Initiative

Observe:

1. Focus on small groups of students or individuals that you would like to meet.
2. Listen to their conversation and think of things you both have in common.
3. Check to see if they seem open to talk with you or have you join the group.

Initiate:

1. Find the right setting: Choose to be involved in activities you enjoy and can meet people who have similar interests. Look for good opportunities to meet people such as one person sitting alone, breaks before class starts, small groups that seem open and inviting, or meal times when people are relaxed and open to talk.
2. Make sure your body language matches your intentions. Social discomfort often is accompanied by a blank expression or limited eye contact—let your gestures and facial expression communicate information about you as well. And be sure to notice the body language of others. The person waiting for a ride who seems to be noticing or acknowledging passers-by is communicating a different message than the person reading who doesn't raise his/her head.
3. Approach people with a gracious attitude and focus on them: What can I learn about this person? How can I be helpful to this person? This group seems interesting and I want to find out about their interests.
4. Prepare ahead of time: Plan a short "commercial" about yourself (where you're from, interests, hobbies, subjects you like at school). Develop lists of questions you can ask others.
5. Take the first step: Approach the person and introduce yourself. Make good eye contact. Begin with some easy comments about the weather or what happened over the weekend. Ask the first question or two and listen to learn about them.

Make Conversation:

1. Start simple: Ask questions, listen, respond to their answers, and exchange information.
2. Ask questions and use their answers to move on to more topics.
3. Be positive: Use positive language and say positive things about the person when appropriate.
4. Exchange information (see the Conversation Starter list below).
5. Ask open-ended questions that require an explanation rather than just yes or no questions.

6. Talk about half of the time. Conversation is more comfortable when it is a balance of talking and listening.

7. Express appreciation: "I've really enjoyed talking with you." "It's been fun getting to know you." "We seem to have a lot in common."

Some people are very outgoing and never seem to have difficulty in developing topics to start conversations. For most of us though, it takes some work to go into new situations and begin conversing comfortably with new people. One way to overcome some of the discomfort associated with making conversation is to develop a list of conversation starters and topics of conversation. Some of the most effective communicators do this and some even carry a list with them as a reminder of what to talk about in case they run out of ideas. The following list may be a good place to start to develop your own list along with a new sense of confidence.

Conversation Starters and Topics

- Talk about the current situation such as: "What do you think of this class?"
- Ask for information (directions, assignments, etc.) "I'm not sure I understand what she's asking; do you?"
- Use current events. "I can't wait until the election is over. These ads keep getting worse and worse."
- Exchange information regarding:
  ○ Classes you are taking or choice of major
  ○ Campus activities and interests on campus
  ○ General personal interests such as movies, music, TV shows, hobbies, sports. "I just started watching this show...it's pretty interesting."
  ○ Previous history such as where you grew up, parents and siblings, vacations, friendships, accomplishments in high school or summer jobs. "Were you in choir last year?" "I like your sweatshirt, are you from there?"
- Talk about feelings: "I like this, this is fun;" "That activity was boring;" "That news story made me sad," and so on. Feelings are a window into the inner person and it helps to share a bit of who you are.

We have talked about a number of ways to make it easier to relate to people in social settings. However, some individuals may deal with more fear than others when it comes to reaching out to others. Perhaps there is shyness or for some students coming from a small rural setting, the university campus is overwhelming and interacting with others is a bit frightening. The next section offers some basic ideas on how to handle your fears as you learn to reach out and meet people. If you struggle with fear that seems overwhelming in social settings, it may be helpful for you to read Chapter 7.

Handling Your Fears

1. Learning to relate socially without fear takes practice so looking for "easier" opportunities to interact with people (such as one-on-one or in small groups) will help you to overcome your fears.

2. If new situations are particularly difficult, it may help to practice initiating conversations by role-playing this skill with a trusted friend, family member, or a counselor in your campus counseling center.

3. Learn some relaxation techniques that will help you manage your anxiety. Deep breathing is easy to learn, and easy to implement when you start to feel nervous. Various relaxation techniques are introduced in Chapter 12.

4. Practice thinking differently. The way in which you feel about the possibility of rejection is determined by how you interpret or frame the experience. If you go into it as a "test" of your character or physical attractiveness, you are likely to personalize and lose perspective. *All or nothing* thinking is another common error—the tendency to see yourself as acceptable or not. All too often, when initiating with potential friends, our self-talk sounds like "She's so popular, why would she ever be interested in me?" or "My life's so boring compared to theirs." Challenge the thinking by examining some of the other explanations or ways of interpreting the situation. This is hard, because old, habitual put-downs come so readily. Take a different angle. Try to think of five different reasons why someone would like to talk with you. When you first begin to experience anxiety in a social situation, say to yourself, "I'm excited about getting to know John, and even though it's a challenge, it will be good practice." Coach yourself with some more affirming and realistic statements about yourself and what is likely to happen.

Hopefully you have found some of these ideas helpful. However, some students find that it is also difficult to continue these interactions and actually make progress toward developing friendships. How do you go beyond the first conversations about surface information and begin to talk about things that are more important? The next section offers some suggestions for strengthening the bond of friendship as you interact with others on campus.

Strengthening the Friendship Connection

1. Share what has been happening in your life and ask the same. This might sound obvious, but becoming friends means gradually keeping our "finger on the pulse" of the other's daily life. This can include keeping up with their classes, asking about their important relationships, or learning about the ways in which they connect with their family.

2. Share entertaining stories—humor is a wonderful bond! Good friends will take time to share things that lighten our days, not just the troubles and concerns.

3. Share more personal information such as dreams, goals, values, and hopes for the future. These topics usually develop over time, but as a college student, you have many opportunities to connect aspects of daily life with future plans and hopes.

4. Find ways to encourage your new friend—notes, kind words, being willing to listen, and so on. As they say, talk is cheap. While early in the friendship you may be saying that you value the relationship, it is your actions, over the long run, that speak of your interest and commitment in the friendship.

5. Show interest in what seems important to your friend. Make time to listen and explore those areas of a friend's life that may not intersect with yours. Too often it feels safe or easy to stay with the realm of your common interests and goals.

6. Remember to share yourself—being open and willing to be known helps to grow a friendship.

DATING ANXIETY

Aside from public speaking, there is perhaps no circumstance that is more associated with anxiety in the minds of most people than approaching a person in whom one is romantically interested and asking them on a date. Then, there is the challenge of actually going on that date, hoping that things will "click" and there will be more opportunities to get to know the person and let them get to know you. The hope is, of course, for continued connection and formation of a meaningful relationship.

There are some excellent resources for dating that are noted at the end of the book. But let's review some of the important considerations in dating, starting with a discussion of some myths about dating. Myths often contribute to the development of unreasonable pressures and expectations, neither of which are helpful when dealing with situations associated with anxiety.

A common myth about dating involves the assumption that there is only one partner out there; the true soul mate. The task of dating is often framed as an attempt to find "the one." Yet, there are, in fact, many potential partners out there. There are people who can bring very different qualities to a relationship. It is important to look at relationships in multidimensional terms. Each of us has a set of needs that are met to a great or lesser extent in any relationship. Implicit in the myth of the single soul mate is the notion that there is one person who can meet all of our needs. There exists no such person. Perhaps, instead, you could approach each potential romance as a step toward finding someone in the future who has many of the qualities you need and admire. Dating and relationships are an opportunity for you to learn more about yourself and what you want and deserve from a partner. If you approach new relationships in this way, rather than looking for permanency or perfection, you are likely to experience less pressure and anxiety.

Another myth about dating follows similar lines, and involves an assumption that we must go about it with a great deal of time, attention, or with expectations that we show our "best" at all times. Infusing the task of dating with a sense of pressure, urgency, and performance expectations can enhance anxiety in an already anxiety-provoking task for many. All of us are familiar with friends or family who began successful relationships in casual or unexpected circumstances.

There is truth in the idea that someone comes along when you least expect it! If you struggle with fears about meeting someone special, it is recommended that you find ways of reducing the demands on yourself and focus instead on building meaningful relationships of all kinds. By realizing that you can only control so many factors in a situation, you'll be better able to step back a bit and let things unfold.

Dating is a process that does involve some skill. The skills already discussed in this chapter, such as how to initiate conversations and how to listen effectively, are important. In dating, it can be helpful to give yourself the time and "space" to increase your social and communication skills. Again, the more you can look at dating as an opportunity to enhance important social and interpersonal skills that will be helpful for you throughout life, rather than as a kind of race to find the perfect mate, the less anxiety will be associated with it.

It's normal to experience self-doubt, fears of rejection, and other concerns when approaching someone you are attracted to. Perhaps the biggest and most common fear is that of being rejected. In order to be best prepared for dating, one must face the prospect of rejection. It must be accepted that more often than not, a given date does not lead to a long-term relationship. It is a common and normal occurrence that one person will be more interested in pursuing a relationship than the other. If, in your case, it is the other who does not want to pursue things further, it is important that you are able to keep the rejection in perspective. In fact, it can be an excellent opportunity to practice some of the thought strategies that are discussed in this book. It is common, especially among the anxious, to take rejection personally and to assume that there is something wrong with us that contributed to the rejection. While that explanation cannot be ruled out, it is more often the case that rejection speaks more to the fit between you and the other. Did you share interests, an outlook on the world, similar attitudes, and lifestyle factors? These are all important determinants of whether dates turn into long-term relationships. It's possible to become so immersed in personalizing the rejection that you fail to truly evaluate your own perceptions of the relationship. It is a rare person who manages to date, rejection free, and finds themselves in a long-term relationship as a result.

Sarah is a senior in college and had been dating Mark for about eight months and viewed him as the nicest, most supportive boyfriend she every had, but was feeling somewhat restless in the relationship and had been talking with her friends about how she wished he was less quiet and more gregarious. However when he told her that he thought they should shift their relationship back to "more of a friendship" and consider dating others, she found herself anxious and tearful. While he told her he loved her and admired her, he wanted to make the relationship less serious as she was his first girlfriend. He also said he wanted to spend more time with his guy friends. Sarah experienced intense worry, wondering if his decision was based on something that wasn't right about herself. She realized that her worry was causing her to doubt whether she, indeed, was "special" or attractive if she wasn't the most special person in Mark's life, and that she seemed to be placing more value on the relationship now than she gave it before. She was connecting her worth as a person with the status of the relationship.

In some cases, anxiety interferes with stable and relatively secure relationships. Worry can cause unrealistic fears about the prospect of rejection or betrayal. While this may sound like jealousy, it is a little different. An anxious student may truly believe that their partner is faithful and trustworthy, only to become plagued, at times, with doubts or distressing thoughts. ("What if he really wants to be with her?") These worries often lead to needless checking or reassurance-seeking which, as we discussed in Chapter 2, often leads inexorably to more anxious thoughts and a reliance on "being sure." For other students, their worry takes the form of persistent doubting regarding the certainty of their own feelings. ("Am I sure I really love her? . . . What if I really don't care for her in the way that she does me?") If either of these sound like you, we encourage you to turn to Chapter 11, and develop your ability to challenge these fears and reduce your unhelpful anxious behaviors (typically, in this context, facing uncertainty by reducing checking and reassurance seeking).

As we discussed earlier in this chapter, preparation is key to building successful relationships. In the context of dating, being prepared means having some idea of what you are looking for. In a sense, dating is a search process. It must have a purpose. For example, are you looking for a long-term romantic partner, marriage and children, a best friend, companionship? Spend time reflecting on your own needs and desires as you prepare for the task.

In addition to what type of relationship you are looking for, it is important to reflect on the characteristics you are looking for in people. Are you looking for people who are exciting, physically attractive, intelligent, kind, talkative, quiet, serious, have a sense of humor, exhibit particular attitudes and beliefs and interests, have certain personality traits, and so on? How important are these various characteristics? People come as a "package" of characteristics. They may have some qualities that you are looking for but not others. Which are most important to you?

There are two sayings that pertain to dating and each appears to have grains of truth. The first, "birds of a feather flock together" is supported by social psychological research and suggests that people who match each other in attitudes, interests, appearance, and other attributes tend to be more attracted to each other. Becoming aware of your own characteristics can give you clues to the kind of person who may best fit with you. The second saying, "opposites attract" has less general support from psychological research. In general, relationships tend to be most successful when there is general agreement and fit on a number of characteristics. However, it can be the case that the other person can meet complementary needs for us. If we are quiet, we may be attracted to those who are talkative. If we tend to be low-key and hesitant, someone who is rather bold or gregarious can be attractive and help encourage us to move in directions we might not otherwise. So, it is also important to be aware of other characteristics that may be complementary.

Finally, it is important to note that what you are looking for in a person may depend upon what you are looking for in a relationship. If you are looking for a serious, long-term relationship for example, you should look for qualities that will endure after the initial thrill and excitement of a relationship wears off.

After preparation, action is necessary. Another basic truth about dating is that you have to get yourself into places where you'll meet people you're likely to be attracted to. This should match your interests. Take a look at what you like to do and get yourself to places where there are others who share your interests. There are a variety of ways of increasing the likelihood of meeting others and they will only be mentioned here. This includes networking among friends, organizations, clubs, and so on and may mean challenging yourself to really try new things, to extend yourself beyond what feels entirely safe and comfortable. Personal ads or face books provide information about others and may provide opportunities of meeting and connecting. However, just as you wouldn't physically go looking for potential dates in highly unfamiliar or suspicious situations, you don't want to place yourself in a forum on the internet that you're not sure you can trust. There are now a myriad of opportunities for meeting new people. Used wisely, these services can be very helpful in linking you with others with similar interests and characteristics.

While dating can be anxiety provoking, it can be approached in ways that diminish a sense of performance pressure. Dating situations can provide an excellent opportunity to practice and increase your social skills. As previously mentioned, there are some excellent resources for helping you master dating skills.

SUMMARY

Fitting in on campus is an important part of what makes college positive and rewarding. Some students find this part of the college experience to be exciting and challenging, while others encounter barriers and frustration. We have discussed the importance of identifying and challenging anxious thinking that stands in the way of reaching out socially. We've also reviewed a number of strategies for building skill sets that will develop confidence and change negative patterns that may have become ingrained. For some students the social aspect of college is painful and these suggestions need to be supplemented with more specific strategies for the anxiety associated with social encounters. The next chapter will provide excellent information and assistance.

CHAPTER 7

Facing Shyness and Social Anxiety

Scientists have found the gene for shyness.
They would have found it years ago, but it was hiding behind a couple of other
genes.

—Jonathan Katz

WHAT IS SOCIAL ANXIETY?

Social anxiety refers to the fear and apprehension that we all experience at times when relating to other people. Almost everyone, from time to time, has felt nervous speaking in front of a group or when meeting someone for the first time. Many people with social anxiety would identify themselves as shy, but some people who would not identify themselves as shy also struggle with this problem. Shyness and social anxiety are related, yet distinct, and we will discuss that later in this chapter.

The experience of social anxiety is associated with the expectation that one might do something humiliating or embarrassing. As a result, it often involves worry in anticipation of social interactions. We fear what might happen in a social or interpersonal situation. It is also associated with the evaluation that one has already done something humiliating or embarrassing. So, social anxiety can occur after the fact, when we review what has already happened in a social situation.

When socially anxious, you fear that others are judging you (or did judge you) negatively. Self-consciousness can be acute, as there is the expectation that one might do something humiliating or embarrassing. You often become inhibited and then regret that others don't see how you "really are." Like other manifestations of anxiety we have discussed, avoidance is often used as a means (albeit unhelpful) of reducing the worry. Who would want to approach someone at a party if they thought that they would say something inane? Who would want to speak up in a group if they thought their voice might shake or they may blush? In social anxiety, there is a sense that one's inadequacies will be painfully revealed in everyday social encounters and situations.

When social anxiety is pronounced, it can make it difficult to interact naturally and form relationships. It can prevent intimacy, dating, and can be a significant factor in the choice to stay in college or leave.

Individuals with social anxiety have many positive characteristics and much to offer their relationships. However, often in the face of paralyzing anxiety, it is difficult for them to interact spontaneously and naturally. Over time, a person may have lost connection with their likeable qualities (which are many!) and lost most if not all self-confidence. Yet, as with other forms of anxiety, there is help for social anxiety. If social anxiety is a problem for you, the strategies in this chapter and in the book can help you deal more effectively with it.

An Example of Social Anxiety

Take Jason, who is struggling with social anxiety associated with going to parties on campus. He finds that he strongly associates his anxiety about parties to an image of others laughing at him rather than laughing with him. When Jason has been able to get himself to go to a party he experiences significant anxiety, especially when he is in a small group of male peers. Jason is self-conscious about his ability to engage in the kidding and banter that often serves as a way of connecting in this situation. Yet, immediately Jason's self-talk includes such statements as "I'll never fit in," "people will think I'm boring." His automatic thoughts include an image of people laughing under their breath as he unsuccessfully tries to make meaningful contributions to the interaction. Memories of being teased by boys when in middle school intrude painfully in his thoughts. He believes that being witty and funny is critical to being accepted and liked, and that he is incapable of acting in a way that won't result in judgment and criticism by his peers. When faced with the situation, he freezes up and is unable to even say what he wants to say. He then has thoughts like "I have to get out of here" or "maybe a beer will help." Jason feels shaky and notices that he is sweating excessively. He feels stiff, rigid, and unnatural. At the end of the experience, he feels defeated and wonders how he'll ever be able to do the things he wants to do.

Jason's experience has many elements that are commonly associated with social anxiety. First, Jason anxiously anticipates going to the party and has specific and powerful automatic thoughts that rattle him. His beliefs create high expectations and turn a rather ordinary social event into a "performance" that will ultimately determine whether he is accepted or not. Second, he experiences strong physical anxiety reactions that further interfere with his ability to be comfortable with himself in the situation. Third, the symptoms impact his behavior. He has urges to flee, and he leaves the party feeling demoralized.

SOCIAL ANXIETY ALONG A CONTINUUM

While Jason's experience may seem rather severe, social anxiety is a normal experience. Everyone experiences it from time to time. It can range in its intensity from quite mild to completely incapacitating. As such, it is important to determine when social anxiety becomes a problem and begins to interfere with your life. If you remember from Chapter 2, Social Anxiety Disorder, as defined by the Diagnostic and Statistical Manual of the American Psychiatric Association (DSM-IV) is a diagnostic term for situations in which:

- there is a marked and persistent fear of one or more social and performance situations
- exposure to the feared social situations almost invariably provokes anxiety
- the person recognizes that the fear is excessive and unreasonable
- the feared social situations are avoided or endured with intense anxiety

Thus, Social Anxiety Disorder interferes with one's life, causes great distress, and persists for at least six months. In actuality, it takes the judgment of a mental health professional to determine if a diagnosis of social anxiety is appropriate. For our purposes, if you are bothered to a significant extent by social anxiety, or if you characterize yourself as a shy person, you can likely benefit from reading this chapter. If you think you may have Social Anxiety Disorder, then you may want to seek an evaluation from a mental health professional. Social Anxiety Disorder may be one of the most common mental health problems in the population at large. A large-scale study[1] of the prevalence of various mental health problems indicate that up to 13 percent of the population in the United States will meet the criteria for a diagnosis at some point in their lives.

GENDER AND CULTURAL VARIATION

The same study noted above suggested that men and women tend to have social anxiety disorder in roughly equal numbers. Social anxiety is found all around the world. Certainly, the experience of social anxiety varies due to cultural norms and customs, but a fear of embarrassment and humiliation appears to be universal. In fact, there may be an evolutionary basis of social anxiety. Evolutionary psychologists believe that human beings developed the capacity to experience emotions because they possess survival value. We considered the fight/ flight response in Chapter 1 and considered its value in detecting and responding to danger. We humans are social animals who live in groups and preservation of the group is important in human survival. Anxiety in social groups, according to an evolutionary view, helps us assess the degree of threat that others represent and helps us to live peacefully together. Some people, for biological reasons, may be oversensitive to social threats, and thus are prone to social anxiety.

Culture also appears to play a role in what behaviors are deemed embarrassing or humiliating and the situations that tend to provoke social anxiety. For example, in Japan, if one has too much eye contact upon initial meeting, they may embarrass themselves. Just the opposite may be true in the United States. Not making sufficient eye contact with someone you have just met may suggest social discomfort, suspicion, or defensiveness.

A recent study[2] found ethnic differences in social anxiety among college students. Hispanic American and Asian American students were found to have higher levels of social anxiety. There may be a number of explanations for this finding including concerns about fitting in, difficulty finding a community of students with similar backgrounds, concerns about racism, among others. A full explanation of challenges and issues faced by students of color is beyond the scope of this book. However, it is important to consider, if you are an ethnic minority student, you may face additional social and interpersonal challenges that result in higher levels of social anxiety.

SOCIAL ANXIETY AND ALCOHOL

In spite of the legal and health concerns associated with drinking, alcohol consumption and alcohol abuse are common in college life. It has long been the impression of many in the substance abuse treatment field that social anxiety contributes to problems with alcohol. Simply put, alcohol can boost social courage by lowering inhibitions and reducing anxious arousal. Research suggests that, in fact, alcohol can reduce social anxiety in many situations.[3] However, it comes with a cost. It can lead to dependence upon the substance and all of the other negative consequences of excessive alcohol consumption (discussed in Chapter 13). Moreover, while it appears that women and men experience social anxiety in equal numbers, more women than men seek professional help for their social anxiety. This finding may, in part, be the result of more self-medication of social anxiety with alcohol in men. If you drink or use drugs and are socially anxious, it is important for you to reflect on the relationship between the two. Often, anxiety lies at the root of a problem with alcohol or drugs and makes it very difficult to stop using.

SOCIAL ANXIETY AND SHYNESS

Shyness is a term that is commonly used to characterize people who are socially reticent and nervous. Unfortunately, there is no consensus on what constitutes shyness. Shyness as it is commonly understood and described, is frequently experienced in childhood and adolescence. For some, it constitutes a period of social inhibition that abates with time. For others, it continues and for some it lasts a lifetime. Shyness is so common that as many of 40% of adults considered themselves shy to a point that they found it to be a problem. Another 40% of people say that they considered themselves shy in the past.[4]

There are similarities and differences between shyness and social anxiety. You can think of shyness running along a continuum from mild social reticence, to social awkwardness, to extreme forms of intense social withdrawal and inhibition that cannot be meaningfully distinguished from social anxiety disorder. Perhaps the major difference is that for many people, shyness can be a passing phase associated with youth. Most people who start out shy "grow out of it." Some learn to live with it and are able to function relatively comfortably in most social situations. However, some have persistent difficulties and exhib-it social anxiety. So, shyness is kind of a "catch all" term that is often used to describe social anxiety and it overlaps significantly with it. We will use the terms interchangeably throughout this chapter. If you have characterized yourself as shy, then many of the points made in this chapter will apply to you as well.

INTROVERSION, SOCIAL ANXIETY, AND SHYNESS

The personality trait of introversion is often confused with both social anxiety and shyness. Introversion has more to do with a preference for solitary activities rather than social anxiety, nervousness, or wariness. Extroverts draw energy from being with others; often "the more the better." Introverts draw energy from activities that are absorbing, whether or not others are involved. Introverts often have sig-nificant friendships and intimate relationships but are not as drawn to activities that involve superficial social contact, such as parties and gatherings. These activities may be avoided because they are not interesting or preferred ones, not because the person fears them. Both introverts and extroverts can experience sig-nificant social anxiety.

EFFECTS OF SOCIAL ANXIETY

How does social anxiety affect you? As with other manifestations of anxiety, social anxiety tends to affect how you feel, how you think, and what you do. You'll remember that we talked about this in Chapter 2. To help yourself with social anxiety, you will need to focus on thought and action strategies. Figure 7.1 describes some of the common experiences associated with social anxiety. You will not likely experience all of those but rather will have your own unique pattern of experiences.

Figure 7.1   Common Features of Social Anxiety

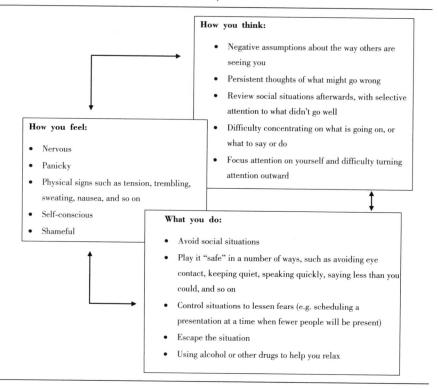

CONTRIBUTORS TO SOCIAL ANXIETY

It is natural to ask the question, "how did I come to be so socially anxious?" Current thinking suggests that there are multiple contributors to social anxiety in any individual's situation. We already mentioned the possible influence of a biological sensitivity to social threat. Negative or traumatic social experiences earlier in life may have contributed. Traumatic events are very stressful at the time that they occur but they often also leave a painful and lasting impression. Socially anxious people often report experiences of having been bullied or teased, particular characteristics or experiences (for example, being "the new kid" or having severe acne) that contributed to a sense of being different, or encountering particularly painful social rejections.

In addition to negative or traumatic experiences, there also may have been factors in the person's family life that played a part. Family interactions provide the early modeling and opportunities for "practice" engaging socially. Some parents do not socialize much themselves (perhaps because they were anxious themselves) and may not have modeled or taught the social and interpersonal skills necessary for the development of social confidence. It is not our intention to discuss all of the possible contributors, though it may be helpful, if you struggle with social anxiety, to reflect on some of the factors that may have contributed in your situation.

SOCIAL ANXIETY AND COLLEGE LIFE

Social anxiety can have a profound effect on one's college career. Below are just some of the situations where social anxiety may appear and be a problem.

- *Choice of classes*: One may experience difficulty in classes where presentations are a part of the course requirements. The fear of speaking in public is very common in the population at large, but can be even more difficult for the person with social anxiety. Aside from presentations, classes that require a great deal of group work can also be challenging. Often people with social anxiety worry about interacting in small groups. Worries can center on a fear of letting others down, or of saying something uninformed or stupid, or of appearing anxious in front of the group. Talking to professors may represent a challenge as well.

- *Life in the dorm*: Dorm life can present a myriad of challenges for the socially anxious. First of all, you are in close proximity to many people much of the time. Privacy is often compromised. An example of how this may be a problem involves what is termed a "shy bladder" (more technically known as *paruresis*). Some people (mostly males) have difficulty initiating urinary flow in public restroom situations or in situations that lack privacy. Clearly this problem can be heightened when living in close proximity to others. In addition, there are opportunities to meet many new people and there can be significant fears of not fitting-in or belonging to the social groups within the dorm. Then, there can be challenges with roommates. You may feel anxious around your roommate or your roommate's friends or have difficulty speaking up and being assertive when necessary.

- *Social life*: Whether or not you live in a dorm, college is typically an intensely interpersonal experience. A significant part of the college experience involves the possibility of establishing and maintaining healthy relationships. Many people find that strong relationships developed in the college years can last a lifetime. Yet, social anxiety can make it difficult for people to establish and maintain relationships. The basics of social interaction (introducing oneself, making small talk) may be quite challenging. As one "gets to know" another, there are increasing pressures to reveal aspects of oneself as the relationship becomes more intimate. For some with social anxiety, it is the initial social contact that is most intimidating, and once that has occurred they feel more comfortable with deepening the relationship. For others, though, the deeper the relationship becomes, the more threatening it feels as there is a fear that revealing oneself to another will result in humiliation, embarrassment, or rejection.

- *Dating*: As discussed in Chapter 6, dating and romantic relationships present challenges for everyone. There is a sense of competition for others one finds attractive, and the problem of finding ways of approaching the other and securing a date.

Then, there is a real possibility of rejection. If one is successful in securing a date, there is the desire to make a strong first impression while revealing enough of yourself to connect in a meaningful way with the other. All of these "tasks" can test your resolve if you are socially anxious.

OVERVIEW OF PSYCHOLOGICAL STRATEGIES FOR MANAGING SOCIAL ANXIETY

There are two areas of focus that have been shown, through research, to be helpful in the management of social anxiety.

1. Thinking strategies involve, as we have discussed throughout this book, identifying, challenging, and transforming anxious thoughts. This requires an examination of how you are evaluating social situations and your own social behaviors. Social anxiety, like other forms of anxiety, is associated with patterns of thinking that may not be accurate or otherwise helpful in navigating the social landscape.

2. Action strategies involve making behavioral changes. For social anxiety, this should involve gradually "facing the dragons" by entering feared situations in order to gain confidence that you can handle them with minimal anxiety. Of course, this "flies in the face" of the natural tendency to want to avoid those situations, and it takes commitment and effort on your part. In addition, it is important to take stock of your communication skills and improve them. This enables you to meet others and interact more easily as well as give presentations and respond more assertively. Don't assume that because you don't know or don't feel comfortable with particular social skills and niceties, you can't learn them. In fact, employers often teach these types of skills to professionals and business people in order to assist them with presentations or client interactions. The bottom line is that we feel more comfortable with any situation that involves the application of skills when we have more confidence in our skills.

In this chapter we will provide an introduction to these strategies. Additional information regarding social and interpersonal skills and dating was reviewed in the previous chapter. If you then feel you need more information, there are several excellent self-help books and workbooks that provide more detailed discussion. A list of resources can be found at the end of the book.

A WORD ABOUT MEDICATION

If your social anxiety is severe, there are a number of medications that may provide help. These include both antidepressants as well as minor tranquilizers. Medications have pros and cons in the management of social anxiety. They can be easy to obtain and to take and they can work quickly. On the other hand, they may have side effects and may be difficult to stop taking. We will not be discussing medication in detail here, but if you have severe social anxiety, you may wish to seek evaluation by a mental health professional and inquire about medication options for social anxiety. If you do consider medication, keep in mind that research on the treatment of anxiety suggests that medication is most effective when combined with psychological treatment strategies.

IDEAS FOR CHANGE

Thinking and Social Anxiety

Thinking plays a central role in social anxiety. This is no surprise. We have emphasized the appraisal of situations, self-talk and automatic thoughts, and beliefs in various parts of this book. When speaking with a group, a socially anxious person might have automatic thoughts that "they think I'm weird" or "they are noticing my discomfort." Negative self-talk might include "I have to get out of here" or "keep quiet." Underneath, there may be beliefs that you don't quite belong or are not smart enough to contribute. These levels of thinking must be identified, challenged, and transformed in order to gain relief.

An important thing to keep in mind when considering the relationship of thinking and social anxiety is that social anxiety affects our attention in two important ways. First, it affects what you notice. Remember the example of Jason earlier in this chapter. He was struggling to make conversation with a group of peers wanting so much to contribute to the humorous banter that seemed to be the communication style of the group. Because Jason is anxious, he is hypervigilant to signs of potential threat in this situation. This may lead him to tune–in to facial expressions that might indicate signs of disapproval. He is essentially trying to "read" the situation. However, we also know from a great deal of psychological research, that people tend to notice things when they are anxious that confirm their fears, and ignore other aspects of the situation that run counter to them. In fact, most nonverbal information that we receive from others is neutral, but it is often interpreted as negative when one is socially anxious. We will talk more about this shortly.

The other way in which social anxiety affects attention is that it turns the focus inward. This can be one of the most frustrating aspects of social anxiety. At the very time when one wants to be paying utmost attention to what others are saying and doing, one is also experiencing painful self-consciousness. At such times, we become painfully aware of ourselves and our perceived shortcomings. Many socially anxious people describe feeling distracted by their internal self-talk, a "judging voice" that comments and criticizes on their every word or reaction.

If you have physical reactions that you are also concerned about, like sweating, blushing, or shaking, you may find yourself monitoring those and worrying whether others will notice or whether they will get worse. For example, Jason may be conscious of feeling stiff, awkward, and uptight while at the same time very much wanting to be natural, loose, and spontaneous.

Becoming Aware of Anxious Thinking

The first step in changing thinking is to become aware of how you are thinking. You need to "hold it up to the light" and examine it. When you are in situations that make you socially anxious, what is your stream of automatic thoughts? You can practice this by imagining a situation in which you experienced social anxiety and recall what you were thinking, as if in slow motion. Try to recall your thoughts as the situation unfolded.

In our example of Jason, he was at a bar with friends who were engaging in amusing banter. He was flooded with automatic thoughts like:

- "I'm weird, they won't like me"
- "I cannot think of anything funny to say"
- "They are noticing that I've got nothing to say"
- In addition, he was self-conscious about his appearance and his symptoms:
- "I feel so stiff"
- "I look so uptight"

Take some time to jot down some of the thoughts associated with a recent episode of social anxiety that you have experienced.

Patterns of Anxious Thinking and Challenges to Them

Social anxiety is typically associated with unhelpful patterns of thinking. You will hopefully recognize some of these patterns from Chapter 6. Below several patterns are noted along with more realistic, healthy perspectives. Do you recognize any of these?

Overgeneralization. Overgeneralization refers to the tendency to jump to a general conclusion based on one item of evidence. An example might include "I couldn't think of what to say with my roommates last night. I always blow it! I'm just no good at talking to people in the dorm." It is important not to make global character judgments based on isolated incidents in which you didn't perform your best.

Catastrophizing. This refers to the tendency to think that if a negative event occurs, it is absolutely terrible and unmanageable. Examples might include "if I blush during this presentation, everyone will notice and it will be a disaster." Another is " what if I can't think of something to say to my date—he'll know that I'm boring." Very rarely are mistakes or negative events actually catastrophic. Sometimes they are not even noticed and at other times the effects on other's impressions of us are minimal or even can be endearing or "humanizing."

Filtering. Filtering refers to the tendency to run events through a kind of sieve and only retaining those that are negative and confirm fears we have about ourselves. You ignore your positive qualities and the social skills that you display; instead you focus on your weak points. Or if someone compliments you, you discount it, thinking, "they only said that to make me feel better." Make sure that you take stock of all the positive qualities you bring to social situations. Many people who are relatively quiet in situations are skilled at making others comfortable, or have good listening skills.

Polarized Thinking. This is associated with perfectionism, a characteristic that we have touched on before. With this pattern, people categorize their behavior and reactions as either completely acceptable or unacceptable without recognizing intermediate possibilities. Examples include "If my voice cracks at the beginning, I will blow the entire presentation." "If I make one dumb comment, they'll never think that I am smart." Rarely does one element of a social encounter determine the entire outcome. In fact, most of the time our behavior in social situations ranges from pretty good to "good enough."

Mind-reading. This term refers to the tendency to guess what others are thinking, based on very little hard evidence and a great deal of speculation. Automatic thoughts that begin with "they are noticing" or "they are thinking" often reflect mind-reading. ("She must think I'm not fun at all.") Keep in mind that the implication here is not that all mind-reading is inaccurate, but that there may be a tendency to engage in more speculative mind-reading when socially anxious. Again, this relates to the selective nature of your attention. Keep in mind that there are other explanations and people may not be thinking at all what you fear they are thinking.

Emotional Reasoning. In social anxiety, this typically involves concluding that you are inadequate because you are feeling embarrassed or humiliated. It goes like this: "I am feeling embarrassed, so everyone must be looking at me and noticing my inadequacy." Emotional reasoning is faulty reasoning. Just because you are intensely embarrassed does not mean that others can see signs of that embarrassment or that something you did is actually humiliating. Now, there are times when "symptoms" of social anxiety can be visible to others, but they are usually not as obvious as one might think or they can be perceived in different ways. For example, sweating may not necessarily be seen as a sign of weakness but rather as a physical condition or simply a difference in the response to room temperature. When anxious, your feelings and self-perceptions are typically not a reliable indicator of others' reactions or your own performance.

Personalization. This refers to taking things personally. It is common in social anxiety to assume that you are the object of scrutiny. There can be a tendency to assume that negative comments or actions made by others are necessarily directed at you. The classic example is someone leaving the room when you are giving a presentation. If you personalize, you assume that their exit resulted from your actions. Again, you want to remember that your anxiety causes you to direct your attention to information that confirms your fears. In challenging this thinking, you want to consider the many other explanations for what happened. In our example this might involve thinking that the individual left your presentation because they had another commitment, or they weren't feeling well.

Fortune-telling. In social anxiety, this typically involves predicting that things will not get better, that because things feel terrible now, they are not likely to change. Examples are thoughts like "I'll always be alone," and "I'll never feel comfortable meeting new people." One of the things we know about anxiety is that it can change. While it may take a great deal of effort and attention, you can feel better.

Using the situations and thoughts that you identified earlier, try to determine whether any of the above patterns of thinking apply to you. Which are the most common in your experience of social anxiety? Jot them down and see if you can generate some challenging perspectives.

Faulty Beliefs

Socially anxious people often hold a number of underlying beliefs and erroneous assumptions. Note how each belief tends to fuel anxiety and how it may be challenged. We've stated these in the extreme as this is the way they often appear in your mind. They may sound dramatic as you read them here, but, in fact, anxious thinking is often characterized by colorful and extreme "self-talk" and one of the challenges in lessening anxiety is to transform such thinking into more moderate and balanced statements.

1. *One must appear perfectly competent at all times.* There is the sense that it is a competitive world and one must always appear competent to be successful. The truth is that no one is always competent and most of us make many mistakes. If one's aim is to be liked and have healthy relationships, competence is an important, but only one of the many attributes that relate to successful interactions.

2. *Others are extremely vigilant and judgmental in social situations.* This is the belief that it is a dangerous social world where others are looking for weaknesses and are ready to exploit them to their advantage. This can be true in some instances, unfortunately. It's possible to find oneself in a group of people waiting with bated breath to pounce on any misstep and put you in your place. In general, however, the social world is fairly forgiving and others are looking to give you the benefit of the doubt. If you find yourself in a judgmental situation, then you have to ask yourself how much that matters to you and whether you want to be there. Do you want to hang around with peers who are so judgmental and what does it say about them that they are so critical?

3. *Others easily notice signs of anxiety, and view them as unacceptable—signs of "weak" character.* This faulty assumption gives anxiety a much bigger role in the way people see us than it deserves. Actually, there is evidence from the field of social psychology that when giving presentations, people who make a mistake tend to be more well received by the audience than those who performed perfectly. In many social situations, people get nervous from time to time and may, in fact, empathize with your discomfort rather then judge it. The irony is that while you fear that your anxiety will create distance and judgment, it often helps to create a connection.

4. *Sharing vulnerability is shameful and unacceptable.* Again, this is the notion that making mistakes, showing that you are fearful, or showing your true self will have very negative consequences. This is similar to the above. In fact, sharing vulnerability and being accepted for who you are, with all of your foibles, is the necessary ingredient for intimacy in relationships.

5. *There are rigid rules for proper and acceptable social behavior and you'd better not break them.* It is true that many of the rigid rules of etiquette in our culture developed as a means of preventing negative behaviors and interactions. Yet, except in the most formal of social circumstances, there are different ways of behaving that are appropriate to a given situation. This seems especially true in the college world where many different styles of dress and social interaction are deemed appropriate. So, let go of some of the pressure and work on being able to be comfortable with who you are. For an expanded discussion of self-esteem and how to build it, check out Chapter 5 of this book.

6. *One must work to impress people to get their admiration and respect.* This is the idea that it is not enough to be you, that you really have to work to be liked. This assumption often leads people to put pressure on themselves to come across better (more well-read, more witty, etc.) when successful interaction is more a matter of letting-go of the effort and being you. While it may be the case that you can benefit from increasing some social skills, most people do better by being themselves. Being comfortable with you goes a long way toward enhancing your ability to connect with others.

7. *Others (not me!) possess the necessary skills to succeed in social situations.* We'll say it once again: People who are anxious are prone to making social comparisons unfavorable to themselves. While there are certainly many very skilled and socially polished people out there, most people lack some skills for social situations. You may tend to underestimate some of the skills you bring to the table and not appreciate the extent to which many of these skills can be acquired through effort.

Changing Faulty Thinking Patterns

In Chapter 11, there is an expanded discussion on how to identify, challenge, and transform your anxious thinking. Take the information that you have gleaned thus far in this book and this chapter and consider the information there. Essentially, to help yourself with social anxiety, you need to identify the patterns that are common for you in social situations. Then, you need to step back and examine your thinking. This involves asking questions about your thoughts and beliefs. By questioning you move toward challenging and transforming your thoughts. With practice, you can think in new ways that make it easier for you to function effectively in social situations.

Action Strategies—Facing the Dragons

So what strategies do you use to do things differently? Essentially these strategies involve facing your fears directly, though gradually, by taking small steps. This involves seeking out situations (yes, that's right, on purpose) that provoke your social anxiety and the urge to avoid. As has been mentioned elsewhere in this volume, avoidance, whether as obvious as not attending a party, or a more subtle form like not saying much in a group, serves to maintain anxiety. When you don't face anxiety provoking situations and use avoidance, you miss out on opportunities to "test" your negative assumptions and experience the worry diminishing on its own (a concept called desensitization). A more detailed discussion of what we call "exposure" strategies occurs in Chapter 11. For now, we will outline the basic features of this approach. Make sure you follow-up with further exploration of this strategy in Chapter 11.

Think of things that you would like to do, but are reluctant to engage in because of your social anxiety. This could include things like asking someone you don't know very well to do something with you, speaking more in a work group for class, inviting someone to your place, or making a difficult phone call. In general, it is recommended that you face the dragons gradually, so it is important to think of all of the things you would like to be able to do and rank order them in terms of difficulty.

Next, it is important to imagine yourself engaging in the behavior. When you do so, you might experience some of the automatic thoughts you noted earlier in this chapter. Think about how you might challenge those. Think of the different ways that the situation may turn out. It will be easy to think of negative outcomes, since that is the way the old anxiety tapes play. But challenge yourself to think of outcomes that are positive or at least more mixed. Finally, make a plan to engage in that activity, in real life, in the near future. When you have, make sure that you reflect on how it turned out with an open mind. Did the outcome confirm your negative thoughts? What are the various ways of looking at what happened? How do you feel about having done it? How were your communication and interactions skills? Are there some skills you might work on? And what skills did you employ—what went well?

Reducing Self-consciousness

It helps to learn to focus attention on things that are happening outside of you. This is not easy. As we have discussed, in the face of social anxiety, thoughts and attention turn inward. As such, it takes special effort to counteract this tendency. As you are trying to do things differently, it is important to willfully try to notice more of the things in your environment beyond the things that you attend to as part of your anxious vigilance. Here's a little exercise. Imagine you are going to a party where there will be very few people you know. There also will be several people who intimidate you. You have avoided these gatherings in the past but consistent with your attempts to overcome anxiety, you decide to try it. Briefly imagine some of the things that you can become afraid of at the party. These should come relatively easily. Now, however, try to imagine a different dimension of the party. Imagine that you are a detached observer of the party. Think about some interesting things that you might want to find out at the party, as if you would be writing a description of it for a local gossip column. Perhaps you would want to observe how a certain person talks to another. Perhaps you'd focus on the surroundings, the décor, or the food. The goal here is to actively "turn the volume down" on your attention to yourself and others' perceptions of you and turn it "up" on the many other aspects of the environment. Choose a few of those and set a goal of exploring them while you are at the party. Practicing this will not only prevent you from engaging in your usual (and unhelpful) patterns of thinking, but also will provide you with new information you can use to effectively challenge and transform your anxiety.

Do I Need to Work on My Social Skills?

It's typically the case that people who are socially anxious tend to *underestimate* their social skills. In fact, there is important research[5] that has found that socially anxious people think that they make a much more negative impression on others than they actually do. As part of their negative self-appraisal, they tend not to give themselves credit when credit is due or recognize that even though they don't socialize in a particular way (e.g. with spontaneous, humorous banter), they possess other valuable skills they offer the situation (e.g. genuine interest in getting to know others, an ability to be nonthreatening and supportive in social interactions).

However, one of the big problems with avoidance of social situations is that, over time, you miss out on opportunities to develop the social and communication skills that would help you deal more effectively with others. If you have been socially anxious for much of your life, perhaps you never learned some basic skills. Now, in college, you find yourself surrounded by social demands and perhaps also have a heightened awareness of the skills that some of your more socially gifted peers possess. While it might be uncomfortable for you, it is important that you "take stock" of your social skills repertoire. The good news is that increasing your social skills will help to lessen your social anxiety. Remember that Chapter 6 provided a discussion of important social skills including suggestions for dating.

Jason Puts the Strategies Together

Identifying his Thoughts. We'll follow Jason's example and discuss some ways in which he can begin to address his problem. First, he has to gain an understanding of his thought processes and their effect on him in social situations. The first task is to *identify* these thoughts. It may be useful for him to do some journaling of his thoughts, ideally by writing them just as they sound in his head, without editing or revising.

Once Jason has come to understand what some of the patterns are in his thinking, it is important for him to reflect on how these thoughts make him feel. In his case, these thoughts are associated with anxiety, vulnerability, and insecurity. In turn, this anxiety results in a "freezing-up" response that adds another layer of difficulty as he is trying to engage with others. The freezing-up response interferes with his ability to relate in a natural and comfortable manner.

In addition to the self-talk and automatic thoughts, Jason needs to gain an understanding of the underlying beliefs that he has about himself and the social world. He does not see himself as funny and thus concludes that he has little to contribute to the interaction. This is combined with a firm belief that being funny is critical for social acceptance in this group. As Jason's thinking doesn't allow for acceptance to come through other means (e.g. laughing with the group and contributing in others ways) he finds himself in a very difficult and anxiety-provoking situation.

Challenge the Thoughts. Jason can either accept his thoughts as they are as immutable facts about himself and the social world—or he can submit them to some scrutiny, much like a scientist. He can *challenge the thoughts*—this is the next step in changing his situation. We have seen that the way one thinks is central to the experience of anxiety, and, fortunately, the way one thinks can be examined and transformed. There are questions Jason can ask about his self-talk such as:

- What is the evidence for or against this thought or belief?
- Might there be other ways of viewing the situation?
- What if the thought is true; how can I cope and what does it mean?
- Are there skills that I can gain that can help me in social situations?

For illustrative purposes, we can start by examining Jason's belief that people will find him boring. He can examine past experiences in social situations. Perhaps there may be some experiences to support the thought, but he can likely find others that don't; times where people either found him reasonably interesting or if not extremely interesting, then likeable. It is often the case when we examine our negative, anxiety-provoking beliefs that the evidence for them is not there, or is *mixed*. Unfortunately, we tend to ignore the mixed nature of the evidence and instead accept and focus on the most negative experiences that support our faulty assumptions.

Let's move on to the second question. We have already begun to answer it. Another way of looking at the thought is to consider that fitting in may have more to do with being likeable and *being oneself* than being funny and interesting. Certainly most people would agree that being funny and interesting helps one be likeable and thus to fit in, but these qualities may not be essential, as Jason's thinking implies. Perhaps he is seeing others in an overly critical and judgmental way, skewed perhaps to some extent by childhood memories of being teased and ridiculed and obviously not accepted by the group from his childhood.

The third question essentially involves the notion of how one would cope with the worse case scenario. In Jason's social dilemma, what if it was indeed true that he wasn't funny or interesting and that he, in fact, failed to fit in because of it? How would he cope? Perhaps examination of this would involve looking at what it means to fit in with a group that has rather strict criteria for membership; that is, being interesting and funny. Does Jason really want to hang out with such a group? Is the rather judgmental nature of this group the norm, or does this group represent the only social possibility, or might this send a message to Jason that it is time to seek out people more like himself?

Perhaps there is a bit of all of these perspectives operating here. The social world is complicated. While being funny and gregarious can be useful, Jason may have other qualities that he "brings to the table" that draw others to him and make him likeable and readily accepted. Perhaps he could work on his sense of humor a bit and spend some time gaining confidence in his conversation skills in order to feel more comfortable. Then, he could try out his new skills in situations of increasing challenge. Jason may never be the proverbial "life of the party," but he could be socially successful by maximizing his positive qualities. Hopefully, this example has illustrated that *identifying* and *challenging* one's perspectives on oneself and social and interpersonal situations can lead to *transformation* resulting in new ways of thinking and behaving.

SUMMARY

To summarize, social anxiety is experienced along a continuum and overlaps with the concept of shyness. Social anxiety can be very debilitating and Social Anxiety Disorder describes the experience of intense and frequent social anxiety. Like other manifestations of anxiety we have discussed, social anxiety is related to feelings, thinking, and behaving. Patterns of negative thinking and avoidance behavior fuel the problem. The hopeful part is that becoming aware of anxious thinking patterns, facing feared social situations, and improving and practicing social skills can lessen social anxiety.

CHAPTER 8

Making the Grade: Academic Evaluation and Test Anxiety

If you can solve your problem, then what is the need of worrying.
If you cannot solve it, then what is the use of worrying.
—Shantideva, eighth-century Buddhist scholar

Testing and evaluation are facts of college life. They provide the most efficient gauge of learning and means of rewarding excellence. Yet, evaluation carries a sharp edge. Some succeed while others fail. Some perform with excellence, and some are deemed average. As a college student, you have become (or are becoming) keenly aware of performance expectations and performance evaluation. There are important outcomes riding on your successful performance in school. Examples include staying in school, retaining financial aid, achieving graduation, distinguishing yourself from your peers, landing that first job, or continuing your education in graduate school. As you know all too well, evaluation of your performance in college involves many "work products" such as papers, written exercises, and class presentations. Although professors are increasingly focused on different learning styles and methods of assessing student performance, the examination or "test" remains the most frequent form of evaluation on the college campus and it's probable you will take many exams during your college career. Unfortunately, for most people, test taking is a source of anxiety.

A sense of apprehension or nervousness prior to, during, or subsequent to an exam is a common experience among students. As we discussed in Chapter 2, some degree of anxiety can be helpful for our performance. It can provide us with increased motivation and the ability to focus our attention on the task. However, the anxiety associated with participating in evaluative and performance situations can hinder performance. In the college environment, such performance anxiety often centers on testing situations, and is referred to as *test-anxiety*. Test anxiety can interfere with both learning and performance and, when severe, can be a factor in the decision to stay in or leave school. This chapter provides a discussion of this common source of anxiety and what you can do to limit its influence on your educational experience. Although the focus of this chapter is on the testing situation, many of the ideas discussed here apply to other situations where you feel anxiety about "performance" evaluation.

TEST ANXIETY—WHAT IS IT?

Test anxiety is an uneasiness or apprehension experienced before, during, or after an examination because of concern, worry, or fear. Nearly everyone experiences some anxiety in situations where their performance is evaluated. Some students find, however, that anxiety interferes with their learning and test taking to such an extent that their grades and their well-being are seriously affected. In fact, test anxiety leads some students to drop out of school entirely.[1]

Amanda entered the classroom feeling nervous and apprehensive. She could feel her hands shaking as she sat at her desk. She tried to clear her head. "This is ridiculous! I've studied for days to be ready for this exam. I know the material." As the professor passed the exam around the room, Amanda felt a wave of anxiety overcome her. She began to feel confused, panicked, and she couldn't seem to focus. As she scanned the questions, she didn't know where to begin. She couldn't seem to remember anything she had studied.

Perhaps you've had an experience similar to this. Maybe you really knew the answers to the questions but could not access them when taking the exam or maybe you've done much better on practice exams than on the real thing. Test anxiety may be a problem for you. Most test-anxious students are well aware of the problem—the sense of dread and discomfort associated with test taking. Most symptoms of test anxiety are experienced during the exam itself, although some may occur when studying or in anticipation of the event. One of the more common experiences is the perception that one is "freezing-up" or having a mental "block." You may find yourself reading the words, only to find that they are meaningless to you. Or, you may feel that you have to reread the words several times to comprehend them. Like other manifestations of anxiety that we have discussed thus far in this book, test anxiety has physical, cognitive, and behavioral "symptoms."

Physical

Let's begin with the physical symptoms. A common physical experience involves a panic reaction. Panic can occur at the outset of the exam or any time during the testing experience. It can occur in response to anxious thoughts ("oh no, I don't think I know these questions"), or it can occur because you are aware that you are anxious, or a combination of the two. In the example above, Amanda was experiencing a degree of panic as she scanned the test and felt that she did not know where to begin. Remember the concept of "fear of fear" mentioned in Chapter 2. Sometimes we can become afraid of our own fear response and the negative consequences that we imagine are associated with the anxiety reaction itself. For example, there are some people who become afraid of their rapid heartbeat, becoming concerned that they will have a heart attack. Others might fear passing out or throwing up during times of high anxiety. If you experience this fear of your own bodily reactions, you may be experiencing panic disorder. Panic disorder was described in Chapter 2 and if this experience sounds familiar, you may wish to reread that section and consider seeking professional assistance, as panic disorder can be treated successfully and quickly.

Back to test anxiety. Typically, a host of physical symptoms occur in addition to intense fear or dread. Some of the reactions you may experience in a testing or performance situation include:

- muscle tension
- excessive sweating
- trembling or shaking
- shortness of breath
- rapid heartbeat or heart palpitations

Does this mean that all physiological signs of nervousness or anxiety are problematic? In short, no. Some degree of anxious apprehension with accompanying physical symptoms is to be expected. Remember, as was discussed in Chapter 2, a mild degree of arousal can help you perform at your best. This is what people are referring to when they talk about "psyching up for the game," and it works to enhance performance.

Cognitive

Cognitive symptoms associated with test anxiety usually include a sense that you cannot concentrate or of being preoccupied with worry. In fact, research has shown that people with test anxiety often experience what are referred to as "task-irrelevant thoughts."[2] Let us explain this idea. One useful way to think about how test anxiety interferes with performance is to think of attention as something that has limited capacity. If you were trying to pay attention to the plot of a television program and a conversation at the same time, it would be difficult to allocate enough attention to these different aspects of your environment without suffering some decrease in performance. That is, you might not comprehend some of the meaning of what you are reading, or only hear some of what is going on, or miss elements of the plot of the T.V. show.

Worrying thoughts are task-irrelevant thoughts and they compete with task-relevant thinking, such as scanning your memory for associations to a concept on the exam, for your attention. Unfortunately, they "squeeze out" some room for the very thinking that is necessary for good performance on exams. One of the keys to better performance is learning to shift your attention away from worries to the job at hand.

Figure 8.1 lists some thoughts, in the form of anxious self-talk, that are often reported by students experiencing test anxiety. A space is provided for you to

Figure 8.1   Common Anxious Thoughts about Testing

Concerns about performance

_____ I should have studied more...
_____ I don't know anything...
_____ What's the matter with me?
_____ I can't think......
_____ I can't figure out what the professor wants...
_____ I'm just not cut out for this...

Concerns about physical symptoms

_____ I feel sick...
_____ It's so hot in here...I'm sweating like crazy..
_____ I feel like I'm gonna throw up...
_____ My stomach is churning...
_____ I am really tense...
_____ I have a headache...

Comparisons with others

_____ I know everyone's doing better than I am.
_____ Everyone else looks calm.
_____ They are done already; it must have been easy for them.

Worries about negative consequences

_____ If I fail this test, I'll flunk the course
_____ I'll never graduate
_____ I'll never get into graduate school
_____ People will think I'm not very smart
_____ People will be disappointed in me
_____ I can't face people
_____ I'm really embarrassed

Thoughts of escape

_____ I just want to finish and get out of here....
_____ How can I leave without being noticed?
_____ I'll ask to use the bathroom and not come back

check which of these often occur in your experience of taking exams, or those with which you identify. As we emphasize throughout this book, it is important to become aware of the ways in which you talk to yourself that fuel, rather than calm, your anxieties.

Behavioral

As has been discussed, the behaviors associated with anxiety usually involve avoidance-type activities. For example, individuals who are anxious about an exam may procrastinate and not study or may put off studying until the last minute. They may find ways to distract themselves from the worry like hanging out with friends, talking in the library instead of studying, or completing other assignments first because they produce less discomfort than studying for the exam. Some individuals go to more extreme avoidance behaviors such as rescheduling an exam or even dropping a course in which the exams seem overwhelming. These types of behavior only reinforce the anxiety cycle and make it more difficult to manage test anxiety. Remember, avoidance only contributes to the cycle of anxiety.

Contributors to Test Anxiety

How did test-taking become so difficult? There are several factors that contribute to the development of test anxiety.[3]

Prior Experiences. Many of you may have had an experience with test taking that was difficult and made a mark on you. When encountering testing situations now, you find that the previous experience continues to bother you. Perhaps you had an experience of a "mental block" or became highly anxious during a test in the past to the point that you felt overwhelmed or extremely uncomfortable. You may have encountered an exam that was much more difficult than you had imagined. Students who have experienced difficulty performing in testing situations can develop what we refer to as "anticipatory anxiety." This type of anxiety occurs in advance of a situation. You may dread an exam weeks or even months before it occurs. Worrying about how anxiety will affect you can be as debilitating as the anxiety itself. As the testing situation approaches, you may find that anticipatory anxiety builds. It may interfere with your ability to study effectively for the exam.

Insufficient Preparation. A lack of preparation can also contribute to high levels of test anxiety. It is important to be able to study efficiently and manage time effectively. In fact, one of the great challenges college students face is structuring and managing time. Problems with time management and difficulties with organization can lead to feeling overwhelmed and highly anxious on the day of the test. The relationship of time management to anxiety is discussed in Chapter 10 of this book. If you believe that you have difficulties effectively managing time, you may wish to spend some time working with some of the ideas discussed in that chapter. You should be aware that most colleges and universities offer information, workshops, and even tutoring in effective time management and study skills. These resources can be very helpful in facilitating the development of organizational and other skills beneficial to managing your test anxiety. And for the many students with attention problems and/or learning disabilities, who find academic tasks even more challenging, the resources available on campus for students with learning disabilities may also be valuable. Testing accommodations such as additional time for tests or using a separate test-taking environment may be available. Poor time management and disorganization can result in a situation in which you are forced to cram at the last minute. Cramming may lead you to be less confident in your knowledge of the material. If you are able to enter the testing situation with a sense of mastery of the material, you will have greater confidence and less anticipatory anxiety.

Anxious Thinking. As we have emphasized throughout the book, negative thought processes contribute to anxiety, and anxiety about testing situations is no exception. Negative thought processes might involve fear of failure or thoughts of being unworthy or inadequate. We live in a culture and in an age in which self-worth is often judged by others' evaluations of our social, academic, professional, artistic, or athletic performances. In an earlier chapter, we addressed the relationship between self-image and appearance. In a similar way, any link between self-esteem and performance standards has great potential for feelings of threat and danger. Many different events in our lives can make us feel as though we have fallen short of some type of standard. These events and their inherent risk of disappointment or failure often lead to worry and anxiety.

Perfectionism. At many points during your reading of this book you'll come across the role that perfectionism and feelings of low self-worth play in creating and sustaining anxiety. Perfectionism is a concept that involves setting standards of performance for self and others that are unrealistically high. A perfectionist is someone who gets 96% on an exam and then feels terrible about the few questions they missed. This is a prime example of "all-or-none thinking." Perfectionists focus on their shortcomings and inadequacies. They rarely compliment themselves and recognize their strengths. For the perfectionist, self-worth is constantly in jeopardy, as failure looms just around the next corner. Perfectionism should not be confused with motivation to do good work or with attempting to do the best job possible. Instead, it involves rigid adherence to extremely high standards coupled with intense striving to meet unattainable goals.

It goes like this. If you are perfect, then others can't negatively evaluate you and you don't judge yourself. You can avoid the failure that appears to loom around every corner. Yet, demanding approval and perfection only sets you up for disappointment. The testing situation can be seen as a way to redeem oneself or compensate for feelings of inadequacy.

Success does involve high expectations. However, placing too much importance on any one academic task can create undue pressure. The more pressure that exists in a situation, the more the climate exists for the experience of anxiety. If indeed the academic task has taken on such a degree of importance, you may see failure as unbearable or devastating. You may then focus more on the negative effects of failure than on what needs to be done to be successful.

Performance Pressure. Many students deal with a heightened pressure to perform. This may be due to pressure from parents, the need to perform well academically in order to deal with financial constraints, or pressure from other outside sources. Research on test anxiety has indicated that students who have high test anxiety do more poorly than low test-anxious students on many learning tasks.[4] While this is not surprising, this may be frustrating news if test anxiety is a problem for you. There's a catch, however: students with high test anxiety only do more poorly when they are given "achievement-oriented" instructions. Sound confusing? Let us explain. When students are told that the academic task or exam is a very important one that measures intelligence or low academic achievement, they do poorly. On the other hand, when the task is presented in a low-pressure manner, as merely an exercise, the test anxious students do *as well and sometimes even better* than their less anxious counterparts. Many of you can relate to this when you think of courses where you did well on frequent quizzes, but poorly on the big exams. What can this tell you? It is very important to *not* overvalue the importance of the test on one's grade and thereby create a "high achievement" or a high-pressure situation. You want to do a good job while reducing the pressure by putting the consequences of a poor performance in realistic perspective.

Catastrophizing. Catastrophizing occurs when test anxious students become concerned that something might go wrong on a test. Thoughts turn to the imagined consequences of failing the test (or doing less than perfectly) coupled with a conclusion that these consequences are very likely to occur. Anxiety escalates with the worry about whether they will do well or not. They imagine not having answers, failing the exam, feeling humiliated, and doing poorly on future exams. This horrific train of thinking can be quite dramatic or involve highly unrealistic or improbable outcomes. Imagination has run away from them before any actual outcomes have occurred. As we have mentioned previously, we call this "catastrophizing"; the tendency to think about the worst aspects of a situation before even experiencing them.

Additional Thoughts about Performance Anxiety

Like test anxiety, other "performance" situations represent a potential threat as we are confronted with the potential for being judged or evaluated.

Figure 8.2   A Recipe for Test Anxiety

A mix of the following:

- You face a situation that you construe as difficult, threatening, or challenging.
- You see yourself as unprepared, inadequate, or incapable of meeting the challenge.
- You are very concerned about the consequences of possible failure.

Source: Adapted from Mann, W. and Lash, J. *Test and Performance Anxieties*, University of Cincinnati; Psychological Services Center and the Student Affairs and Services, http://www.uc.edu/cc/Test.html, retrieved on September 20, 2006.

Again, anxiety is a natural, adaptive human response to a situation we perceive to be threatening to our wellbeing. In performance anxieties, a key threat is the loss of our self-esteem. When we face demands to perform, we risk the possibility of failure. Failure can lead to a loss of confidence and be a blow to our sense of esteem in the eyes of other people. Other performance situations may include presentations in class or athletic or artistic performances. In fact, most athletes and artists experience performance anxiety at some point in their careers.

Figure 8.2 describes a "recipe" for performance anxiety. The level of distress or discomfort you experience is related to the intensity of each of the ingredients. Thus, high levels of test anxiety will occur if you view the situation as very difficult, you lack confidence in your abilities, and yet see the outcome as tied directly to your self-worth or your potential for success in the future. Here's some advice:

- Try to reframe the testing situation as important but not overly threatening.
- Be reasonably confident that you are prepared for the exam. Work on your preparation to increase your confidence.
- Don't let consequences associated with failure loom overly large or affect your sense of worth as a person. Work on "decatastrophizing" the situation.

Let's take a look at how to accomplish these goals.

IDEAS FOR CHANGE

If you are experiencing the kind of worry and anxiety described in the previous sections, you can do several things to diminish performance anxiety. Note that we said "diminish." Test anxiety is not something that must be eliminated entirely; just reduced to a level that is manageable and enhances, rather than hinders, performance. Before discussing strategies and perspectives that can help diminish anxiety, it is important for you to reflect on your situation. Let's return to the story of Amanda described at the beginning of the Chapter. Which of the variables just discussed reflect her situation? Which reflect yours?

- Are you *underprepared* for the test? She noted that she studied for days. Perhaps this was adequate preparation although we would need more information about her study habits and how she managed time to answer this question.

- Have you had *previous experiences* with tests that have gone badly? It is possible that now that she is in the situation, she is reminded of previous difficult experiences, memories that further fuel her anxiety response. It is also possible that such recollections on previous experiences led to anticipatory anxiety that interfered with effective preparation.

- Do you *lack confidence* in your abilities even when you are prepared? Amanda seems to be experiencing a crisis of confidence. She thought she was prepared but now feels bewildered as she examines the material on the test.

- Do you engage in *perfectionistic*, or *all or nothing* thinking about your performance? Perhaps Amanda has put a lot of pressure on herself and feels that she must achieve a high standard to be worthy. She may see herself as either a success or failure with little in between in terms of self-evaluation.

- Do you *lose perspective about the importance* of the test and create undue pressure? Perhaps Amanda feels that this test is the true indicator of her worth, or her potential, or of her ability to be successful in the future.

Work on Your Preparation[5]

With the many demands for your time presented by college life, it is easy to back yourself into a corner. Try not to put yourself in a position where you must attempt to learn weeks of material the day before the test. The last minute is not the time for optimal learning. If you can make progress with your time management skills, you can more efficiently spread the workload for any given course over the semester or year. There are those individuals who can pull an "all-nighter" and be successful. But, as someone with test anxiety you will feel better if you do not put yourself in that position.

Pull together all the information you have been presented thus far that will be covered on the exam and focus on the main themes and concepts. Learn them well. Research on the psychology of memory suggests that material is better remembered if it is *integrated* with other material as opposed to remaining a collection of disconnected facts. When studying for the test, ask yourself what questions may be asked and try to answer them. Integrate the ideas from the various types of class material such as lectures, notes, exercises, texts, and supplementary readings.

If you are unable to devote time to studying all of the material given throughout the time period for the exam, focus on the most important concepts and ideas. Identify and challenge "all or nothing" thinking and remind yourself that while it is not likely that you will perform excellently on the entire test, your score may reflect a mastery of most of the material.

Here are some additional suggestions to help you be more efficient in your study habits and arrive at the exam prepared.

- Develop a study schedule
- Study in a location free of distractions
- Consider the use of "flashcards" and quiz yourself
- Learn how to take good notes and review them after each class
- Make outlines and summary sheets to help integrate material
- Determine the most important information and give that extra attention
- Consider a study group with other, highly motivated students
- Take advantage of campus resources for writing, study skills, and test-taking skills
- Obtain tutoring if needed

In general, organized, self-confident students with efficient study habits may actually spend less time studying than others who receive lower grades. The emphasis on preparation may sound a bit repetitive and obvious, but nothing can help reduce anxiety like confidence. In fact, if you overprepare a bit, your responses become more automatic, and your performance will be less affected by anxiety.

A Word about Overstudying

In Chapter 2, we discussed that in addition to avoidance, a common behavioral response in the face of anxiety is to overcontrol or overcompensate. If one can achieve complete control over a situation or work extra hard to make sure that the bad things that one fears won't happen, anxiety can be reduced. The problem with such a strategy is that it becomes associated with other problems. A person drives himself or herself so hard that they are exhausted. Other satisfying parts of one's life are sacrificed, such as relationships and enjoyable activities. Overpreparing and overstudying are attempts to cope with performance and test anxiety that, paradoxically, can actually heighten one's sense of anxiety. Overpreparation and overstudying are usually the result of highly perfectionistic expectations of performance.

Consider Thomas, who has been preparing nightly for two weeks for a philosophy exam. He has read and outlined each of the chapters and lectures. He has gone over them many times and has been able to recall from memory the concepts and ideas to the envy of those in his study group. Yet, he cannot let go of lingering doubts that he is missing something and finds himself going over and over the same material. He feels tremendous pressure to be the best, as he has always scored at or near the top on exams. Yet, now in college, he finds that the material is much harder and the competition seemingly much stiffer. If only he can try harder, he can feel more secure. Thomas' situation is surprisingly common. Some students exhibit a highly perfectionistic and driven style that hides deep insecurities about their ability to succeed.

Other students exhibit anxieties that manifest as persistent doubting in the face of uncertainty. In some cases, this also can result in studying that goes well beyond what is needed for excellent performance, or is much more detailed and painstaking than necessary. The need for a sense of "good enough" or certainty can cause them tremendous distress as, for them, this feeling is never obtained. If you are a student who experiences persistent doubting, finds it difficult to stop studying, or feels compelled to read or write repetitively or in seemingly non-sensical ways, you may struggle with a degree of obsessive-compulsive disorder or OCD. OCD was discussed in Chapter 2 and is highly amenable to psychological treatment. If this experience is similar to yours, you may benefit from reflecting on ways to work on your perfectionism.

Shift Your Perspective

As is discussed throughout this book, anxiety management involves identifying and challenging negative or unhelpful thoughts. When you are facing a testing situation, take a close look at what you're saying to yourself about the examination. The underlying source of test or performance anxiety is the fear of failure. You're likely to find that your thoughts reflect some of those "ingredients" of test anxiety we talked about earlier in this chapter, such as interpreting the test as overly threatening or risky to your success, and lacking confidence in your own abilities. You can begin to control this fear or change the expectation by changing the way you think and talk to yourself regarding the exam.

Remember the concept of catastrophizing? You need to decatastrophize to help you reduce performance pressure. It is important to realistically consider the consequences of doing poorly on an exam. Rather than a catastrophe, performing poorly on a test is more realistically a challenge that must be addressed in some manner. Many students who suffer from test anxiety will jump on the "worry train"; that is, from a poor test performance to a poor course grade, to ruined GPA, to poor chances with a job or graduate school, and on and on. For perfectionists, the catastrophizing often takes the form of turning a slightly less than stellar performance (but not a poor one) into possible failure. The truth is that a bad grade signals a problem that needs attention, and it is important not to lose sight of the fact that you are in college to learn. The results of evaluation help you correct your course and learn more effectively. In addition to course content, there is also an opportunity to learn about yourself and how you define expectations for yourself and how you can tend to build pressure and anxiety in performance situations.

If you receive a bad grade, it is important to examine what went wrong. You can obtain the correct answers and study your work. The truth is that one test rarely ruins a course grade, let alone a career. You may need to study more or with a different strategy, or acquire some additional time management, organizational, or study skills. In most cases, your performance will improve as you address your anxiety and gain additional study skills. If this cannot be accomplished within a reasonable period of time or with hard work then the worst that will happen is reevaluation of your goals (possibly a change in major or a shift in career direction). That's not likely, but it is important to think of it too as a problem that can be solved with a satisfactory outcome.

Here are some examples that can help Amanda (and you) to practice more positive and realistic self-talk: "This is just one exam, my future is not on the line. Besides, the exam is only a part of my course grade. If I don't do as well as I'd like, it doesn't necessarily mean other bad things will happen. I can learn from mistakes I make, and I don't have to be perfect to be worthwhile."

While it may seem that changing the way you think about tests should be easy, it does take some work. Fortunately, as you practice identifying and challenging your negative thinking, it becomes easier and more automatic. You may even find that your improved perspective of the test-taking experience actually helps you enjoy studying and certainly may improve your performance. Here are some more perspectives:[6]

- Remind yourself that a test is only one test—there will be other opportunities to show what you know.
- Try to show as much of what you know as you can.
- Avoid thinking of yourself as either a success or a failure.
- Reward yourself after the test—do something fun.

Practice Relaxation Strategies

In a later chapter we will examine strategies for reducing arousal using various relaxation strategies. So, consider this a brief introduction to a basic, yet important strategy. When anxious, we often breathe shallowly, through our chest, rather than deeply, through our diaphragm. Learning to breathe deeply and slowly can help you to relax. To help yourself learn to breathe deeply, place your hand on your stomach and inhale in a way that makes your abdomen expand (as opposed to your chest). It is often referred to as "belly breathing." Breathing through your nose may help. It is not necessary to take in a lot of air (as in the "deep breath" we are instructed to take when we see a doctor). Slowly exhale. Practice taking deep breaths over a period of 10–15 minutes. Consider it a skill that takes some practice. It may take a little while but it is an important skill that can reduce some of the uncomfortable physiological reactions that occur during panic. When you are preparing to start an exam, focus on taking 2–3 deep breaths, and your body will start to relax. Breathing is an excellent initial relaxation skill. Other strategies can be added to it for a more comprehensive set of skills, and this will be discussed again later.

Take Good Care of Yourself[7]

Consider that your mind is a tool. A good tool needs to be sharpened and handled with care in order to be most useful when it is needed. Students preparing for tests often neglect basic biological, emotional, and social needs. Good self-care is vital to the effective management of anxiety. Here are some suggestions:

- Practice habits of good nutrition and exercise. Continue your recreational pursuits and social activities—all these contribute to your emotional and physical well-being. It is tempting to let go of basic self-care, recreation, and socializing when preparing for exams. By all means, it is important to curtail fun around exam times, but don't neglect it completely.
- Balance intense study time with breaks. People tend to reach a point of "saturation" after a few hours of continuous study. A short break can help you recharge your intellectual batteries.
- Get good sleep—fatigue interferes with optimum performance. For some of you, this may mean working hard to recognize the difference between being well prepared and having a sense of certainty that you covered absolutely everything in great detail; in this case, good self-care means "letting go."

Rehearse the Performance

Have you ever seen elite athletes studying the course, examining the playing field, or walking the track just prior to an event? In all likelihood, they are visualizing their performance. They are activating mental and muscle memory in an attempt to "rehearse" their performance. This mental imagery can help in reducing anxiety. It is important to make a deliberate attempt to alter imagery that is associated with perceptions of threat. This involves three steps. First, it is important to become aware of anxiety-related imagery. Next, you should develop new, more adaptive patterns of imagery and fantasy and finally, practice, practice, practice your new images.

Here is an exercise in *coping imagery*. It involves actually imagining yourself experiencing some anxiety but then coping effectively with it. This type of imagery exercise can help you gain confidence in your ability to work through anxiety. It helps you feel prepared for difficult experiences that come your way during the exam.

This should take about 15 minutes but feel free to spend more time if you like. Read through the entire description of the exercise before you start. You may also find that jumping ahead to some of the material in Chapter 12 may be helpful.

Find a place where you can be very comfortable and not be disturbed. Take some time (5–10 minutes) to become very calm, using some of the relaxations strategies described in Chapter 12. When you are relaxed, close your eyes and visualize the testing situation. Imagine approaching and then entering the place where you will take the test. Imagine all of the sights and sounds you are likely to experience, the other students, the room itself, the professor, and so on. Imagine yourself experiencing some anxiety. Imagine the physical sensations that would accompany this anxiety along with some of the negative thoughts that might enter your mind. Imagine these experiences along with the exam itself, which should be visualized as a challenging one. Then, begin to imagine yourself relaxing by taking some deep breaths. Picture yourself using positive self-talk to reduce pressure and counteract any catastrophic thoughts you may be having. As you do so, imagine your thoughts turning away from your worries and more and more toward the exam. Imagine yourself feeling confident and good about being able to perform at your best.

The above exercise should ideally produce some mild to moderate anxiety at first. That's ok—it is a clue that your imagery exercise is effective. It provides you with an opportunity to put into practice the ideas that are discussed in the chapter, prior to the exam. It might take some time and repetition to make the most of this strategy. Each time, try to develop a more vivid image and add to your repertoire of coping strategies.

In-vivo Practice

In-vivo means literally "in life" and refers to real-life practice. The next step beyond practicing in imagination is to simulate actual testing conditions and consider taking practice exams. Try to simulate the actual testing experience as much as possible. Work within the same time frame that will exist on test day. Try to practice with some of the same environmental conditions, such as not having notes, turning the cell phone off, and sitting in an upright chair. Consider using the library or a classroom to simulate some of the other conditions of the actual exam.

On Test Day

The following specific suggestions for test day are adapted from the website of the University of Illinois Counseling Center:[8]

- Eat a healthy breakfast. This should involve a moderate amount of food: too large a breakfast can make you sleepy and too little can leave you without the energy needed. If you are prone to 'caffeine jitters,' avoid caffeine as it can enhance feelings of anxiety. If you feel you must have caffeine to function effectively, then at least moderate your intake on test day. Consider your activities just prior to the test. Avoid last minute cramming as it can interfere with your grasp of the "big picture" of the course. Last-minute studying rarely adds useful material to your knowledge base. If possible, engage in a relaxing activity for the hour or so before the test so that you arrive for the test with a reduced state of tension and stress.

- It is often helpful to arrive early at the testing location. This can help you relax before the test begins and enable you to select a good seat away from distractions.
- You may want to avoid classmates who generate anxiety. Others will understand your need for some space. You can check-in with them after the exam.
- If waiting for the test to begin provokes anxiety, then consider bringing in some recreational reading material, such as a novel you are reading or a magazine or newspaper.

During the Test

After the exam has been handed out and before you begin responding to the questions, consider the following:

- Review the entire test and pay special attention to the instructions to ensure that you understand them clearly. Think of how you can organize the time efficiently. If you find that some parts of the exam appear easier or more familiar than others, consider working on those parts first. That will help you build a sense of mastery and momentum for the remainder of the exam.
- For essay questions many students find it helpful to construct a short outline. Begin your response with a sentence that summarizes your response. Then, with the remainder of your response you can fill in details that communicate what you know. Provide responses that are short and to-the-point for short-answer questions. If you are struggling with a question involving a written response, show what knowledge you have on the subject—write what you can. If you are struggling to remember jargon or terminology, show what you know with your own words.
- For multiple choice questions, make sure that you read all the options first. Eliminate the most obvious ones. Consider relying upon your first impression if you are unsure of the correct response. Mark the question in some way with a check mark or other symbol, and then quickly move on. You can always return to those questions that you are most unsure of if time permits. Pay special attention to qualifying words such as "only," "always," or "most." It may be helpful to develop a habit of underlining or circling those.

While it is important to work quickly and efficiently, there is no need to rush through the test. Wear a watch or position yourself in the room where you have a clear view of a clock and check the time frequently as you pace yourself. If it begins to look like you will be unable to complete the exam, attend to those portions that you feel confident in responding to well. If, then, you have any extra time, you can return to the questions that you marked earlier.

After the Test

At this point it is important to take care of yourself and reward yourself for your effort. If you promised yourself a reward, make sure you follow-through with it whether you believe you did well or not on the exam. It is tempting to dwell on the mistakes or to try to reassure yourself, but resist this and relax for awhile. You've earned it!

SUMMARY

Test anxiety can be a distressing and debilitating problem, but one that can be overcome by cultivating a number of strategies. Helping yourself with your test anxiety can provide valuable insights for coping effectively with the many situations in which performance is evaluated. Remember to put the test-taking experience into perspective and to practice the strategies found in this chapter and later in this book. If you reduce the physical tensions, task-irrelevant thoughts, and self-defeating behaviors, you will be well on your way to managing test anxiety.

CHAPTER 9

Planning for the Future

True vocation is where the world's deep need meets your deep gladness.
—Friedrich Buechner

Surely a man has come to himself only when he has found the best that is in him, and has satisfied his heart with the highest achievement he is fit for.
—Woodrow T. Wilson

Steven Covey, the author of the best selling book, *The 7 Habits of Highly Successful People*, offers powerful lessons in personal change.[1] His second highly acclaimed method is to "begin with the end in mind." By beginning with the end in mind, an individual has a roadmap, a guide for the journey ahead that provides direction and motivation. Let us, then, begin with the end in mind. This chapter will deal with the important topics of discovering career options, career planning, and decisionmaking, and dealing with the stress and anxiety related to financial issues that are often a part of the college experience. College is a formative time when many decisions are made regarding career direction and future plans. In addition, financial pressures impact college life and planning for many students, and are a frequent source of anxiety among students. Although you may, at this time, be most interested in how to deal with what's happening on campus in the present, taking time to examine your needs and face your worries will pay off in a much more successful transition to the world outside.

CAREER ISSUES

Most college students have concerns regarding a career and plans for the future. In a large national study of the top ten concerns of college students, two of the ten issues that caused distress for both men and women included uncertainty about the future and concerns about career decisions.[2] One of the most significant issues a student struggles with at this time in life is finding meaningful lifework and a sense of direction and purpose for the future. This involves a process of finalizing a choice of major, looking at lifework alternatives, deciding on a suitable option, and ensuring that your curriculum prepares you for your desired choices. Individuals who are indecisive about this process and lack direction often experience significant stress and anxiety when contemplating life after college.

It sounds like a simple process—pick a career and set a course for the future. However, in our current economy these choices have become complex and confusing. A recent report by the U.S. Bureau of Labor Statistics showed over 146 million jobs in the U.S. economy.[3] These numbers are projected to increase in the future and this presents a staggering amount of choices for individuals as they sort through the maze to find lifework that fits.

And what about staying open and exploring the options? In an earlier chapter we discussed the importance of exploration during the process of learning about one's identity and discovering appropriate lifework. However, this openness needs to be balanced with the ability to make good decisions along the way. If a college student continually explores, frequently changes majors, and never sets a course, it is difficult to finish college—let alone find direction for a career. Career direction, as we have seen, involves exploration, discovery, choosing a major, narrowing career information to areas that can be researched, finding an appropriate internship or practical work experience, and then linking what we know about ourselves to appropriate career options.

Career Indecision

For some students, this whole process feels overwhelming and frustrating and they find themselves in a state of *career indecision*. Career indecision and the anxiety associated with this problem can be paralyzing to college students during a time in life when important career decisions need to be made. Individuals who are confused, uncertain, and incapable of making these kinds of decisions about careers report that they have higher levels of anxiety than those who have more career certainty.[4] The ability to think clearly and make good decisions has a great deal to do with this process. When a person has difficulty processing information about self and career options, the emotions and behaviors that emerge can make it difficult to move in a positive direction to carry out career tasks and accomplish desired goals. This can result in difficulties such as lack of confidence, fear, helplessness, frustration, and guilt.[5]

Box 9.1   Career Indecisiveness

1. Lack of student readiness
   - Lack of motivation
   - Indecisiveness in decisionmaking in general
   - Inaccurate career beliefs
2. Inadequate information
   - Lack of information about the process of career decisionmaking
   - Lack of self-knowledge
   - Inadequate knowledge about careers
   - Uncertainty about how to obtain career information
3. Information that is not consistent
   - Unreliable information about self or careers
   - Problems with internal conflicts (unsure, frustrated, confused)
   - Problems with external conflicts (parental expectations, lack of opportunity)

Source: Lounsbury, J.W., Tatum, H.E., Chambers, W., Owens, K., and Gibson, L.W. "An Investigation of Career Decidedness in Relation to 'Big Five' Personality Constructs and Life Satisfaction," *College Student Journal*, 33 (1999), 646–652.

Career indecision is a problem on many college campuses. In a study of career decisionmaking in first-year college students, researchers assessed the difficulties that contribute to indecision in the career development process. The researchers identified three factors that contribute to career indecisiveness: 1) lack of student readiness, 2) inadequate information, and 3) information that is not consistent.[6] The list in box 9.1 illustrates these factors and offers reasons for each.

Feeling Out of Control

When individuals find themselves in a state of indecisiveness other difficulties can surface. Feeling out of control is another difficulty associated with indecisiveness. Some college students feel fairly confident about the process of making career decisions and feel that they have control over many aspects of the process. Individuals who believe that they have control with regards to their career choices apply problem-solving skills and begin to work toward finding an appropriate career. These types of individuals demonstrate much less anxiety than those who feel they have little or no control.[7] A sense of control and some certainty offer many positive benefits such as increased levels of life satisfaction and motivation that helps obtain success in college.[8,9]

On the other hand, many students do not feel a sense of control about the process of finding a career. Many factors can impact an individual's sense of control, including the condition of the economy, the individual's abilities, and the need for these abilities in the job market. Individuals who feel they have no control on any of these processes may not be capable of making important steps forward toward finding appropriate lifework.

It is obvious that the nature of an ever-changing global economy is a formidable obstacle for students and one of the reasons why there can be anxiety when making decisions that will impact the future. Career decisionmaking is a complex task that involves a number of important issues for college students. Making decisions about careers involves the ability to assess interests and values, evaluate abilities, examine issues related to identity, and the willingness to think about the way one makes decisions.

Self-defeating Behaviors

We began with the end in mind by examining the importance of the process of career development—learning about oneself and career options. When individuals work through the career process and find lifework that is meaningful, there is a deeply satisfying reward and a chance to make a difference in the world. On the other hand there are many students who feel unable to navigate this complex process.

The previous chapters in this book have addressed the anxiety associated with living in an environment that routinely involves evaluation through weekly tests and papers, the pressure to earn good grades, and the expectation to complete a degree. It often seems that there are enormous amounts of material to master and inadequate amounts of time available to accomplish this.[10,11] In the midst of

Box 9.2   Self-defeating Behaviors

1. Inactive but not concerned—continuing to do what they do even when there may be negative consequences.

   Oh, it's too early in the semester to decide on a major. I'll think about it next year.

2. Sudden change in strategy without preparation—make a decision without being prepared for setbacks.

   Since talking with my friend, I just switched majors. I'm not sure what extra courses I'll need to take in order to graduate but I don't care. I'm just so glad I finally made a decision.

3. Defensive avoidance—procrastinate or rationalize and ignore the consequences.

   I don't care. There are too many choices for majors and I just don't have the time to think this through. Maybe someone will just tell me what to do.

4. Hypervigilance—living in an almost continual state of panic.

   I've got to make a decision. I've got to go over my four-year plan again. Maybe I can figure something out today. Who can I talk to? I feel so nervous and overwhelmed.

Source: Whitman, N., Spendlove, D., and Clark, C. *Increasing Students' Learning: A Faculty Guide to Reducing Stress among Students (Report No. 4)* (Washington, DC: Association for the Study of Higher Education; ERIC Document Reproduction Service No. ED284526, 1987).

these academic expectations, students are expected to make decisions that set the course for their future. This stress impacts an individual's ability to make good decisions and move forward to implement these decisions.

Most individuals find their way through this maze even though it can feel quite overwhelming. However, some students falter and exhibit self-defeating behaviors. The list in box 9.2 illustrates some of these behaviors.

Obviously, none of these coping strategies are helpful to the student and may result in ever-increasing levels of anxiety. For highly distressed students, there is concern that this heightened anxiety may impact their ability to make appropriate decisions along the way and this in turn will lead to negative consequences such as settling on a major that is unsatisfying or not being able to make necessary decisions and dropping out of college. Research shows that those students who are able to find a good sense of direction regarding their career, experience higher levels of satisfaction in college and the motivation that helps to make the college experience successful.[12]

FINDING DIRECTION

We have discussed the need to make important career decisions during the college years. However, a very important question arises for most college

Box 9.3   Steps to Career Direction

1. Learn about Yourself
   - Take a couple of vocational assessments to help you identify your interests, personality type, values, and abilities.
   - Talk to others about who you are and what you are good at: parents, friends, faculty members, mentors, former employers, and others who are important to you.
   - Develop ideas of possible career areas and journal about what you might like to do.
2. Learn about the World of Work
   - Search for careers using the internet (your career center can help with this).
   - Read about careers of interest and employers in your area.
   - Do some informational interviews with people in these career areas to find out what they like about their careers.
   - Get practical experience in career areas such as volunteer work, part-time jobs, summer jobs, and internships.
3. Develop a Job Search
   - Write a resume and have a career counselor review it.
   - Create a timeline and practical steps for your job search (see Job Search Activities for seniors in Chapter 4).
   - Write a good cover letter.

students—how do I find career direction? Most campuses have a career center or some resource for assisting students in their search for career direction. Your career center will have the most up-to-date lists of employers and employment opportunities in your area. In addition, most colleges offer vocational testing as low-cost or no-cost options for their students. Box 9.3 offers a brief outline of the essential steps related to career direction. However, working directly with a career counselor is your best option for finding direction regarding your career.

MAKING DECISIONS

Making important decisions about the course of one's life can seem overwhelming and can be a major source of anxiety throughout college. One way to deal with this is to look at the immense task of deciding one's career and break it down into smaller decisions. College students sometimes tend to think that they need to make one or two major decisions that will set the course of their entire future. In reality, life involves making many smaller decisions that lead to new opportunities and other decisions. Instead of worrying about making an immense decision, making thoughtful mini-choices actually gives better life-direction in a rapidly changing world. The decisionmaking process in box 9.4 is a good method for dealing with the many decisions that are a part of college

---

Box 9.4   Decisionmaking Process

1. Put into words the decision you are trying to make.
2. Think about outcomes—what you would like to have happen as a result of this decision.
    - Do you have specific goals?
    - What might this decision lead to?
3. Develop a list of at least three options—three directions you could choose.
    Example: I could 1) go to graduate school, 2) get a yearlong internship after college, or 3) work a temp job until I have a better understanding of a career I would like.
4. Research each possible choice and find out what is involved in making a decision in the direction of each option.
5. Ask for advice. Parents, professors, and trusted friends can provide insights that may help you and give you confirmation in a certain direction.
6. Develop a list of pros and cons about each option and compare these to the outcomes that you listed earlier.
7. Make a decision and move forward.

experience. It might be helpful to use this process for some simple choices and then try it out on a more significant and weighty decision.

Because having good sense of direction for the future is critical to your development and well-being, it's important to be open to seeking assistance. Most college campuses have a career development center that offers free or low cost career counseling and a wealth of resources to assist students in this process. Students who take advantage of these resources early in their college careers will benefit most from these services.

FINANCIAL CONCERNS

Anxiety on campus is also connected to concerns about finances. A growing problem on college campuses today is the high cost of education. In a recent article in the *New York Times*, the cost of college tuition payments were compared to home mortgage payments.[13] Over the past several years there have been substantial increases in college tuition but these increases have not been accompanied by proportionate grants or other financial subsidies for students and their families.[14,15] Certainly, the stresses of college tuition, student loans, and the pressure to find employment to compensate for the debt incurred during college is of increasing concern to students, parents, and college personnel.

The perception of financial problems as students begin college can influence the way they experience college.[16] Day-to-day stress regarding finances and one's ability to stay in college is a constant concern for many. An increasing number of students find it essential to access part-time employment in order to stay in school. This escalates a student's workload and the level of stress required to meet the growing demands.

These problems have serious implications for students and their families. For many students, the financial strain makes it difficult to stay in college. National studies show that many students leave school for financial reasons.[17,18] In addition to difficulties in remaining in college, financial pressures sometimes impact students' capacity to perform well academically. Research indicates that financial difficulties can be linked to decreased performance on exams as well as emotional distress.[19]

The financial pressures for college students are very real and appear to be increasing. From the 20 years between 1980 and 2000, tuition and fee revenue for higher education rose 117%. Students, families, states, and institutions of higher education are all impacted by economic conditions that make college increasingly difficult to afford. These economic difficulties result in increased pressure for students to map their careers early and to prepare for jobs that will provide an adequate return on their investment.[20,21] This growing sense of competition to find professional employment is another significant source of stress for students.

So how do these financial stressors affect the quality of life for students on the college campus? Cathy Small, an anthropology professor at Northern Arizona University, says that today's students are more professionally focused and motivated than previous generations partially due to these high education bills. A large portion of today's college population lives with a constant realization of growing debt and the need to find employment to offset this debt. This realization pushes many students to decide on a career path early in order to be able to find a job quickly upon graduating.[22]

These are the financial realities. However, most students will stay in college because a good education is now, more than ever, linked with finding a good career. So what are some practical ways to deal with these realities? The advice from the experts is to find out all you can about financial aid available to students. The most costly mistake that students and their families make is not taking advantage of what is available. There are resources available to help you investigate the possibilities. Your financial aid office on campus is a great source of information and most institutions have staff members who can discuss options one-on-one. In addition, there is a great deal of information on the internet. Even though you are already in college, the following list (box 9.5) offers some general suggestions to consider.

Box 9.5   Investigating Financial Aid Options

1. Begin by estimating all the costs associated with your education (tuition, books, supplies, room and board, transportation, and personal expenses).

2. What is the timetable for applying to scholarships or financial aid? Determine the timetable and stay on schedule.

3. What are all the options that your college offers—financial aid, merit scholarships, need-based aid, scholarships related to your major?

4. What other sources of aid are available—federal and state grants and loans, scholarships in the community, grants or scholarships based on your field of study?

5. Consider how the financial aid will be credited to you and what your cash flow looks like.

6. Determine what other sources of income you have such as parental support, summer jobs, on-campus employment, or part-time employment.

7. Develop a plan and stick to a budget. Review the amount of debt you have and repayment options. Learn about changes in your financial aid package such as increases, changes in financial status, and so on. Resist the impulse of using credit cards—credit card debt is a huge trap for some college students.

8. Consider discussing your financial situation with a professional who can offer some guidance and practical suggestions.

IDEAS FOR CHANGE

This chapter has offered several suggestions and resources for dealing with the stresses created by these two issues. For many students dealing with planning in the areas of career or finances, anxiety can become overwhelming. In Chapter 1 we discussed the importance of our thinking processes in managing anxiety. In Chapter 7 we examined patterns of thinking commonly associated with social anxiety. We identified several cognitive patterns or errors that serve to intensify anxiety. Let's return to that concept as we look at ways to deal with anxiety related to the issues addressed in this chapter. Remember our aim is to first identify, then challenge, and finally transform anxious thinking.

Identify

One of the cognitive patterns that often seems to be associated with these issues is *catastrophizing*. These types of thoughts might include self-statements like:
"I chose Psychology as my major but I have no idea of what I'll do for a career. What if I can't find a job in that field? What if I can't pay back my student loans? I'll go broke!"

Students struggling with anxiety often struggle with two other cognitive errors—*overestimation of threat*—believing that negative events will most likely happen and that they will be overly harmful or distressing and *underestimation of ability to cope*—assuming they do not have the ability to cope with whatever situation they will face. Those cognitive errors might sound like this:
"I'm just sure that my GPA will keep me out of any decent kind of career. I absolutely cannot interview with this company because explaining my GPA will be too difficult and I won't get the job anyway."

Identifying cognitive errors such as this is the first step toward dealing with anxiety. What would you do? How would you deal with these types of thoughts? Let's use these examples and apply the next steps in our strategy for overcoming anxiety.

Challenge

- "I chose Psychology as my major but I have no idea of what I'll do for a career. What if I can't find a job in that field? What if I can't pay back my student loans? I'll go broke!"

Challenge that Thought. I like my major and I don't need to look at this in such a catastrophic way. I will get into a career I like because other graduates in my department have.

- "I'm just sure that my GPA will keep me out of any decent kind of career. I absolutely cannot interview with this company because explaining my GPA will be too difficult and I won't get the job anyway."

Challenge those Thoughts. I'm over-reacting and making too much of this GPA thing. My GPA is a problem but it won't necessarily keep me out of a good career. In regards to the interview, I know I can do this interview because I've done other difficult things throughout college. I will just find a way to explain my GPA.

Take some time to reflect on your own situation using the Thought Worksheet in box 9.6.

Box 9.6   Thought Worksheet

Identify anxious thinking as you ponder important decisions regarding your future or about the financial realities of college. Challenge those thoughts: How can you respond to these thoughts? Ask questions like: How likely are these fears to play out as I imagine? What if they did occur? How would I cope? Is there a more balanced view? What would I say to others in this situation?

Transform and move forward: What are some new perspectives you can apply to your fearful thoughts about your future, finances, and life decisions?

Transform

Take it one step further and begin to change the negative thoughts into positive beliefs and actions. In the first example the individual may have a faulty belief that there is only one *right* career and he/she will have to find it or just end up doing some mundane work. This core belief can be changed and he/she can move forward with some positive actions.

- I know there are many options for careers. I will do some research on careers in Psychology and I will meet with a career counselor to talk about options. Perhaps I can talk with someone in my Financial Aid office about school loan repayment so that it's not such a big concern for me.
- In the second example, the individual may be overestimating the problem with his/her GPA and underestimating the ability to cope with the problem. The student may have a core belief that he/she simply cannot change things because he/she *messed up* in the freshman year and didn't get good grades. These thoughts can be transformed in this way:

  I know my freshman year was not my best but I've worked hard since then and I've really pulled my grades up! I will take that interview and I think I can find a way to explain my situation. I'm going to write out a paragraph explaining my poor performance in my freshman year and then illustrating my progress since then. I have proven I can succeed and I think the employer will see my value once I explain this.

SUMMARY

These examples illustrate the power of examining and altering the ways in which our anxious "lens" may be distorting our perceptions of our abilities and

choices. We hope that you are beginning to see that developing these skills for changing anxious thinking can be applied to many issues associated with anxiety, both in college and beyond. In this chapter we explored the stresses associated with thinking about and planning for the future, as well as coping with financial realities of college life. Taking charge of this part of your life by addressing your concerns will prevent anxiety from interfering with your forward progress. The college years are a time of significant decisionmaking that must occur simultaneously with many academic demands. Fortunately, guidance is available through on-campus services.

PART THREE

Managing Anxiety and Related Conditions: Solutions and Effective Approaches

CHAPTER 10

Time Management

God gave me a certain number of tasks on earth.
Right now, I'm so far behind I may never die.

—Bumper Sticker

The bumper sticker reminds us that sometimes life can seem truly overwhelming. Time can be both an enemy and a friend, increasing or decreasing our anxiety depending on the situation. Thus far we have focused on the problem of anxiety and why many people in the present society feel anxious. We focused on the many sources of anxiety unique to college students and we offered a few suggestions for facing and overcoming anxiety at this time of life. The next few chapters will offer more in-depth discussion of strategies that have been shown to be effective in coping with and overcoming anxiety. We will begin with time management—an effective strategy for lifting layers of stress associated with college life.

Colleges and universities are rich, exciting places. It is difficult to find any other institution or geographic place for that matter, that can match a campus for social and intellectual stimulation. College is a lush, multi-layered opportunity to experience the abundant wealth of life. However, as we have also discussed, college is filled with expectations, deadlines, academic challenges, and multiple choices for involvement and social activity. Time can easily slip away and deadlines can come crashing in at the most inopportune moments.

Much anxiety can result from an inability to organize our lives effectively. When individuals feel overburdened, there may be a sense that it just is not possible to do all that we have to do in the amount of time allotted to us. Students often feel they have insufficient time in which to accomplish their academic work.[1,2] Feeling that we have insufficient time can make us hurry and worry. This type of mindset makes it easy to put things off in the face of seemingly endless outside pressures and the need to accomplish a great deal. However, it is possible to get a grip on this situation and to make the most out of the college experience. Time management is about time, but it is also about making choices and making room in life for all the options available to us.

First, an important component of time management is *planning*. It is truly the case that a little planning goes a long way. Here is a three-step process of planning: set goals, establish priorities, and identify your personal "energy cycle" so you know your best working times.[3] Many college students find it difficult to plan. Planning takes time and can actually rob us of time needed to study, sleep, make friends, and so on. However, time management experts tell us that even taking a small amount of time for planning can make our work much more effective and efficient and ultimately that will give us back the time that we need.

SET GOALS

Let's begin with the first step in the planning process—the concept of setting goals. This is not a new concept for most college students. The process of choosing a college and getting accepted involved some evaluation of desires, interests, and some process of setting goals. Setting goals related to time management is a similar type of procedure. It is often helpful to sit down and think about what you would like to accomplish in college and your first couple of years after you graduate. What future career goals have you determined? What GPA does this require? How would you like to develop socially while on campus? Are there certain clubs, leadership positions, or volunteer opportunities that you would like to explore? As you review these goals you can begin to determine some time management goals. Perhaps that means reviewing the time needed for homework, labs, writing papers, and participating in group projects. Then think about the social activities and campus involvements that are important to you. These can also be categorized into segments of time. As you think about how to best use your time and set goals in each area, it may be helpful to consider the ways in which you currently use your time. Take the Personal Time Survey[4] below as a basis for estimating the time spent in a variety of normal day-to-day activities.

Personal Time Survey

1. Number of hours of sleep each night   _____ × 7 = _____

2. Number of hours per day getting dressed, grooming, etc. _____ × 7 = _____

3. Number of hours for meals/snacks per day   _____ × 7 = _____

   (if you make meals yourself include preparation time)

4. Total travel time on weekdays   _____ × 5 = _____

   Total travel time on weekends   _____ × 2 = _____

5. Number of hours per week for regularly scheduled   _____

   functions (clubs, church, sports, exercise, get togethers, etc.)

6. Number of hours per day for errands or chores, etc.   _____ × 7 = _____

7. Number of work hours per week   _____

8. Number of class hours per week   _____

9. Number of average hours per week socializing, dates, etc.   _____

                                          Total for the week   _____

Now, subtract the total from 168   168– _____ = _____ *

*The remaining hours are the hours you have allowed yourself to study!

Surprising isn't it. We actually do have more time than we may have realized we have. What's good about completing this survey is that it reminds us that our schedule is under our control and that developing a flexible, adaptable schedule means that even in the demanding life of a college student there is time to build in the things are important to us—even study time.

ESTABLISH PRIORITIES

Step two in the process of planning is to begin to establish priorities. You've set some goals. You know some of the things you want and need to accomplish. However, what gets difficult in college is that many of these goals compete for our time and it's difficult to sort out what to do first or what kinds of things should be the most important use of our time. One way to balance these demands is to set some priorities. The Time Management Matrix that follows (figures 10.1 and 10.2) is a great way to prioritize the demands of your day (week, month) into four categories based on importance and urgency.

Figure 10.1   Time Management Matrix

	Urgent	Not Urgent
Important	(Manage) • Crises • Pressing problems • Medical emergencies • Deadline-driven projects • Last minute preparations for scheduled tasks	(Focus) • Preparation/planning • Prevention • Values clarification • Academic work/assignments • Relationship building • Exercise • Recreation/relaxation
Not Important	(Avoid) • Interruptions • Phone calls/ instant messaging • Some social events • Video games	(Avoid) • Excessive web surfing • Escape activities/procrastination • Irrelevant email/phone/ calls/messages • Some shopping • Mindless or excessive TV watching

Source: Adapted from Covey, S.R. *First Things First* (New York, NY: Fireside, 1994).

The Time Management Matrix helps to categorize activities. Some things are important; some are unimportant. Some things are urgent; some are not. The matrix asks you to make decisions about the activities of your day. It provides a quick way to organize a day and to begin to recognize what activities to attend to and what to avoid. When you are done you will have placed the activities of the day in one of the four boxes.

The Important and Urgent category is reserved for the activities that need to be done first. That's because they are urgent (like a paper that is due the next day) and they are also items that you have endorsed as high priorities (the paper is in your major and you need to get a good grade). If you find yourself with too many assignments and papers in this quadrant, you probably aren't managing your time effectively. Unfortunately, although these activities are ones that should absorb our focus they are often pushed aside for more trivial activities or are resisted due to procrastination. The topic of procrastination will be addressed in more detail later in this chapter.

The Important but Not Urgent category are activities that you have identified as matters that involve values and personal meaning. These are activities that we often put aside but they are important to us and should be areas of focus. They may include such things as physical exercise, planning, building meaningful relationships, and other activities that are based on individual values.

The two final categories are areas in which we often lose time or waste time. We are often unaware of the amount of time we spend here. We often give our time to activities that seem important at the time but they do not contribute to our goals and the things that we truly value. These can be the everyday interruptions that absorb time and energy (phone calls, emails, endless conversations, etc.) These may also include inefficient use of time. You know the kind of situation in which you go to the library to study and you get involved in trivial conversations rather than the studying that you need to do? Here's another example. Have you ever been to a meeting for a group project that went awry? You know the kind where everyone talks and no one takes charge and soon the time is

Figure 10.2   Time Management Matrix Worksheet

	Urgent	Not Urgent
Important	(Manage)	(Focus)
Not Important	(Avoid)	(Avoid)

gone? The project is further behind and you feel frustrated. These kinds of situations can take away time that we need to give to better or more efficient pursuits.

The Not Important and Not Urgent category includes activities that take our time and we get little from them. Things such as unimportant phone calls, long and mindless sessions with video games, and trivial email conversations can absorb time and energy. A great deal of time can be lost in this category. Use the matrix on the previous page (figure 10.2) to see how it works for you. It is a way to identify activities that steal our time and rob us of more beneficial, enjoyable and, yes, more productive pursuits in our lives.

In Stephen Covey's *The 7 Habits of Highly Effective People*, one of those habits is "Put First Things First."[5] This is another helpful way to set priorities. He suggests that you take time each morning to develop a *"To Do"* list. Write it out and then put the tasks of the day in rank order based on what seems most important to you. This list would include classes and study time but also appointments, exercise, college games, theater or music events, clubs or organizations, special speakers and intramural games. It looks like a busy day!

IDENTIFY YOUR PERSONAL "ENERGY CYCLE"

The final component of the planning process is to identify your personal "energy cycle." It is important to find the times when you have the most energy so that you can know what times of the day and week you will do your best work. We all seem to have a biological cycle that regulates our energy level. Some people think clearly and have the most energy at 7:00 in the morning. Others just begin to hit their stride at 10:00 at night. It works best to plan study times and times of intense thinking and problem solving for times when you know your mind is sharp and you are physically energized. Sometimes this means adjusting your sleep schedule (which may be different from your roommate's schedule) to accommodate your natural times of energy. By utilizing your best biological times for intense activities, you will work more efficiently and your work will be more productive and successful. Then times spent socializing or doing less intense activity can be scheduled for times when your energy is at a lower level.

HELPFUL TIPS FOR TIME MANAGEMENT

Most resources on time management provide a list of "tips" that seem to have an uncanny resemblance to each other. It looks like we know how to manage time, if we only would. It reminds us of a joke—"I . . . bought a book on time management to read when I find the time."[6] Here are is a list of useful suggestions:

1. Set Goals—As we discussed our goals are the reason for managing our time. We want to achieve the goals we set for ourselves. Goals give purpose, direction, and value to our lives. In setting goals, we can develop goals that are short term (while in college) long term (5 to 10 years after graduation), major goals (career, life partner, graduate

school), and minor (what activities to do for the semester or the year). We can even think in terms of goals for a day, for a week, for a month, or for one's college career and beyond. This is a place to think big and a place to be practical. Effective time management involves breaking down our goals into smaller, more manageable pieces and acknowledging our achievements along the way. This is key to getting our assignments done and accomplishing stressful tasks throughout the semester, but applies to the larger goals as well. The prospect of a job search after graduation will not cause undue anxiety when the various tasks and responsibilities have been tackled gradually.

2. Spend time planning—Goals are about directions, values, and meaning. Planning is about how to accomplish our goals. Frankly, these are the top two stars of time management and the others are members of the supporting cast. Planning involves developing both some long-term plans and some short-term plans. It helps to think about your college experience as a four-year long (if everything goes according to plan!) experience and plan your course of study from beginning to end (hopefully, you will have an advisor to help). The truth is that it is difficult to graduate on time if you plan a semester at a time. It is more important to plan a year at a time and at some point have a plan developed for your four years of study—semester by semester until graduation—or at least as far into the future as the published schedule will permit. In fact, most academic departments do have four-year plans that you can use for planning. You are already engaging in short term planning as you attend your classes, study the syllabi, and develop a calendar of due dates. Some students find it helpful to put all the course assignments on a master calendar (remember to set markers along the way so you know you are making progress on the plan). Think about planning for the semester, the month, the week, and the day. Even though planning the day is the bottom rung on the organizational ladder, it is important. It might even be that nicely planned days lead to an accomplished year.

3. To Do List—We mentioned the "to do" list earlier. As simple as this idea is, it is essential in order to build good time management skills. It is also a surprisingly effective small tool. It is certainly no waste of time in the morning to take a few minutes to organize your day by writing out the tasks of the day and then ranking them in terms of importance and urgency. Then, remember "first things first," keep the high priority items in focus and the most important and urgent ones first. Beginning your day this way will go a long way toward putting you in charge of the rest of your day.

4. Get a good night's sleep—Sometimes in college it's difficult to remember that sleep is important. Try to establish a schedule—as hard as that is—and try to stick to it—as hard as that is. Partying can mess up a schedule, so when that happens the best advice is to get back to your schedule as soon as you can. Every person's need for sleep and sleep schedule is different so it's important to recognize your own needs and seek to meet those needs. Sleep contributes to good grades and an overall sense of well being. If you are finding it difficult to sleep it may help to talk to your resident director or to discuss your difficulties with a counselor in the college counseling center. Lack of sleep can lead to a variety of problems and that can be prevented with your own planning or with some outside help. Once you find a good sleep schedule, it's good to maintain about the same schedule on weekends as you do on weekdays.

5. Use your spare time wisely—One of the authors rides a shuttle bus daily to work. It takes about 20 minutes each way. So there are 20 minutes in the morning and 20 minutes in the evening in which small bits of work can be accomplished. So those travel minutes actually buy time for other activities at home and on weekends that do not

have to be devoted to work. This is like being given an extra three hours or so each week to plan other rewarding activities. Your campus might have a similar opportunity as you take classes in different buildings on different campuses. Another way to seize some extra time is to find a nook and read, plan, review notes, or study between classes. Sometimes 10 minutes don't seem like much, but finding 10-minute segments throughout the day can really add up. For example, writing a paper can seem overwhelming when you look at the whole project. However, in just 10 minutes you can come up with a draft of an outline and then move on to your next activity. When you come back to the paper you will have a framework so that you can begin writing.

6. Be flexible—Managing time isn't meant to lock you in, make you more anxious, or stifle your creativity. It is meant, as we have said previously, to help you organize your days and weeks so that you are able to participate in the rich opportunities that your campus offers. In order to do that, planning needs to be flexible to accommodate the busy and unexpected aspects of college life. Professors can be unpredictable; elevators in the dorms fail; the Anthropology class has the opportunity for a behind the scenes visit to the Natural History Museum; and sometimes you have unexpected opportunities for tickets to concerts, drama events, or sporting activities. It's good to plan and leave room in your life for the spontaneous, the unanticipated and out-of-the-blue events that throw the plan into disarray. That's all part of the adventure of campus life.

7. Steady wins the race—Honestly, life isn't a 100-meter dash. It is in actuality more like a marathon. Occasionally, even in a long distance race, we have to sprint for a bit as circumstances dictate or as we choose. The wise course of action, most of the time, is to keep up, keep pace, and stay steady. Although many students resort to cramming and last minute hastily written papers, the accumulated knowledge that colleges and universities seek to pass on as well as critical learning skills are the beneficiaries of a steady attention and focused concentration that span the academic term rather than neglect punctuated by panic.

8. Learn to say "No"—Time management and exercising choice require saying "No" to invitations and opportunities that can provide enrichment but also may prove to be costly. You might have the opportunity to take an additional class with a favorite professor, but if you do, it means missing that requirement that leads to graduating on time. You can volunteer at a humane shelter 40 hours a week if you like but you would have little time to study. You might be invited to a great party, but you may not complete the term paper that is due in the morning. All of these demand self-discipline and the willingness to give up a short-term pleasant experience for a long-term goal. Saying "No" becomes a part of a lifelong skill of making decisions that are meant to enrich a person's life. Yet, there are times when your planning can actually get in the way. Sometimes you might have to say "No" to the established plan to grab an opportunity that comes around only once in a while. You might consider missing a study session to hear a presidential candidate who has come to town for the day, for example.

9. Schedule in breaks—It may seem obvious but taking breaks is an important part of good time management. None of us can go for very long without taking time to be refreshed and rejuvenated. This may mean taking some time to hike in the woods, talk with a good friend from home, go shopping, take a nap, or whatever kind of activity that will give you energy and a break from the routine. Whenever your schedule begins to "own" you it's time to take control and take care of yourself. Yes, college is demanding and there is a lot to do. However, you will only be at your best and enjoy

this experience if you have a sense of balance. Finding that rhythm is important and it will help to get you through the entire four, five, or more years that comprise your college career.

10. Conquer procrastination—Hmmm, wonder why we put off procrastination until the end. Oh well, never mind. Procrastination is a big problem for many college students. Actually procrastination is closely tied to anxiety. There are a number of issues to consider regarding procrastination. Please read further if you find yourself putting things off and feeling frustrated with the results.

PROCRASTINATION

Procrastination goes hand in hand with anxiety and is associated with a number of problems, including poorer health, delays in seeking attention for health problems, perceived stress, and fewer wellness behaviors.[7] Procrastinators seem to continually trade tomorrow for today. Procrastination can be understood in terms of delayed versus immediate rewards. When we procrastinate we choose activities (chatting with friends, watching television) that are immediately rewarding. In addition, we are reinforced with the immediate reduction in anxiety or discomfort we experience when facing the real tasks at hand. Activities that are less immediately rewarding, like doing homework or planning your time bring more long-term satisfaction, though this reward may not be realized for months or years down the road. In the moment, they are often noxious and anxiety-provoking. So these types of activities are often put aside.

Frequently, when choosing the immediately pleasing activity, there is a sense that we can somehow be relieved of our long-term commitments. Unfortunately this is not the case. They later loom up and nag at us. If an individual were somehow able to "do the math," perhaps using some measure of stress, it would be clear that acting today rather than tomorrow (or the next day or the next) is stress relieving. Once one has developed a pattern of avoidance and the work piles up, of course, it becomes harder and harder to tackle and the work seems more and more unmanageable.

Factors Contributing to Procrastination

Perfectionism. Perfectionism is a strong contributor to procrastination. To be a perfectionist is to be disappointed if things are not done perfectly. Yet, to do things perfectly requires toil and difficulty, and the likely outcome that the product will not be "good enough." In a sense, the perfectionism is a set up for disappointment and anxiety, so we are much more likely to avoid these unpleasant tasks. Think of doing a paper for a class. The perfectionist may have difficulty getting past the first page, writing and rewriting in an effort to get it just right. Let's say you are beginning the task well before the deadline. Given your extremely high standards and the prospect of long hours of anxious effort, you put off the assignment. Your anxious thinking likely sounds like "This is so huge...I'll never get it done." Then, you may "pull an all-nighter" or otherwise work like crazy to get it done at the last minute, hardly the optimal circumstances for completing your best work. But even though you got it done, you find yourself feeling disappointed. Like any anxious avoidance, you're left with a sense that perhaps you really weren't up to the task. That is, you didn't give yourself an opportunity to prove your anxious thinking wrong.

Saying "Yes". How can simply saying "yes" contribute to procrastination? Ask your self this. Do you feel that you are so occupied with small, busywork that you cannot find the time to complete work that is more important? Often, people who are overburdened with commitments to others answer this affirmatively. We are more likely to honor commitments made to others than to ourselves. Saying "yes" too often to others can result in a pile of commitments that are unrelated to your goals and perhaps more in the service of the goals of others. We're not suggesting that you stop giving, but to be mindful of all of the demands on your time and say "no" to people more of the time in the interest of getting your important work done.

Rationalization. Sometimes we are just not very honest with ourselves. We play games with ourselves with the mistaken belief that they will help us get things done. Sometimes we know we are procrastinating. We go out to a party rather than study for a test. However, other times, we kid ourselves by engaging in activities that appear to have some redeeming value or we "prepare" ourselves for the unpleasant task with one that is less unpleasant, but a task nonetheless. Here are some examples. We might wish to clean up our room before studying, with the rationale that less clutter will result in better concentration. Or, we might go for a walk or hang-out with friends, in an attempt to "get in a better mood" for the task we face. The bottom line is that when there is important work to be done, you are either doing it or not doing it. Watching T.V. to "relax" or reading fun magazines as a "warm-up" to required reading can be associated with immediate gratification. In effect, it can make you feel better while you are procrastinating. The bottom line here, as has been said before in this book, is that it is important to be aware of how you avoid things that you are afraid of or that frustrate you.

Underestimating the Scope of the Task. Some projects are simply too large to complete in any reasonable period of time. As such, we tend to avoid them, becoming quickly overwhelmed once we try to begin. Yet, often we tend to think of the "whole" of a project when we try to undertake it. Building a house, for example, has an obvious beginning and end but there numerous steps in between. In the same way, a large project can be approached by breaking the overall task down into smaller components, to be tackled one at a time. This makes the process much more manageable.

Managing Projects

Let's look again at the example of writing a paper for class, a 20-page expectation that seems overwhelming. A procrastinator will most likely put this task off until the last minute. All throughout the semester the anxiety will build and when it's time to write the paper the anxiety will seem insurmountable. Some individuals will pull an all-nighter but others will ask for an extension on the deadline and continue to procrastinate.

The outcome, however, could be quite different. By identifying the anxious thinking that is attached with the avoidance, you can begin to challenge it. Rather than "I'll never be able to put this project together.... I don't have any idea what he's asking," you might give yourself the message that "I don't really know exactly what I'm supposed to do with this, but I can get started with outlining most of the sections. I'll probably get a clearer idea as I go along."

Applying good time management strategies will also be helpful. You could approach the task by taking a 10-minute block of time early in the semester to write a rough outline of the paper. Although this may not seem like much, it's actually a huge leap forward, as with your actions you've already begun to test some of your anxious and likely unreasonable assumptions. Then in another 20-minute block you could begin doing research. Another short block of time could be used to refine the outline. Then, when you sit down to actually write the paper, the goal could be to write one section (such as the introduction) at a time, with some regular breaks built in. As the blocks of time add up, the paper will be taking shape and the actual time spent writing before the deadline will be much less intense. As was said before, acting today is much less stress-producing and it will actually make you feel good about yourself and the work you do. By transforming your thinking, setting goals, breaking down tasks and pushing yourself to try them in the face of uncertainty and anxiety you begin to dismantle the habit of procrastination.

SUMMARY

Time management is a shortcut way of saying you can develop the skills you need in order to become the architect and engineer of your accomplishments and achievements. It is a way of exercising your values, setting direction in your life, and giving purpose to your behavior. Setting goals and planning are the primary recommendations for gaining control of your time. Others such as developing the habit of organizing your day with a "to do" list, identifying your energy cycle, using your spare time effectively, and avoiding procrastination, for example, are recommendations of how to accomplish goals and further planning. Colleges and universities are rich in social and intellectual stimulation and with the newfound freedoms college life offers, it is important to develop time management skills so that you can take advantage of the opportunities the campus offers, manage your anxiety, and at the same time confidently move in the direction of obtaining your degree.

CHAPTER 11

Thinking and Action Strategies

There is nothing either good or bad, But thinking makes it so.

—Shakespeare

Things do not change; we change.

—Henry David Thoreau

We hope that by the time you reach this chapter you are feeling hopeful that what you learn in this book will really make a difference in your life. Before you began reading, you may have felt relatively alone with your problem with anxiety. Now you know that anxiety is a common problem among college students like yourself, that other competent students suffer with it, and that it is manageable. Knowing that others have had similar struggles can make a difference in understanding and addressing your own problem.

LEARNING TO MANAGE ANXIETY

This chapter and the following one on lifestyle strategies will describe some of the most helpful strategies and techniques as they apply to you as a college student struggling with anxiety. As we mentioned at the beginning of this book, you get out what you put in the change process. This is true for a lot of things in life, and very true for overcoming anxiety. You have made a big step forward already by taking the time to learn more about your experience. The next step is to put the ideas and strategies you've learned to work. As you've noted in previous chapters, putting these into practice takes time and effort, but has the promise of significant improvements in anxiety and your self-confidence.

Throughout this book we have focused on two important types of strategies—thinking and action strategies. In previous chapters, we've discussed how these strategies can be applied to deal with a number of anxieties, including those about tests, social relationships, and others. This chapter offers more in-depth explanations of the most effective thinking and action strategies available. Thought and action strategies form the basis for a cognitive-behavioral approach to anxiety. We know from a great deal of research that these cognitive-behavioral strategies produce positive change.

THINKING STRATEGIES

Let's turn again to some of the simple and effective ways to change the kinds of thoughts and beliefs that help fuel anxiety. We will focus on the three elements of facilitating change in our thinking that have been discussed throughout the book: identify, challenge, and transform.

IDENTIFY

Self-talk. We have the power to change our thinking, yet this is difficult if we do not gain awareness of what and how we're thinking and how it is related to our anxiety. Throughout this book we have discussed the fact that anxious individuals tend to evaluate situations as more threatening than nonanxious individuals. So it is important to build awareness of the ways you perceive situations where there is threat. One of the best ways to do so is to "listen" to your anxious self-talk. This self-talk provides the cognitive fuel for anxiety reactions.

Anxious self-talk can lead to paralyzing feelings of fear and the associated urges to flee or avoid facing difficult situations. When anxious, our thoughts spring to the possibility of danger or impending catastrophe, resulting in distortions or exaggerations relative to the situation at hand. We call this *erroneous* or faulty thinking. Remember, everyone experiences the distorted "lens" when anxious or upset; the difference is that, when you're more anxious than usual or chronically worried, the thinking becomes more automatic (habitual), frequent, and intense. Essentially, we begin to alter, more constantly, our beliefs about our surroundings and ourselves. The thoughts may be, "I can't do this, this test is too hard, I'm going to flunk out of college" or "I never should have come to this party, I don't know anyone, I'm going to embarrass myself and never fit with this group." When one is anxious, these pop into one's head "automatically," in a kind of shorthand form. It's as if you experience the thought as "Test—too hard—fail," or with the second example, "Party—don't know anyone—rejection." Can you imagine how you'd feel if someone else was saying these things to you ("you really shouldn't go with everyone, you'll just embarrass yourself," "this test is too hard for you, I bet you're going to flunk it")? You'd feel terrible, of course. If it occurred only once, you might be able to shrug it off and not take it personally, but what if you heard this day after day? Yet we engage in this type of self-dialogue day after day when we're anxious.

Now, at this point, many students find themselves wanting to *not* think about these situations and the feelings that arise. But we're telling you that instead of avoiding or distracting you want to actually *concentrate* on what happens to you in these moments; in particular, the kind of self-talk you engage in at these times. Think for a moment about a recent experience that was very anxiety-provoking for you. Replay the situation and try to "get inside your head" to hear what you said (see the example in box 11.1). It's very important that you don't judge or criticize your self-talk. Its hard enough to experience these anxious thoughts, you certainly don't want to beat yourself up about them. At this point in the process, your job is simply to recognize and observe them.

Box 11.1   Annie's Self-talk

> *Annie has a 20-page paper due. She feels a great sense of dread and is overwhelmed with anxiety whenever she thinks about getting started. She feels like its just so hard to push herself to get to work. She thinks "I can't write this paper. I don't even know where to begin. This paper is far too difficult for me! Perhaps I should consider dropping this course."*
>
> What is happening to Annie here? She is giving herself self-defeating messages and is doing so over and over, every time she thinks about the assignment. She is, in essence, telling herself that she is not capable of writing this paper.

<u>Strategy</u>: *Recognize your self-talk and see it for what it is. This is the first step in making a change in your thinking that fuels your anxiety.*

Cognitive Errors. There are some common patterns that occur in anxious thinking; these are sometimes called cognitive errors. By now, these should be somewhat familiar to you. We provided you with a brief introduction to the concepts in Chapter 1 and talked about them in detail as they apply to social anxiety in Chapter 7. In Chapter 8 we devoted significant attention to the error of catastrophizing as it applies to test anxiety. You want to learn to identify cognitive errors because, when you're very worried or worried often, they become ingrained as your typical thought pattern. When this happens, you begin to believe these erroneous messages and self-statements. Not only are these usually inaccurate, they can be extremely negative, discouraging, and self-defeating.

Some of the more common cognitive errors are listed along with examples to help you recognize them.

- Overgeneralization: This refers to the tendency to jump to a general conclusion based on one item of evidence. Example: "I can't get this assignment done. I never seem to be able to succeed in anything I do!"

- Catastrophizing: This refers to the tendency to think that if a negative event occurs, it will be terrible, unmanageable, or have tremendous negative consequences. Example: "I can't seem to figure out what assignment to do first. I know I won't get all my assignments done in any of my classes. I'll probably fail the entire semester." "I'll never get the attention of that recruiter."

- Filtering: This is the tendency to run events through a kind of sieve, in which all but those that are negative or confirm our fears are filtered out. In our "anxious minds," we actually tend to pay more attention to those aspects of a situation that seem to support our worry. Individuals who encounter this cognitive error will tend to focus on their weak points and ignore their positive qualities. Example: "My roommates see how boring I am. They must think I'm a real loser."

- Polarized thinking: This cognitive error is characterized by a pattern of extreme thinking—either all good or all bad. Example: "If I make even one mistake in this assignment my professor will think I'm stupid."

- Mind-reading: Mind-reading refers to the tendency to guess at what others are thinking, based on very little hard evidence and a great deal of speculation. Example: "I'm so nervous. Everyone in this line can see how I'm blushing and sweating. They must think I'm a fool!"

- Personalization: We all know this one. It refers to our taking things personally. It is reflected in a tendency to assume that negative comments or actions made by others are directed at you. Example: "She looked at me in such a critical way. She must think I'm worthless." In reality the other person could have a sour look on their face for any number of reasons (e.g. a headache, lack of sleep, receiving bad news, etc.)

- Fortune-telling: This typically involves predicting that things will not get better. Example: "I will probably flunk out of college;" "I'll always be alone;" or "I'll never fit in."

Strategy: *Look at some of your most negative thoughts. Do you see any of these cognitive errors? Label them and see them for what they are.*

Challenge

We've already shared some of the strategies for challenging anxious thoughts in our discussions of the various ways in which anxiety manifests in previous chapters. Remember, challenging your thinking is different than engaging in "positive thinking." Instead of just saying positive things to yourself (like "everything will work out just fine"), you will be training yourself to think more realistically. That is, you will be examining your interpretations and assumptions from a more balanced perspective. This section will offer a more detailed review of challenge strategies and also some new material.

Imagined Consequences. Now that you've identified some of your negative and erroneous thinking, let's take it a step further. This involves challenging the imagined consequences associated with your most anxious moments. In moments of intense anxiety, we tend to jump ahead and imagine outcomes and consequences. Unfortunately, these are usually quite negative. We don't imagine these deliberately; instead, they tend to occur instantaneously and automatically. For example, the worry "I can't get started on this assignment" might be followed by an imagined consequence like "I'll probably fail the class." That's pretty extreme but this is often the way we think when worried. Notice that we are referring to "imagined" consequences. This is not to say that the consequences you fear are not real, but as we will be discussing in more detail, they are at least less likely to occur than you might at first imagine.

These Imagined Consequences Occur as a Result of Faulty Cause-effect Chains. Anxious thinking often involves thought cycles that include a number of specific events that have to happen in a sequence for there to be the negative outcome or consequences you picture. For example, perhaps you are anxious about going to a party where you fear you may not know anyone. The imagined consequence is that you will be humiliated. Take a moment to think of all of the smaller events that must occur in order for you to end up humiliated. At the party, you have to actually find yourself with nobody to talk to. You have to assume that people will show no interest in you or, worse yet, will be judgmental and critical. Then, you actually have to do something that can be construed as humiliating. While this chain of events is certainly possible, it is very unlikely. The bottom line is that many times we skip from the thought to the final outcome, without regard for the myriad of smaller events that have to take place. Remember the worry process from Chapter 2? Anxious thoughts often lead to increased physio-logical arousal and anxious sensations. We experience more intense levels of anxiety due to the threats implicit in these imagined consequences. That is, our nervous systems are responding to the danger associated with our imagined outcome, not just the immediate concern.

See the following diagram that illustrates this.

Party—Automatic Thought ⟶ Imagined Consequence—Humiliation

The actual chain of events that must occur for humiliation to occur:

Party → Nobody to talk to → Nobody shows interest → Several attempts to approach people → People are critical and judgmental → I do something humiliating → Humiliation Experience → Anxiety

The bottom line is that is it unlikely that all of these events will happen in this sequence and result in your humiliation.

It is important to *challenge* this type of thinking. One simple way to do this is to use a *Thought and Consequence Sheet* that follows. We have provided a few examples with some space for you to add your own examples. Here is a list of common anxious thoughts, along with imagined consequences that are associated with them.

<u>Thought</u>	<u>Imagined Consequence</u>
I'll never get through this assignment	I'll probably fail this class
What if this major doesn't work out?	I'll end up a loser
I can't joke around like the rest of the guys	Everyone will think I'm boring

In the spaces provided, fill in some of your own examples from situations that make you anxious.

_____   _____

_____   _____

_____   _____

<u>Strategy:</u> *Look for the imagined consequences in your thinking and write them down. Become more aware of the faulty cause-effect chains in your thinking. Recognize that it is highly unlikely that the chain of events will occur that links your initial thoughts and your feared outcomes. Even if some of the events happen, the consequences are typically not realistic.*

Testing Hypotheses. Whenever you have one of the automatic thoughts that you described in the previous exercise, you are, to use the language of science, putting forth a hypothesis. In effect, you are saying, "if I can't think of a witty thing to say, everyone will think I'm boring." And given that it is a hypothesis and not a confirmed fact, it is testable. How could you test this hypothesis? As a start, you could review some of your experiences. Were you at a social gathering where you couldn't think of something witty to say? How did others really respond to you? Do you really have evidence that others thought you were boring? Most likely this was not the case. We're asking you to think about what really happened in these past experiences, not what you perceive, through your anxious lens, to have occurred. Remember, you may have walked away from situations in the past with what you believe is "evidence" of your fears. Too often we engage in "filtering" or "mind reading" as we review anxious experiences in our past. The goal is to examine what the facts were in the situation, not what your feelings led you to believe. Let's go back to the example of Annie. If she examines the other large papers and assignments she's completed in the past year, she sees that although she almost always has difficulty initiating the tasks, they typically feel far less daunting once she's started. She realizes that it's been helpful for her to review her ideas with her professor, or hear what others in the class are doing.

Because, as we have mentioned in earlier chapters, avoidance or escape are such common responses in the face of anxiety, you may have chosen to leave the social setting because of your fear that everyone would see you as boring. If avoidance or escape is involved, we really aren't fairly testing our anxious assumptions and interpretations. Again, think of way in which worry works. By engaging in anxious behaviors, we tend to only find proof of our anxious beliefs (I left the party just in time, before I was humiliated; I made it through class because I got that seat right by the door). In the approach we are discussing here, we are encouraging you to test the theories that you generate when you are anxious. This involves deliberately examining your experiences and assumptions with the more logical and realistic way you appraise situations when you're not anxious. It will also involve actively placing yourself in situations where you'll face what you fear. We will be devoting significant time to the notion of facing one's fears in a later section. For now, we want to drive home the message that many of the anxious hypotheses that are generated never come to pass. That is because they are based on faulty premises. We'll go so far as to say that most of the consequences that anxious people fear do not come to pass. Notice that we said "most." You can clearly cite instances from your life of a worry that came to pass, or your worst nightmare that came true. Still, in those situations, you want to challenge your perspective with questions like "Was it as bad as I thought it was going to be?" "How can I cope with it now that it's happened?" "What can I take from this bad situation that will help me in the future—what have I learned?"

Strategy: *Don't accept your negative thoughts at face value. Test your hypotheses in a logical manner.*

Examine the Probabilities. We're doing some hypothesis testing, remember? Examining the Probabilities is an important thought strategy that forces us to use real facts and evidence to test our fearful assumptions. People who are anxious often feel like they need to be 100% sure that bad things won't happen in their lives. They may try to ensure that they have covered all of the bases by being vigilant for signs of threat or danger or control situations in order to feel safe. In contrast, nonanxious people walk through life with faith and hope rather than trying to control all the events of their lives. They recognize that while there is no certainty of safety, they can reasonably expect that things will turn out alright most of the time. What can be learned from this? In order to better manage anxiety, it is important to develop the habit of thinking through the probabilities of negative events occurring. Often the things that anxious people worry about seem quite likely (to them) that they will occur. That is, the imagined consequences and faulty cause-effect chains occur automatically and are, in an instant, rated as likely to happen.

Many anxious thoughts pertain to circumstances that could occur but have, in fact, a very low probability of taking place. A fear of flying is a good example. Let's say you are someone who worries about flying. When approaching an upcoming airline trip, you may have intrusive images of plane crashes you've seen on T.V. or elsewhere in the popular press. These images are vivid and come to mind easily. They are coupled with thoughts like "it is stormy today...there is turbulence...there is a good chance I could die on this plane." How would you counter this line of thinking? By examining the available evidence. Let's begin by evaluating the probabilities associated with the safety of commercial air travel. If we attend to the known probabilities, we should be more worried about other types of transportation such as automobile travel. Aviation has been so safe that a passenger who takes a domestic jet flight every day would have to fly, on average, for 36,000 years before succumbing to a fatal crash.[1] For another perspective on the safety of air travel, go to an international airport and watch the planes take off and land, note their frequency, and keep in mind that planes fly at this frequency day in and day out, year after year, with very few crashes. Lessening the fear involves challenging your assumptions by examining the real probabilities; you are, in essence, pushing yourself to believe the facts, not what your feelings tell you. In this example you are introducing new thinking about the relative safety of flying and perhaps even the benefits of flying to your destination.

Now, let's take a worry and apply these new approaches. We've provided you with a form for you to use in box 11.2 than can serve as a guide.

Strategy: *Recognize the probabilities attached to consequences and use them to generate alternative consequences and provide you with more realistic types of thoughts.*

Transforming Thoughts and Beliefs

You've become more aware of your thinking in particular situations and are generating more realistic alternative consequences. This is good. But how can you transform your thoughts and beliefs in ways that will reduce your tendency to be anxious and worried? This involves consistent stocktaking of your anxious moments, your appraisals, and the meanings you've ascribed to them, particularly about yourself. Transforming steps include catching yourself, finding balance, and developing better core beliefs.

Catch Yourself. We have learned a great deal about anxiety and how anxious people view the world around them. Now that you know these things about yourself you can begin to take a new approach. Maybe it will feel like you are catching

Box 11.2   Identifying and Challenging Anxious Thoughts

Complete this in as much detail as possible when anxious—these questions are here to assist you in taking a "snapshot" of your anxious thoughts and assist you in challenging them.

Situation:

Identify the Thoughts (fearful self-talk, "what-if's)

What exactly do I fear would happen?

How does the situation play out in my mind? What consequences am I imagining?

What am I saying about my ability to cope with this fear?

Challenge the Thoughts: (answer these questions)

What evidence do I have to support my fear?

What is really likely to happen? How probable? What is a more realistic consequence? An alternative perspective (challenge)?

What would I think about this matter if I weren't so anxious? How do others whose perspectives I trust view this?

What evidence supports my more realistic appraisal of the situation?

yourself from falling. Have you ever had the experience of almost falling down a flight of stairs? At the last moment you catch the railing and hang on to steady yourself. As you look down the steps you feel a sense of relief that you did not take that plunge! Similar to this experience, you can begin to transform your thoughts by catching a mental railing and not taking the plunge into worry. Stop—realize that you are starting to fall into a negative pattern of thinking—and step back to reconsider and move toward a more effective and realistic mode of thinking. Try to make this a more frequent and habitual pattern. Take time to reflect on anxious episodes and try to view it in a different way. Ask yourself these questions: What exactly do I experience as threatening in these situations? What am I telling myself (self-talk) about this situation that results in the meaning it has for me and results in my experience of anxiety? How often is my anxiety fueled by meaning I give situations? This initial step in which you *catch yourself* will help you to begin to transform your thinking patterns.

Find the Balance. The purpose of challenging imagined consequences, testing hypotheses, challenging faulty cause-effect chains, and examining probabilities is that it provides us with *balance.* Instead of always evaluating things in a threatening manner and letting automatic thought patterns go unchecked, we need to come to a more balanced way of looking at the world. This is a world that doesn't require us to be so vigilant and watchful of threat; a world where we aren't so stressed. For example, we used the illustration of being afraid to go to a social gathering because we may say something stupid. We recognized that we may not say the most intelligent or poignant statement at the gathering, that we might not offer a lot to the conversation, but that we are not at all likely to say the most "stupid" thing either. Others may not be awed by our intelligence, but may be likely to view us as having common interests or being a good listener. Recognizing this allows us to find a more balanced way to view the social gathering. It is freeing to realize that you can go to the party and it will probably be fine because it will not be a horrifying experience. In fact, it might just be a normal event in which you get to know some people. That's balance!

Develop More Affirming Core Beliefs. This final step in transforming thoughts and beliefs is a bit more challenging. This step involves digging deeper to the source of our thought patterns—our core beliefs. As we review our thought patterns we need to ask this question "Does the nature of my self-talk reflect any themes regarding the way I view myself and others?" "Are there some beliefs at the core of my thinking that I need to better understand?" Here is an example that may help to explain this important concept.

Angela has been fretting for weeks about going to a party at the neighboring dorm. The party represents a significant event for new freshmen looking to meet new people. Although Angela's roommates are very nice and they have agreed to go together, they seem to feel comfortable joining in with new groups and "going with the flow." They are hoping to meet a lot of new people and have a great time partying. Angela worries that there will be a lot of rowdiness and that she'll end up alone, looking inhibited and strange. She wonders if she will be able to talk to new people or if she will just freeze up. She imagines the other girls drinking and flirting and that she'll look so "out of it" in comparison. Every time she thinks about going she begins to feel physically ill and quickly changes her thoughts to other things. Angela considers herself shy and woefully inexperienced.

Can you help Angela? First, it would be important to help Angela *identify* her anxious thought patterns. She seems to have some *self-talk* about not being able to relate to others due to her shyness and inexperience with drinking and dating. We could help Angela *challenge* her self-talk by asking her to consider her hypotheses. One of these is that she'll go to the party and not be able to think of anything to talk about. How could she test this hypothesis? She seems to have made friends with her roommates and they have offered to go together to the event. It's obvious that she will be able to talk with them even if she does not find anyone else to whom she can relate. While they are far more comfortable than she is talking to new people, she is not likely to be "ditched" by all of her friends. So we have helped Angela to challenge her hypothesis and disprove it.

But what about Angela's core beliefs; can you think of what some of them are? Angela may hold the belief that she should be an extrovert, that her introversion is not normal and that people only really like socially outgoing people. So at the core, Angela believes that she must be engaging and gregarious in order to be accepted.

This core belief impacts how she feels about herself and it also impacts the ways in which she relates to others. In this example it would be important for Angela to realize that she has this core belief and to see how it can be changed. Angela can look at the friendships that she currently has and recognize what her friends like about her. Angela's friends have often told her that they think she is kind, caring, and a good listener. These are wonderful characteristics! And, furthermore, they don't seem to judge her for her relative lack of experience with many social experiences. In order to change her core belief, Angela needs to realize that we don't all need to be extroverts. She has some very desirable qualities that other people appreciate. She can adjust her attitudes about the party based on a change in her core belief—it's okay to be introverted and people will still like her. Now she can strategize how she will talk to one or two new people rather than feeling like she needs to be as lively or talkative as others.

<u>Strategy:</u> *Examine your anxious thoughts and see what core beliefs are reflected in them. Make sure that you attend to all the evidence that contradicts your negative core beliefs. What are alternative ways of thinking about you? How would those guide your behavior? Try the exercise below in box 11.3.*

Box 11.3   Transform: Examining Core Beliefs about Myself

Situation:

Anxious thoughts and imagined consequences:

If true, what would these say about me? If bad things happened in the way I fear, what would that mean about me as a person?

What interpretations and assumptions am I making about my capabilities?

What is the core fear/belief about myself revealed in my anxious thinking?

How can this be challenged? What evidence do I have that it is true? Not true?

What are other ways of viewing the situation? Other ways of seeing myself?

If I adopt these more affirming ways of thinking about myself and my situation, in what ways might that guide my behavior?

Source: Adapted from Greenberger, D.G. and Padesky, C.A. *Mind Over Mood: Change How You Feel by Changing the Way You Think* (New York, NY: Guilford, 1995).

ACTION STRATEGIES

We have focused a great deal on thinking strategies but action is also necessary! Real transformation of our attitudes, thoughts, or beliefs occurs as we repeatedly disprove our old ways of thinking and act in ways that are more closely aligned with our more realistic perspectives. New ways of thinking require evidence to support them. We need feedback to give our challenges staying power. This feedback comes from taking new action. If you can behave in new ways in threatening situations, you can discover that feared consequences fail to occur. Or, that if they do occur, you can see that it is possible to cope with them in a manner that strengthens you and makes you more able to face challenges in the future.

There is an old saying that goes something like "it is easier to act your way into a new way of thinking than to think your way into a new way of acting." A common myth is that we have to build up a "critical mass" of self-confidence before we can take the risk of behaving differently in life situations that we fear. When facing anxiety, we don't wait until we feel comfortable or safe. If we did so, few efforts at change would get past the stage of wishful thinking. Dispensing with this myth can open up the path to recovery from anxiety.

New actions may feel awkward at first. You will likely feel uncertain and tentative. You have undoubtedly felt this way when learning new skills, for example driving (especially when learning to drive a stick shift!). When first learning to drive, you had to focus a great deal of attention on the task. Now, driving likely feels automatic. The truth is that rarely do things go smoothly the first few times—it usually takes us a while to feel comfortable. This is a fact of life that cannot be avoided. If you struggle a lot with the need to have things go smoothly and predictably, we hope that you attended to some of the information on perfectionism earlier in the book.

The bottom line is that in order to modify your anxious behaviors, you have to be willing to face some uncertainty, to allow yourself to not be 100% sure that things will go ok. If you think about it, this is not any different than the way in which you approach most of the things in your life that you are *not* afraid of. If you can accept ambiguity, uncertainty, and a certain amount of personal clumsiness as a fact of living, you can begin to build confidence by behaving in new and different ways in any number of situations.

Exposure—A Strategy for Facing Your Fears

A very important approach for taking action to combat your fears is a technique called "exposure." The term exposure refers to the process of facing your fears. As we've discussed a number of times, this is in direct contrast to the avoidance and other anxious behaviors that actually fuel your worry. If you are like most people struggling with a degree of anxiety, you likely have become adept at controlling your environment or avoiding situations that bring on anxiety. This is a natural part of the fight/flight reaction, but one that can be countered.

Let's talk about how exposure works and how it can be a significant part of your "toolbox" for managing anxiety. Exposure works in a number of ways. First, it helps you learn that facing the situations you fear does not result in your imagined consequences. On the rare occasions that feared outcomes arise, exposure can help you learn that, in fact, you can cope with them and survive the unthinkable. Second, repeated and gradual exposure to feared situations will actually help you experience less physiological arousal with each encounter. Perhaps most importantly, exposure helps you build confidence that enables you to eventually participate fully in the situations that you have avoided.

Let's say you tend to avoid all social gatherings. By doing so, you do not have the opportunity to learn that you can get through these situations without disastrous consequences. Catastrophic expectations cannot be proven wrong when you avoid anxiety-provoking situations. By pressing yourself to attend social gatherings you can learn new ways of thinking and behaving.

You might be thinking, though, that there aren't any guarantees that you can go to a party without a social disaster resulting. This is true. If you have had a difficult experience at a party in the past, it will be hard to face situations that place you at risk for a similar occurrence. However, it is our experience, and one that is supported by a good deal of research, that the vast majority of exposures result in positive learning. People are often pleasantly surprised to discover that a situation that they have dreaded for so long was not so difficult at all. Taking action leaves you feeling stronger, more in control, and empowered against your anxiety that so often feels like it has power over you.

Exposure work, as we often refer to it, involves some discomfort. It provokes a degree of anxiety. Experiencing some anxiety is crucial for the success of exposure, as it helps you cope with it. Through gradual provocation of anxiety, you learn that anxiety can't actually harm you and it helps you take a new look at the situations that you fear.

Beyond shedding light on whether your fearful thoughts are likely to be true, exposure helps your body respond differently. With repeated and planned exposures, your body begins to act more calmly in situations that have made you anxious in the past. The process by which this occurs is known as "habituation." This refers to the process of getting used to the things that previously caused you fear. For example, let's say that there is construction going on in the proximity of your home that involves loud hammering. Initially, the noise might result in a startle response. Your body may have reacted with increased heartbeat and respiration among other changes and you had the accompanying thought, "what is going on?" As you understood what was going on and the noise became more repeated and predictable, your anxiety response diminished even though the situation that provoked the anxiety in the first place continued unchanged.

Figure 11.1   Exposure and Habituation

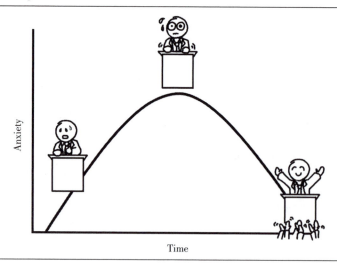

Figure 11.1 demonstrates the relationship of exposure and habituation. When you put yourself in a challenging situation with respect to your fears (exposure), anxiety climbs, as depicted on the left side of the diagram. As you stay in the situation, anxiety reaches a peak and begins to decline with habituation. Anxiety is overcome with further habituation until you no longer experience discomfort and distress. Habituation is a natural process that takes place with exposure, but you may not have experienced it given your tendency, when anxious, to avoid or escape fear-producing situations before habituation can occur. To make the most of an exposure experience, you must stay in the situation long enough for anxiety to peak and then decline. Many people find that exposure does not generate as much anxiety as they anticipated. In fact, it is important to note that anticipatory anxiety, the anxiety you experience before entering a feared situation, is often stronger than the anxiety experienced during the exposure.

Two things happen with repeated exposure. First, the peak level of anxiety decreases. In other words, with repeated exposure, the situation becomes less threatening. Second, habituation occurs more quickly. In this way, the exposure process helps to contribute to mastering one's fears of situations.

Now, let's spend some time discussing how to actually engage in exposure as a tool for overcoming your fears. Exposure can be approached in different ways. Exposure to real-life situations is referred to as *in-vivo* exposure. If you have a fear of small group gatherings and decide to participate regularly in a study group, you are engaging in in-vivo exposure. If you decide to work on introducing yourself to people that you don't know at parties by attending parties and purposefully approaching others, then you are engaging in in-vivo exposure.

An important consideration in exposure work is to approach it *gradually*. It is important to generate what is called a *hierarchy* of feared situations. There may be some situations that are easier than others. For example, if you have a fear of speaking in groups, then perhaps speaking in a small group is easier than in a large one. Or, speaking in a group of friends may be easier than in a group of strangers. In planning exposure, it is important to keep in mind which situations you fear the most and which you fear, but less so. Consider the following steps that summarize what we have covered thus far about exposure.

- Identify the fears that you would like to work on.
- Rate the anxiety associated with each fear as mild, moderate, or severe.
- Rank order the fears on the hierarchy from mild to severe.
- Begin by working on the lowest fear on the hierarchy.
- Enter and stay in the situation long enough for habituation to occur.
- Do not avoid or escape the situation prematurely.
- Reflect on what you learned from the experience in terms of the thought strategies discussed earlier.
- Repeat the exposure in the same situation until you achieve some mastery.
- Move on to the next fear on the hierarchy, repeating the steps above.

Here is an example involving fears of speaking to others in class and speaking in front of the class:

Amount of Anxiety	Situations I Fear
Severe	Speaking in front of the entire class
Somewhat Severe	Presenting in front of a small group
Moderate	Sharing my opinion or answering a question in class
Somewhat Moderate	Sharing my opinion in a small group
Mild	Talking with a group of five to six people in my dorm
Almost None	Talking with one or two roommates

Now, use the spaces below to note how you can apply exposure to a situation that you fear:

Amount of Anxiety	Situations I Fear
_____	_____
_____	_____
_____	_____
_____	_____
_____	_____
_____	_____

There are situations that are difficult to encounter in real life, either because they occur very infrequently (giving a talk in front of a class, taking a big exam,) or are, at first, too difficult to expose oneself to (asking someone out on a date, discovering that you have let someone down). When one cannot purposefully expose oneself to fear for these reasons, it can be useful to confront the fears or worries in imagination rather than in real life. We call this process "imaginal exposure." It is very similar to the imaginal coping approach discussed in the chapter on test anxiety.

The key is to create an imaginary scene that resembles a real life situation as closely as possible. There should be key attention to details of the real life situation using all five senses (sights, sounds, tastes, sensations, smells), if possible. Ideally, the situation should arouse enough anxiety that it is difficult to sustain the imagery at first. Sticking with the imagery enables habituation to occur.

Exposure to Worries

Much of the experience of anxiety involves worry about things that might happen in the future. These also often involve situations that are unlikely to happen and/or difficult to expose oneself to in real-life. For example, you may be riddled with unreasonable fears about your boyfriend being in a car accident, or whether you'll get cancer. Other examples might include worries about the health or well-being of loved ones, worries about your finances, worries about your grades, or worries about your friendships. In Chapter 4 (box 4.1) you were encouraged to note some of your most frequent worries. It may be useful to reflect back on that exercise as you move through this section.

At first it might seem strange and maybe even a little unkind to contemplate actually thinking about your worries on purpose. When one is plagued by rumination and worry, it often feels as though one's thinking is out of control. Yet, it is for precisely this reason that practice in provoking anxious thoughts can help you master them. This process can provide you with an opportunity to practice some of the thought strategies we have covered earlier along with the process of habituation. In this instance we will be applying habituation to thoughts rather than to actions. Let's discuss how to use the principles of exposure to focus on specific thoughts or images associated with anxiety, repeatedly, until new perspectives are generated and habituation takes place.

Take the following steps to engage in exposure to worries:

- Generate a list of your most troublesome worries.
- Create a hierarchy based on the degree of anxiety associated with each worry from mild to most severe.
- Begin with the first worry that you have identified, and concentrate on your anxious thoughts. Think of the most troublesome aspects of the worry. Ideally, you should experience some anxiety when you do this. Stay with this for awhile, focusing on the outcomes that you fear most.

- After awhile, especially if the anxiety begins to fade, begin to think of alternatives to the worst. Use the thought strategies discussed earlier to challenge the thoughts. Aside from the worst-case-scenario, what other alternatives may occur. Also examine how you would cope if the worst did occur.

- Once you have finished with this worry, move on to the next one on your hierarchy.

Try this using the worksheet below:

Amount of Anxiety	My Most Troublesome Worries
_____	_____
_____	_____
_____	_____
_____	_____
_____	_____
_____	_____

SUMMARY

The experience of anxiety is closely tied to how we think about situations and whether we face or avoid situations that we fear. It is important to become aware of thought processes that contribute to anxiety, challenge these perspectives, and transform this thinking into more balanced and self-affirming perspectives. However, new action is also necessary to change thinking and generate the "evidence" needed to support new perspectives. Exposure is a key strategy in overcoming anxiety, and involves gradually facing feared images and/or situations. Engaging in repeated exposure "quiets" our anxiety reaction to situations and helps us support new ways of thinking.

CHAPTER 12

Relaxation and Lifestyle Strategies

There is no need to go to India or anywhere else to find peace.
You will find that place of silence right in your room, your garden or even your bathtub.
— Elisabeth Kübler-Ross

Never eat more than you can lift.

— Miss Piggy

Going to college involves a radical change in lifestyle for most students. It is typically the first time that a person is out on his/her own, having to manage many aspects of life that were at least, in part, managed by one's parents or other family members. It is now a well-known fact that lifestyle choices relate to health over the lifespan. The popular press is filled with stories of the health perils of smoking and drinking and not getting enough sleep, living life with little time devoted to relaxation, among other lifestyle factors. It is also well established that individuals under stress tend to make poorer lifestyle choices. When stressed, we are more likely to engage in problematic behaviors in an effort to cope. College students experience a doubly difficult set of challenges. If it is the first time one is living on one's own, new lifestyle habits must be developed at the same time that one is experiencing a great deal of stress. There are specific challenges to living a healthy lifestyle, such as ready access to high-calorie and relatively non-nutritious food, easy access to alcohol and drugs on many campuses, an irregular and ever-changing class schedule, and many others. This chapter is devoted to discussing healthy behaviors that help buffer one from the stresses of college life and most certainly help to reduce anxiety.

RELAXATION TECHNIQUES—AN INTRODUCTION

Learning to deeply relax is a key component of anxiety management. We often think of relaxation in relation to activities, such as unwinding in front of the television or hanging out with friends, or while sitting on the beach. For many, such activities are indeed relaxing. But relaxation can be much more if practiced regularly and in a more structured and intentional way. In this chapter we will introduce various forms of deep relaxation. We will encourage you to consider investigating one of these forms on your own.

In 1975, Benson and Klopper first described *the relaxation response*.[1] They noted that the bodily changes that occurred in deep states of relaxation were the exact opposite of those produced by the *stress response*. They found that, during deep relaxation, there were decreases in heart rate, respiration rate, blood pressure, muscle tension, and metabolic rate.

Researchers were quick to find that 20–30 minutes of daily practice of relaxation can produce changes that last long after the period of the relaxation. That is, the result of these consistent relaxation exercises was a generalization of effects to the remainder of one's life. In other words, put in consistent time with relaxation practice and you will become calmer all of the time!

Relaxation has become a cornerstone in psychological treatments for a variety of physical ailments and what are called psychosomatic disorders; that is, physical conditions that have a psychological component to them. A few examples include headaches, gastrointestinal disorders, chronic pain, hypertension, and insomnia. In addition to providing help for physical problems, it can be a valuable addition to the toolbox for coping with anxiety as well.

There are a number of relaxation techniques that can help you manage anxiety and also improve your concentration, productivity, and overall well-being. We'll provide you with some of the more popular strategies here. However, a counselor or psychotherapist can be an excellent resource for further relaxation training. He or she can offer more detailed instructions and coaching and can help find strategies that are best suited to your personality and lifestyle.

GENERAL GUIDELINES FOR RELAXATION

The following are general guidelines that apply to the many different approaches to relaxation.

Find a quiet, relaxing place, where you will be alone for at least 10–20 minutes. Use of relaxation strategies is most effective when there are no distractions and when there is sufficient time to engage in the strategy. As a student, you may feel like you have no place to be alone! However, try to identify places like the library that are relatively quiet and private.

Practice once or twice a day. Regular practice is essential in order to obtain the optimal benefit from relaxation exercises. Because relaxation is a skill, it requires practice. Like any skill, there is a period of learning and you should not expect to feel fully relaxed until you have developed more proficiency in the method of relaxation.

Stick with a technique that works best for you. Not every technique will work for every person. The most effective relaxation strategy for you is one that you really enjoy and one that you will use from day to day. Relaxation should not be a chore but rather an enjoyable activity. As such, feel free to try some different methods and see which seems most fitting for you.

Be patient! Don't worry if you don't notice a major change immediately. In fact, you will likely need to practice for a few weeks before you begin to feel the benefits of any relaxation strategy. Like any skill, relaxation does not feel natural at first. You will devote a fair amount of attention to simply learning how to do it, and this concentration is actually counter to calmness for most people. So in order to benefit, you have to learn the skill well enough for it to become largely "automatic." That can be accomplished quite quickly with regular practice because relaxation techniques are, fortunately, relatively easy to learn.

Below are brief descriptions of the more common relaxation methods. The instructions are detailed enough to get you started. We recommend that you try them all on for size. However, to receive maximum benefit, it is important to seek information from the resources provided at the end of the book.

PROGRESSIVE MUSCLE RELAXATION

Progressive Muscle Relaxation (often referred to as PMR) has become a very popular strategy in many treatment programs for anxiety in recent years. This method is based on the relationship between muscle tension and psychological tension. As we discussed in Chapter 2 of this book, as part of the fight/flight response, skeletal muscles tense when the body prepares to deal with an emergency. A moderate amount of tension in the muscles makes them more efficient and able to execute movements that can help us in dangerous situations. Yet, in modern life where few of us are involved in having to run from situations or defend ourselves physically, we derive little if any benefit from this association of tension and negative emotions.

Research by Edmund Jacobson in the 1920's revealed that tense muscles were associated with many forms of emotional distress.[2] He theorized that mental relaxation would follow relaxation of the major muscle groups of the body. Progressive relaxation, as it is typically practiced, involves several basic features. You are taught to tense a muscle (such as a hand or arm muscle), hold it tight for about seven seconds, and then release the tension by relaxing the muscle completely. This results in a muscle that is more relaxed than at the beginning of the tense-release cycle. Below are some introductory instructions to get you started.

- Wear loose, comfortable clothing. Sit in a favorite chair or lie down in a comfortable spot.
- Begin with your facial muscles. Frown hard for 5–10 seconds and then relax all of your facial muscles.
- Work other facial muscles by scrunching your face up or knitting your eyebrows for 5–10 seconds. Release. You should feel a noticeable difference between the tense and relaxed muscles. Focus on the difference between the tense and relaxed muscles.
- Move on to your mouth and jaw. Then, move on to other muscle groups—shoulders, arms, chest, legs, and so on—until you've tensed and relaxed individual muscle groups throughout your whole body.

Here are some specific instructions for the various parts of the body.

Eyes. Close your eyes tightly. Hold them closed for 10 seconds, and then slowly open them. Relax. Notice the difference between the eyes open and closed.

Forehead. Raise your eyebrows as high as you can. Hold them there for 10 seconds, and then release them. Relax. Then, make a frown, lowering your eyebrows as far you can. Hold for 10 seconds. Release the tension and notice the difference between tension and relaxation in these muscles of the face.

Nose. Wrinkle up your nose. Hold for about 10 seconds. Release the tension slowly and relax while noticing the difference between tension and relaxation.

Mouth. Press your lips together as tightly as you can. Feel the tension in your chin and in your cheeks. Hold 10 seconds. Gradually release, noting the difference between tension and relaxation. Relax.

Tongue. Move the tip of your tongue up against the roof of your mouth, behind your upper teeth, pressing hard. Hold for about 10 seconds, and then let go. Relax.

Neck. Press your head back against the top of a high back chair or against the surface on which you are lying down. Hold for about 10 seconds, then release while noting the difference between tension and relaxation.

Shoulders. Shrug your shoulders as high as you can. At the same time, extend your arms stiffly behind you and angled outward, with your palms facing back and thumbs pointing down. Hold for about 10 seconds, and then relax your shoulders while noticing the sensations associated with tension and with relaxation.

Chest. Take in the deepest breath you can, expanding the chest and tensing the muscles that are involved in breathing. Hold it about 7–10 seconds. Slowly exhale while concentrating on the difference between tension and relaxation in these muscles. Relax.

Arms. Hold your arms straight out in front with your palms facing down. Bend your hands upward at the wrist, until your hands and forearms make a 90° angle. Notice the tension in your forearms. Hold for 10 seconds and then let go. Relax.

Hands. Extend both arms in front, palms up. Make tight fists and hold for 10 seconds. Notice the tension in your hands. Release and relax.

Stomach. Push your stomach muscles out as far as you can. Hold for 10 seconds. Release. Now draw in all your stomach muscles, keeping them tight for 10 seconds. Release. Notice the feeling of relaxation in these muscles.

Thighs. Press your upper legs together and tighten your thigh muscles. Hold for 10 seconds. Slowly release the muscles, letting them relax, while noticing the difference between tension and relaxation.

Feet, Ankles, and Lower Legs. While sitting on the floor with your legs straight out in front of you, put your feet together and point your toes forward. Notice the tension in your feet, ankles, and lower legs. Hold for about 10 seconds. Now using your ankles bend your feet back toward your body as far as possible. Hold for 10 seconds. Relax while noticing the difference between tension and relaxation in these muscles.

Once you are able to master the strategy of progressive muscle relaxation, you will note that the complete relaxation of the major muscle groups of the body can be associated with a profound inner sense of relaxation.

MEDITATION

Meditation has received wide publicity in recent years. However, meditation is centuries old and practiced by people worldwide. Aside from being enduring and widely practiced, it is also very well researched within Western psychology.[3] Several methods of meditation are effective in reducing arousal and producing feelings of inner calm. Fortunately, techniques of meditation are generally easy to learn. All of the various forms of meditation share common features. First is the arrangement of the body in a comfortable position that can be sustained for a period of time. Second is the maintenance of physical immobility. Finally, attention is directed to an object, sound, or process in the body. This may sound easy to you, but the key to successful meditation is in sustaining the focus, rather than initiating the focus. In other words, meditation is easy to learn but more difficult to practice.

Meditation runs against the grain of some of the features of life in Western culture related to anxiety and stress. First off, meditation requires you to sit quietly and engage in simple, and rather monotonous activity. For many of us, it is difficult to imagine spending time doing nothing as a path to enlightenment. Meditation is also associated with the concept of "passive attention."[4] In Western culture, we typically think of ourselves "trying to do something" in order to improve ourselves. In meditation, expending active effort actually defeats its purpose. One orients, in meditation, toward "being with" or "flowing with" the object of one's attention. We experience moments where we are totally absorbed in experiences, such as when listening to music, while enjoying nature, or while reading a book. At such times, we are not analyzing the experience or trying to change it. We are literally flowing with or being with the experience. It is this state, or psychological posture, that one is attempting to experience while meditating.

Another challenge in learning meditation but one that provides great benefit in relieving anxiety is transcending self-evaluation. In meditation, you are not concerned with how successful you are in completing the activity in a particular way. Simply put, the language of success and failure does not apply to meditation. One is not a good or poor meditator. If you are attending to the object of meditation, then you are meditating. If you are attending to how well you are doing, then you are likely not attending to the object of meditation. Below are some general guidelines that will help you give meditation a try.

- Choose a quiet room free of distractions.
- Wear loose, comfortable clothing and sit or lie in a relaxing position. It is important that your position does not restrict your breathing. If you are unfamiliar with Yoga postures, it is good to provide your back with support. You should be in a position that you can sustain for at least 20 minutes without discomfort.
- Close your eyes and concentrate on a calming thought, word, or object.
- You may find that other thoughts pop into your mind. Don't worry, this is normal. Try not to dwell on them. Just keep focusing on your image or sound.
- If you're having trouble, try repeating a word or sound over and over (known as a "mantra"). Some people find it helpful to play soothing music while meditating.
- Gradually, you'll begin to feel more and more relaxed.

These brief instructions are provided here to get you started and give you an idea of what the process of meditation involves. There are many varieties of meditation and it is a practice that can be explored and deepened for a lifetime. In the Resources section at the end of the book, resources are provided that enable further exploration of meditation.

VISUALIZATION/IMAGERY RELAXATION

In Chapter 8 we discussed an exercise that used your imagination to rehearse ways of coping successfully with stressful testing situations. In addition to using visualization and imagery for rehearsal and coping, it can be very beneficial as a method of inducing relaxation. In this technique you focus on a mental scene or sustained image rather than on an object or on your body. As an example, many people find the beach a quiet and comforting image.

- Sit or lie down in a comfortable position.
- Imagine a pleasant, peaceful scene, such as a lush forest or a sandy beach. Picture yourself in this setting, noticing the natural beauty of the scene and using all of your senses to experience it.
- Focus on the scene for a set amount of time (any amount of time you are comfortable with), then gradually return to the present, letting the scene slowly fade out.
- Try to engage all of your senses with the images. In addition to the visual mode, imagine how the scene would sound, smell, taste, and even feel tactilely while you are in the image. The following is a scene involving a beach that can serve to get you started with a script. Feel free to use a similar strategy to develop imagery of other comfortable and quiescent places.

Imagine that you are walking alone along a beautiful beach. There are few, if any people around. You feel soothed by the warm sun that shines down on your head and shoulders. You hear the waves coming in and going out, and coming in and going out. The waves are rhythmic and add to the calm you are feeling. You can feel the slight scent of salt in the air, and the air feels clean and clear. You notice your breath and you feel with each and every breath you are more and more calm. After awhile, you find a comfortable spot on the beach and lie down on the soft and warm sand. You notice a beautiful blue sky above you and large puffy clouds gather above and float by. You take in all of the sights, sounds, smells, and sensations and experience a sense of peace and inner calm.

This is just one example of what you can do with imagery. You can take any pleasant and relaxing experience you have had or observed and work it into an imagery exercise. Imagery relaxation is not for everyone. You might find it tedious if you are someone without a vivid imagination. If you do enjoy this method, combining it with the breathing exercise that follows may be even more beneficial.

DEEP BREATHING

One of the easiest ways to relieve tension is deep breathing. The way in which you breathe is strongly associated with the level of stress and tension that you experience. What is this association? Your breathing changes when you become tense: it becomes shallow and rapid, and occurs high in your chest. When you are relaxed, you breathe lower in your chest, from your abdomen. In this way, oxygen permeates "deep" into the diaphragm. As it turns out, it is difficult to be anxious and to breathe deep from your abdomen at the same time. Learning to control your breathing by maximizing abdominal breathing and minimizing shallow breathing will serve as an important tool for relaxation. Furthermore, because breathing is so "portable," it can be used in just about any situation and in a short period of time. Here are some instructions for beginning to practice deep breathing.

- Lie on your back with a pillow under your head. Bend your knees (or put a pillow under them) to relax your stomach.
- Put one hand on your stomach, just below your rib cage.
- Slowly breathe in through your nose. Send the air as low and deep as you can. Your stomach should feel like it is rising and your chest should feel like it is moving only slightly.
- After taking in a full breath, pause briefly, and then exhale slowly through your mouth, emptying your lungs completely and letting your stomach fall. Allow your body to let go with the breath.
- Repeat several times, keeping your rate of breath slow and comfortable, until you feel calm and relaxed. Practice daily.

Once you are able to do this easily, you can practice this technique almost anywhere, at any time. Again, it can be combined with imagery for good results.

The methods described above constitute more formal methods of promoting a deep sense of relaxation. These have been the focus of psychological research demonstrating their effectiveness in achieving relaxation. However, there are certainly many other less structured ways that one can promote relaxation. If use of one of the above methods is not feasible for you, or you have the opportunity to engage in other activities that promote relaxation, by all means explore other activities for inducing relaxation. Other activities to consider include getting a massage, taking a long hot bath, taking a slow relaxing walk, lighting scented candles, and painting or doing some creative and relaxing form of art. Remember, though, that one of the benefits of more formal methods of relaxation is that they can easily be practiced daily and in a number of contexts. And they don't cost anything!

LIVING A HEALTHY LIFESTYLE

Chronic stress and anxiety can impact your immune system, lowering your resistance to getting sick. It can also help you manage the effects of the stress of life as a college student. It can result in a healthier you and one that is more productive. Several lifestyle issues are discussed here. This section is intended to help you evaluate areas that apply to you and to reflect on changes that may improve your life and reduce your level of anxiety. Take an honest apprais- al of your lifestyle choices. Which of these are health enhancing? In contrast, which are not in alignment with your health and personal goals? What things can you change right now? Keep in mind that change requires a commit- ment and does not have to be perfect. Any change that you can make in these areas will likely pay dividends for your health and well-being and for reduction of your anxiety. There are many resources available that promote healthier living, and we urge you to explore some of the resources noted at the end of the book.

Healthy Eating

There are special challenges that you face regarding healthy eating as a college student. If you live in a dormitory, chances are that food is relatively available to you. However, there also many unhealthy foods that are high in calories, fat, and processed carbohydrates. If you live off-campus, you may not have the time, skills, or facilities to cook, meaning that you often depend upon restaurant food, fast-food, or on ready-made foods that lack good nutrition.

Perhaps you are familiar with the term "the freshman 15." For many years this phenomenon was considered an inevitable part of college life, attributed to the freedom of living on one's own, stress associated with the transition to college life, and the ready-availability of food in residence dining halls. As it turns out, more recent research on nutrition among college students suggests that the over- all weight gain among freshmen is about four to five pounds.[5] The freshman 15 myth is problematic in that it can contribute to weight preoccupation among some students and contribute to eating disorders.

This is a book about anxiety and not nutrition, but we want to emphasize, as with other lifestyle issues, good nutrition is good for the nervous system. Eating well will increase your physical, mental, and emotional stamina. Fueling yourself with nutrient-dense foods can boost your immune system, help you maintain a

Box 12.1   Nutrition Tips

- *Don't skip meals*, especially breakfast. Consider getting a small dorm refrigerator and stock it with healthy foods. That way, good food will be readily accessible.
- *Include one fruit or vegetable at each meal.* Finish breakfast with a glass of juice, add a sliced tomato to a sandwich, include a salad with dinner, and snack on a piece of fresh fruit in order to ensure an adequate supply of fruits and vegetables.
- *Eat smaller amounts* of things that you really like. Balance higher fat food choices with lower calorie options like vegetables and fresh fruit.
- *Limit late night snacking.* Fueling your body throughout the day will reduce late-night cravings that can lead to a high intake of calories.
- *Drink wisely.* There is no substitute for drinking plenty of water. Watch colas and coffee because too much caffeine can heighten anxiety as well as contribute to other problems like insomnia, headaches, or stomach upset. Alcohol is simply non-nutritious and packed with calories and, of course, interferes with you using your brain in the way you want to for maximum performance as a student.

healthy weight, and help you feel better about yourself. Those of you who eat better and sleep better respond to stress more effectively. Box 12.1 summarizes some keys to good nutrition.

Physical Activity

Physical activity provides immediate stress relief as well as long-term stress management. Just 20–30 minutes of walking a day, for example, can give you more energy, help you put things in perspective, improve your sleep, sharpen your mental productivity, and boost your self-confidence. Our bodies are made to move and everyone can find some type of activity that is enjoyable. Colleges and universities are great places to get fit. There are typically a myriad of activities (e.g. intramural sports, fitness programs) and facilities to help. If you experience anxiety about exercising in public or in a new situation, you may want to take a class where instruction, support, and goal-setting are involved. Just walking a little extra between classes can help. Breaking up long periods of studying with a walk, a jog, or an activity like Frisbee can be very beneficial.

Sleep

Consistent sleep is important to our optimal functioning and our sense of well-being. Although we all need varying amounts of sleep, too little sleep affects our immune system and our ability to learn and remember information. Sleep is as important as nutrition and exercise when preparing for peak performance. College life presents a very significant challenge to good sleep; namely the absence of a clear sleep-wake schedule. There may be some days where you must get up early for class and others when you can sleep in. There may be nights when you get to bed at a reasonable hour and those when you are awake until the wee hours of the morning. Yet, sleep studies have consistently shown that one of the most important contributors to healthy sleep is a consistent wake-up time. Even if you get the same number of hours of sleep each day but at disparate times, your sleep tends to be less efficient and restful. Your body will function more effectively when set to a regular "clock."

If you are having persistent problems with sleep, you may be experiencing *insomnia*. Students with insomnia may find their sleep nonrestorative, they may awaken frequently during the night, or wake up earlier than desired. However, most often it is the case that the student experiences persistent difficulty falling asleep. A number of factors may trigger a period of insomnia including changes in the environment (e.g. noise), a change in the sleep-wake schedule such as jet lag, stress, illnesses, and the misuse of alcohol, caffeine, or other substances. It is also important to note that sleep difficulties can be a symptom of depression, which often goes hand in hand with anxiety.[6] If you are struggling with sleep, you should read Chapter 13 that addresses the topic of depression.

While any number of factors my initiate sleep problems, persistent insomnia can develop when anxiety arises regarding one's ability to sleep. Students with insomnia will anxiously anticipate bedtime and can become readily agitated when not able to control the onset of sleep. This can be a vicious cycle. The more that the student worries about and tries to control sleep, the more aroused they become. Paradoxically, this lessens the likelihood of sleep. Not unsurprisingly, the intervention for insomnia addresses anxious thinking, sleep interfering behaviors, and managing physical arousal. This is achieved through:

- *Relaxation therapy* that can help calm the body and mind to promote the onset of sleep. Any of the relaxation strategies discussed in this chapter can be helpful. It is important to have a night-time routine where you gradually reduce activities and exposure to anxiety-provoking situations. Then, introduce the relaxation into the routine.

- *Sleep restriction*. People with insomnia often spend a great deal of time in bed, tossing and turning, in an attempt to sleep. Sleep restriction involves actually restricting sleep to a few hours at first and then gradually increasing the hours. This may at first seem counterproductive. If you cannot sleep why limit your sleep? This strategy operates on the assumption that if you have insomnia, you are not sleeping very well anyway. It is more important that you get a few hours of better quality sleep than poor quality sleep spread over a longer period of time.

- *Reconditioning* involves associating the bed and bedtime with sleep. People with insomnia often read in bed or watch television. Unless one is reading dull books or watching boring shows, this leads to an association of the bed with mental and physical stimulation. Reconditioning involves using your bed only for sleep. In reconditioning, the person is advised to go to bed only when sleepy. If unable to fall asleep for a period of time, they are encouraged to get up and stay up until sleepy before returning to try again. During the time a person is trying to recondition, they should avoid naps and ensure that they go to bed at the same time each day.

- *Challenge anxious thinking concerning sleep.* In insomnia, anxious thinking often involves catastrophizing about the consequences of achieving less sleep than is desired. One worries about performance the next day or worries that serious health consequences will result, or that a bout of insomnia forebodes a longer period of time with poor sleep. "I'll never get to sleep, what's wrong with me" or "I have to sleep or I won't be able to get anything done tomorrow." Perspectives that can be helpful include recognizing that the consequences of lost sleep are not typically as severe as imagined in the middle of the night! Yes, limited sleep usually results in some physical discomfort along with some decrease in performance on tasks that are repetitive and mundane. Certainly one should avoid operating machinery or driving long distances if one is experiencing insomnia. Generally, bouts of insomnia improve as stress abates and only infrequently result in a more chronic problem. Finally, the body wants to sleep! After a night or two of less than optimal sleep, the body's natural mechanisms will make it difficult to stay awake. Recent research has indicated that these efforts to reduce anxious thinking used in combination with the other strategies above are an effective initial intervention for insomnia.[7]

- If you find that insomnia is persistent, you should consider making a visit to the student health service at your college or university and discuss the problem with a physician. The short-term use of a sleep medication may be indicated in some cases. It may also be helpful to seek assistance through the college or university counseling center. In Chapter 14 we discuss how to seek professional assistance.

Tobacco

Tobacco can impact your sleep, ability to fight infection, and overall health. While tobacco use is seen by some as an anxiety reliever, it's negative effects have been well studied. We're sure you've heard them many times before. Is this the time to address this problem? Quitting tobacco use takes time and practice. To find assistance with quitting tobacco use, see the resources listed at the end of the book.

SUMMARY

College life presents a significant challenge to a healthy lifestyle. Yet, setting aside time for relaxation and making healthy lifestyle choices can have a profound affect on anxiety and stress. When stressed, our behaviors often move in more problematic directions as we attempt to cope with the challenges we face. Attending to relaxation and a healthy lifestyle can pay great dividends in managing anxiety and it can contribute to overall health and well-being.

Addressing Other Concerns

The significant problems we face cannot be solved at the same level of thinking we were at when we created them.

—Albert Einstein (1879–1955)

There are no big problems; there are just a lot of little problems.

—Henry Ford

Anxiety, although prevalent, is not the only concern on college campuses across the United States. The many stresses intrinsic to college life contribute to a wide range of personal problems and mental health issues. Counseling centers across the nation are seeing increases in the severity of the psychological symptoms for which students are seeking treatment.[1] We will not attempt to provide an exhaustive list of other concerns. Instead we would like to introduce some recent research on issues that are significant on most college campuses today. While we hope the material in this book will benefit you in managing anxiety, we want you to be informed about other concerns and conditions that are presenting with greater and greater numbers on college campuses.[2] In addition, this chapter offers some practical information and suggestions on how to address these issues and how and when to seek help.

DEPRESSION

Throughout this book we have emphasized that college is a time of new beginnings. The changes and challenges confronting students often contribute to problems with mood and depression. For many students, a potent mixture of depression and anxiety is experienced.

Like anxiety, depression is a complex experience that usually arises from a combination of situational, biological, cognitive, experiential, and genetic factors. These causal variables appear to impact everyone differently. Some students may have a strong genetic component to their depression, while others, with no family history, may experience depressive symptoms in response to significant stresses they face on campus.[3] Gender is also a significant variable, as women tend to experience depression at rates almost twice that of men.[4]

Everyone, and we mean everyone, has the "blues" or the "blahs" now and then. Periods of mild or brief depression are extremely common, if not universal, responses to stress. They may indeed be "adaptive" in the sense that they are self-limited experiences that involve facing images, thoughts, and feelings that one would normally avoid.[5] Grief and loss reactions are examples. The sadness or despair experienced during these times typically lead to some level of personal reorganization where we begin to rebuild and restructure our lives. The transitions that begin and end your college life often are accompanied by losses or difficult adjustments in relationships, and depressed mood sometimes results.

Periods of sadness or dysphoria also occur in response to many other stresses and developmental challenges that occur in college. Mood difficulties can arise in the context of illness, conflicted relationships, insomnia, and many other situations. (We reviewed many of these in Chapters 3 and 4). When these depressed moods stretch out for a time, the symptoms often become more pointed and quality of life can be affected. You might be more withdrawn from your friends, more irritable, less communicative with family, less interested in activities, and have difficulty attending class or completing assignments regularly. You may experience a general sense of lower self-worth, lack of motivation, and loss of self-confidence.

These periods of depressed mood are highly responsive to short-term counseling and the good news is that your college counseling center staff is well prepared to help. Clinical depression is a more serious and often persistent condition. Take a look at this list of symptoms:[6]

- Sadness, anxiety, or "empty" feelings
- Decreased energy, fatigue, being "slowed down"
- Loss of interest or pleasure in usual activities
- Sleep disturbance (insomnia, oversleeping, or waking much earlier than usual)
- Appetite and weight changes (either loss or gain)
- Feelings of guilt, hopelessness, or worthlessness

- Thoughts of death or suicide, or suicide attempts
- Difficulty concentrating, making decisions, or remembering things
- Irritability or agitation
- Sadness or tearfulness
- Chronic aches and pains not explained by another physical condition

Experiencing one, two, or even three of these symptoms is not necessarily suggestive of clinical depression. Five or more, however, tied to a duration of two weeks or more are a cause for concern and reason to see a counselor or physician for an assessment.

The American Psychiatric Association reports that one out of four young adults will experience a depressive episode by age 24, and nearly half of all college students report feeling so depressed at some point in time that they have trouble functioning, and 14.9% meet the criteria for clinical depression.[7] Consider a campus of 10,000 students and the numbers can be staggering. Clinical depression, like milder mood difficulties, is amenable to treatments including counseling, medications, or a combination of both. A number of therapeutic approaches, including cognitive-behavioral therapy and interpersonal therapy, have been shown to be effective. But treatment is critical. While some students may experience depression for only several weeks, initial episodes typically last for months and can persist for years. The cumulative impact of these serious symptoms can have a devastating effect on a student's social and academic functioning.

Good self-care and personal and behavioral changes are crucial regardless of severity. You can help yourself with the mood swings that accompany college life in a number of ways. Consider the following, adapted from the National Mental Health Association:[8,9]

- Carefully plan your day—take control of your day by planning and knowing you can do it. Keep organized as much as possible and don't succumb to the urge to skip classes. Regular attendance will keep additional stress at bay.
- Plan your work and sleep schedules—don't put off important tasks, studying, and other class assignments until late at night robbing you of sleep so that you wake up each day exhausted.
- Participate in an extracurricular activity—find something you like, find the organization that promotes your activities of interest and join others with similar interests.
- Seek support from other people—a college roommate, a friend, a family member, or a college counselor. Be sure to stay in touch with your family, friends, and professors.
- Try relaxation methods—exercise such as walking, meditation, or any activity that you find relaxing.
- Take time for yourself everyday—don't forget to take care of yourself and don't give in to negative thinking.
- Work toward recovery—if you find out your blahs are getting deeper and longer, then seek help at the counseling center or some other mental health agency.

These are all strategies for helping yourself. What if you want to help a friend? The first thing to remember is to get other people involved in helping too. Mostly, encourage your friend to seek out the college counseling center if the symptoms are serious enough to affect daily activities. Otherwise, offer emotional support with plenty of time for conversation and gently insist that your friend stay involved socially in activities available on campus, as well as attending classes. Gentle, persistent encouragement can help them re-engage and step back on the path to improvement.

IF YOU ARE THINKING ABOUT SUICIDE

If left untreated depression can lead to suicide. Suicide is the third leading cause of death for those aged 15–24 and the second leading cause of death of college students.[10] Suicide has been called a "permanent solution to a temporary problem." If you are feeling extremely depressed your problems may not seem temporary but rather may seem overwhelming. You may be feeling hopeless, as if things will never get better. But most things do get better if you wait them out and get help for the feelings you are experiencing. Here are some things to consider if you are having suicidal thoughts:

- Suicidal thoughts and feelings are a symptom of depression. Having thoughts of ending your own life do not necessarily mean that you truly want to die. Rather, they may mean that you have more pain than you feel you can cope with right now. The pain of depression can be intense and you may feel that it is too much to bear for long periods of time. When we are depressed we truly don't see things in the way we do when we feel better—you have to try to trust that things won't always feel so despairing.

- Give yourself some distance between thoughts and action. Try making a contract with yourself. Perhaps you can agree to wait 24 hours and not do anything to harm yourself during that time.

- There are people who want to support you during this difficult time. There can be relief from your pain and there is help available. It is important, in any way possible, to increase your connections with people who will listen. Even if it may not feel like it right now, there are many people who welcome the chance to support you during this time. They won't try to argue with you or judge you. They will simply listen and be there for you. Find someone now.

- Reach out to just one person to start. In the front of your phone book is a number for a crisis line. Calling can get you connected with a trained counselor who can listen. Your college counseling center can be a resource. If you call after hours you can typically be directed to a number to call for immediate assistance. Finally, you can always call 911. Serious suicidal thoughts constitute a legitimate emergency. Trusted friends, family members, a member of your faith community, a doctor, or a counselor may be helpful.

HOW TO HELP A SUICIDAL PERSON

All talk about suicide should be taken seriously. The sad truth is that many people have died when others thought their talk of suicide was exaggeration or an attempt to get attention. It is true that ambivalence accompanies many thoughts about suicide. It is also true that many people do not really wish to die but are desperate to communicate the distress they are in.[11] Many, however, have died "accidentally" in making a gesture to call attention to their deep despair. Suicide is truly often a "cry for help." What can you do to help someone, a friend, who is suicidal?

Let's consider some actions that are not helpful. Here is a list of Don'ts[12]

- Don't judge them.
- Don't show anger toward them.
- Don't provoke guilt.
- Don't discount their feelings
- Don't tell them to snap out of it.

What is helpful?

- Foremost, take the person seriously. Be a patient and compassionate listener. As soon as you can, involve other people. Your resident director or other residence personnel are trained to help. If the person has made a suicidal gesture (taken some medication, cut themselves), call 911 immediately and get anyone nearby to come to help.
- Be encouraging and available—if they are talking to you, then go to him or her if you can, and if you can't go, find a way to get someone else to be there. Encourage him or her to go to the counseling center or another mental health agency.
- Stay with the person until others arrive to help, or walk the individual to the counseling center. It is critical that they receive immediate attention from someone who is trained to assist.
- Finally, be available to talk to the person after they have visited a counselor. Continue to involve him or her in social and academic events.

These general recommendations are meant to help you get the person to seek help. The counseling center staff is prepared and has, because of the unfortunate number of college students who are suicidal, well-established procedures for helping. Remember, most suicidal people are in crisis for very brief minutes, hours, or days—if we keep them alive, then help is available and they can find a way out of their despair.

GAY, LESBIAN, AND BISEXUAL STUDENTS

In a recent large-scale national survey of college students, over 70% indicated they had been sexually active with one or more partners during the preceding year. In this same sample, 4% of men and 3% of women indicated they had at least one same-sex partner.[13] Similarly research in the United States, France, and England indicates that the rate of adult homosexual behavior is between 2% and 6% of the population, with rates being higher for male than female homosexuality.[14] While some students enter college with a clear recognition of their sexual orientation, others find college a time when their preferences are revealed. While worries about sexuality are common, anxiety can be particularly acute for students struggling to come to terms with their sexual orientation in the campus environment. Concerns regarding acceptance, possible discrimination, or changes in relationships can lead to social anxiety, depression, and social withdrawal. Developing an understanding of one's identity is an important component of this issue. The college counseling center is often a good place to find resources, support, and a safe environment for help in understanding one's sexual identity. They are likely to have information about local support groups, organizations, and other helpful resources.

SEXUAL VICTIMIZATION

College can be a wonderful time of life, but sadly, there are those who experience trauma and grief on the college campus due to rape or sexual assault. National surveys of college students in the United States indicate that at least 13% of college students report that they have been forced to have sexual intercourse against their will at some point in their lifetime. More female students (20.4%) than male students (3.9%) reported experiences of rape. A startling number of students (2.6%) reported their first experience of rape as occurring before the age of 13 years. However, among college students, 3.6% noted that their first experience of unwanted intercourse occurred at age 19 or older.[15] Statistics from the Justice Department's National Institute of Justice (NIJ) and Bureau of Justice Statistics (BJS) from 2000 indicate that college women are at greater risk for sexual victimization than women their age not attending college, with a victimization rate of 27.7 rapes per 1,000 female students (this included completed rapes and attempted rapes).[16] In addition, as many as 3% of the college women surveyed in the study reported attempted sexual contact without force. The majority of completed and attempted rapes occurred after 6 p.m. at night. For completed rapes, nearly 60% that took place on campus occurred in the victim's residence, 31% occurred in other living quarters on campus and 10% occurred at a fraternity. However, particularly for sexual contacts and threatened victimizations, incidents also took place in bars, dance clubs, nightclubs, and work settings. Of the sexually assaulted women, 90% knew the person who victimized them, and fewer than 5% reported the incident to the authorities.

These sad statistics about rape do not speak to the horror and devastation that may occur in the aftermath of a rape. While physical injury does occur, emotional and psychological trauma is even more common and long-lasting. These very real threats and actions result in a wide range of responses, including the intense anxiety, hypervigilance, and intrusive memories associated with post traumatic stress reactions. Lowered self-esteem and feelings of self-doubt often occur, resulting in social withdrawal and depression. Some women may experience fears about the possibility of pregnancy. Individuals who have experienced a sexual assault need support, empathy, and counseling in order to find healing and a restoration of a sense of normality. The college counseling center provides this for many but some students may need to look off campus for specialized treatment in a rape crisis center. The important thing is to seek help for yourself or for a friend whose life has been impacted by rape.

ALCOHOL AND OTHER DRUGS ON CAMPUS

A great deal of attention has focused on problematic drinking on college campuses. The most common and prevalent health problem on college campuses across the United States is high-risk alcohol and other drug use.[17] Heavy drinking (men equaled five or more drinks in a sitting in the past two weeks; women equaled four or more drinks in a sitting in the past two weeks) has not only individual consequences but ones that affect the colleges as well. These include academic, social, and societal problems that range from poor neighborhood relations to tragic personal stories of violence, sexual abuse, and even death. It is well know that high-risk behavior can have devastating consequences.

Most college students would not consider themselves to be heavy drinkers. However, one significant study showed that more than 40% of college students were estimated to be heavy drinkers.[18] While more students seem to be drinking heavily, there is a corresponding rise in the number who abstain. The latest statistics available show an increase in heavy drinking by college students during an eight-year period from 19% to 22%. Pointedly, the number of students who reported drinking to get drunk rose from about 39% to an alarming 48%. Students abstaining during the same period increased from 16% to 19%.[19]

Interestingly, drinking rates vary considerably among campuses. Students in the Northeast and Midwest report higher drinking rates than students in other parts of the country.[20] Demographics are varied as well. Men drink more heavily than women.[21] Students involved in fraternities and athletics tend to be heavier drinkers than other student groups.[22] Ethnicity seems to affect drinking rates as well. White students are more likely to be heavier drinkers than students from other ethnic or racial groups. White students, for example, report heavy drinking rates of about 50%. Hispanic students, on the other hand, report heavy drinking rates of about 34%. Asian/Pacific Islander students report about 26%; Native Americans about 33%; African-American students about 21%.[23] Lastly, as a group, students at historically and traditionally black colleges and universities report drinking less than students at predominantly white colleges and universities.[24]

Consequences

So what are the consequences of heavy drinking and the behaviors associated with it? The consequences of undisciplined alcohol use present a disquieting statistical and personal portrait based on statistics from a survey of college and university students in the United States:

- Each year, 1,400 college students die from alcohol-related causes, and 1,100 of these deaths involve drinking and driving.
- 500,000 students suffer nonfatal injuries.
- 400,000 students have unprotected sex.
- More than 10,000 students are too intoxicated to know whether they consented to sexual intercourse.
- 1.2–1.5% of students attempt suicide because of alcohol or other drug use.
- More then 150,000 students develop a health problem related to alcohol.
- 11% of students damage property.
- 2.1 million students drive while under the influence of alcohol.[25]

These health consequences mirror academic problems directly related to heavy alcohol use. About 25% of college students report academic problems related to heavy drinking. These include, for example, lower grades, poor performance on tests, inadequately prepared papers, poor class attendance, and not keeping up on assignments.[26]

The reputation of the college is often tarnished. Neighborhood relationships often become strained due to vandalism, noise, vomiting and urination in public, and poor retention rates. The college may develop a reputation as a "party school," with the resulting effect of attracting more students who repeat the patterns and problems associated with heavy drinking. Fraternities, for example, have been found to attract students who are seeking a heavy drinking environment.[27]

Students who drink moderately or abstain report a number of problems associated with other students who drink heavily. These include:

- 60.0% had study or sleep interrupted.
- 47.6% had to take care of a drunken student.
- 20.2% had been insulted or humiliated.
- 10.5% of female respondents experienced an unwanted sexual advance.
- 19.0% had a serious argument or quarrel.
- 15.2% had property damaged.

- 8.7% had been pushed, hit, or assaulted.
- 1.0% of female respondents had been a victim of sexual assault or acquaintance rape.[28]

Other Drugs

Drugs other than alcohol have different degrees of popularity on campus. A survey conducted by the Monitoring the Future (MTF) organization polled 1,350 students and found the following percentages of drug use on campus:

- Marijuana: 35.6%
- Ecstasy: 9.2%
- Hallucinogens: 7.5%
- Amphetamines: 7.2%
- Tranquilizers: 5.1%
- Cocaine: 4.7%
- Barbiturates: 3.8%
- Inhalants: 2.8%
- Methamphetamine: 2.4%
- Heroin: 0.4%[29]

While drug use is less frequent than the use of alcohol, the consequences are similar to those identified with heavy drinking including violence, sexual assault, hospitalization, and death.

EATING DISORDERS

In an earlier chapter we discussed at length the pressures that college students face to "look good" according to this society's standards of physical attractiveness. Unfortunately, this pressure contributes to another problem on college campuses—eating disorders. Eating disorders are considered prevalent and difficult to treat.[30] While estimates vary widely, approximately five to ten million people are suspected to have eating disorders in the United States. Given this fact, there is an irony in our public policy regarding eating disorders. They are underfunded for both research and treatment purposes. Recent statistical evidence for the prevalence, research support, and treatment costs demonstrate the disparity regarding different mental health problems (figure 13.1). These startling statistics need to be more widely publicized to drive legislative action, influence more adequate insurance coverage, and inform the continuing dangers of the social norms to be thin.

Figure 13.1 Prevalence and Cost Comparisons

Diagnosis	Prevalence	Research Funds	Treatment Costs
Eating Disorders	Est. 10 million	$12 million	$5K annual
Alzheimer's Disease	Est. 4.5 million	$647 million	unknown
Schizophrenia	Est. 2.2 million	$350 million	$6K annual

Source: National Eating Disorders Association (2006) http://www.nationaleatingdisorders.org

Figure 13.2 The "Indicators" for Anorexia Nervosa

1. Refusal to maintain body weight at or above a normal weight for age and height

2. A strong fear of gaining weight or becoming fat, despite being underweight

3. Having a distorted image of one's body weight or shape

4. Placing undue importance on body weight or shape in self-evaluation

5. Denying the seriousness of low body weight

6. Having an absence of consecutive menstrual cycles

Eating disorders are complex, treatable mental disorders with severe physical symptoms and side effects as well. The causes of eating disorders are considered to include biological, psychological, and sociocultural forces acting in concert to develop the particular diagnostic symptoms for each affected person. The two most common eating disorders are anorexia nervosa and bulimia nervosa but include many other unspecified types as well (see figures 13.2 and 13.3). Eating disorders can affect women and men and are not limited to age, sex, socioeconomic category, or ethnicity. A recent poll of college women sponsored by the National Eating Disorders Association suggests that as many as 20% of female college student respondents believe that they have suffered from an eating disorder at some point. While eating disorders are more prevalent for women, about 10% of those diagnosed are males and the symptoms for males are similar.[31]

There is a wealth of information regarding eating disorders and we recommend you visit the website of the National Eating Disorders Association for updated information and resources (see Resources). This short section is meant only as the briefest introduction to this significant mental health problem. Because of their prevalence on campus, the college or university counseling center is

Figure 13.3   The "Indicators" for Bulimia Nervosa

1. Repeated episodes of binge eating. A "binge" is characterized by:

    a. eating, in a short period of time, an amount of food that is definitely larger

       than most people would eat during a similar period of time

    b. the eating feels out of control

2. Behavior to "compensate" for the binge eating in order to prevent weight gain.

    Examples can include self-induced vomiting; misuse of laxatives, diuretics,

    enemas, or other medications; fasting; or excessive exercise.

3. Placing undue importance on body shape and weight in self-evaluation.

prepared to work with individuals who come for help. Our purpose here includes dispelling myths concerning eating disorders for college students.

Myths

There are a number of false beliefs that can prevent those with eating disorders from seeking the help they need and can prevent friends and loved ones from encouraging and supporting them to seek help. The counseling center at George Mason University has produced a succinct and clear description of myths surrounding eating disorders and our description below is adapted from their website.[32]

Myth #1. College women are at low-risk because they are intelligent and well educated.

While estimates vary considerably (5–20%), college women are at substantial risk for eating disorders.

Myth #2. Men don't have eating disorders.

It is estimated that approximately 10% of those diagnosed with eating disorders are male. The consensus among treating professionals is that the clinical symptoms for males and females are virtually the same. Among both males and females, certain sports involve greater risks including gymnastics, running, bodybuilding, rowing, wrestling, horse racing, dancing, and swimming as these sports often include weight requirements.

Myth #3. Dieting ensures weight-control.

Paradoxically, repeated dieting can be associated with higher weight gains. It seems that when we lose weight we lose both fat and protein but when we regain weight we regain mostly fat. Here is the bad news. After about two years, more than 90% of dieters regain all the lost weight plus an additional 10 pounds. After five years as many as 98% have regained the weight plus 10 pounds.

Myth #4. Eating disorders aren't fatal.

In fact, anorexia nervosa "has the highest premature mortality rate of any psychiatric disorder." It is estimated that 1% of teenagers in the United States are anorexic and that as many as 10% of those die. The ultimate cause of these deaths is physiological, brought about by the abuse of chemical substances such as laxatives and diet pills resulting in physical and neurological damage such as "gastric ruptures, cardiac arrhythmias, and heart failure."

Myth #5. You can tell if someone has an eating disorder by his or her appearance.

Studies of women with bulimia nervosa reveals that about 70% are of normal weight; approximately 15% would be considered overweight and the remaining 15% are underweight. What these statistics remind us of is that an eating disorder is a psychological disorder with a set of symptoms that extend beyond the physical. These psychological symptoms include distorted body image, obsession with losing weight, distress over body size and shape, perfectionism, and emotional difficulties. Such symptoms are often not reflected in a simple observation of a person's weight.

Myth #6. An eating disorder is such a secret and shameful issue that it is impossible for friends and loved ones to know and help.

It is a fact that someone may engage in eating disorder behaviors such as binging/purging for years before anyone is aware of a problem. One way to be of more help is to be aware of the warning signs of an eating disorder. These include frequent use of bathrooms right after meals, vigorous exercise, preoccupation with body weight and constant weighing. Further, there are warning signs associated with medical care that might signal a problem as well. These include hair loss, complaints of sore throat and bloating stomach, fatigue and muscle weakness, tooth decay, and edema (swelling or puffiness of parts of the body usually in the feet, ankles, leg, face, and hands).

Eating disorders are treatable and the earlier the diagnosis the more successful and timely the treatment can be. In the United States, there is an identifiable and unsettling preoccupation with the size and shape of the human body. Thinness is the recognized and honored norm, especially for women but for both genders, particularly among male athletes. In exposing some of the myths associated with eating disorders, it is hoped that sufferers may be encouraged to seek the psychological and medical help necessary to regain control of their lives.

SUMMARY

Throughout this book, we have mentioned the idea that college students are not immune to the cares and woes of the larger society. The concerns outlined in this chapter highlight that reality. The issues of depression, sexual victimization, heavy drinking, use of drugs, and the struggle with eating disorders do not begin nor end at the border of a college or university. An important objective of this chapter is to alert you to resources and ways of managing the difficulties that have been discussed. Depression can be treated but it needs to be recognized first. There are excellent resources for students and friends of students. Reaching out to find those resources is the first step. Some issues do require the help of a professional. The next chapter will offer a number of important guidelines as you look at getting help from a mental health professional. Chapter 14 is intended to help you as an independent adult to make informed decisions about your own mental health and what type of care may be most beneficial for you.

CHAPTER 14

Helping Yourself and Letting Others Help You

All of us are much more human than otherwise.

—Harry Stack Sullivan

HELPING YOURSELF AND SEEKING HELP

We can probably safely assume that you picked up this book because anxiety is a significant issue for you and you would like to see that change in some way. Perhaps you were looking for some insights and suggestions that would help you overcome or at least reduce the negative impact of the anxiety on your life. Hopefully, along the way, you have learned how better to describe your anxiety and how your experience relates to that of others who struggle with this problem. We trust that you better understand your experience of anxiety and recognize whether your experience is in the "typical" range or whether you may be dealing with a diagnosable anxiety disorder that requires professional assistance. This book was designed to provide some useful strategies for helping you more effectively manage your anxiety, whatever the level of severity.

Box 14.1   Professional Help

We strongly recommend you seek professional help if you are experiencing any of the following:

- Constant, chronic worry that causes significant distress, disturbs your social life, and interferes with classes and work.

- Persistent worry and nervousness in social situations or avoidance of common social situations for fear of being judged, embarrassed, or humiliated.

- Panic attacks or persistent worry/anticipation of another panic attack, intense feelings of terror or impending doom, or avoidance of daily situations due to fear of experiencing panic or a sense of being out of control.

- Irrational fear or avoidance of an object, place, or situation that poses little or no threat of danger. This may include plane travel, insects, heights, driving, and elevators among others.

- Performing uncontrollable, repetitive actions, such as washing your hands repeatedly or checking things over and over. These may also involve repetitive mental behaviors (counting, praying) that feel necessary and persistent.

- Ongoing and recurring nightmares, flashbacks, or emotional numbing relating to a traumatic event in your life that occurred several months or years ago.

Source: Adapted from Anxiety Disorders Association of America "What is an Anxiety Disorder?" http://www.adaa.org/stressoutweek/what_is_an_anxiety_disorder.asp (accessed on October 5, 2006).

We have also addressed the relationship of anxiety to other common problems faced by college students. Perhaps you identified to a greater extent with the descriptions of problems such as depression, alcohol abuse, or an eating disorder. In any case, you may be asking "Do I seek help beyond this book? Are their other self-help resources that can assist me? Should I consult a mental health professional? If so, what professional should I seek, and how do I go about that?" This chapter will address these questions. You can start by examining the questions posed in Box 14.1 above.

SELF-HELP OR PROFESSIONAL HELP?

Self-help Organizations

Self-help generally refers to groups or meetings that involve people who have similar issues or problems. Typically, they are facilitated by someone who is struggling with the problem or some other individual who is not professionally trained. Self-help groups and organizations assist people with a variety of problems today. Perhaps the largest and most recognizable self-help group is Alcoholics Anonymous (AA). Self-help groups are frequently operated on an informal, free-of-charge (or for a small donation), and nonprofit basis. They provide support and education as opposed to active psychological treatment and are voluntary and usually anonymous. Many people find that self-help groups are an invaluable resource for recovery and for empowerment. Similar to the AA concept, there are self-help groups for people struggling with anxiety disorders. The Anxiety Disorders Association of America (ADAA), an organization that we have mentioned throughout this book, can help you locate specialized support groups in your geographic area. Keep in mind, though, that the resources listed in ADAA pertain to people who are suffering from an anxiety disorder. Self-help and support groups for anxiety disorders can empower people to help themselves, and others, on the path to recovery. Self-help groups can provide a safe place to talk about the pain of struggling with anxiety and diminish the sense of isolation that often accompanies these problems. Good self-help groups provide mutual support, a safe and compassionate environment, as well as updated information about anxiety and the anxiety disorders.

Consulting a Professional

Despite your best efforts to help yourself without professional assistance, it may be necessary to seek help to most effectively deal with your problem with anxiety. As we stressed in Chapter 2 of this book, everyone experiences anxiety at different times. Most of the time those feelings come and go. While we may be upset about these feelings, they may not interfere with our ability to do what we set out to do. In general, if your anxious feelings persist for an extended time and their intensity interferes with your daily activities in the ways we've talked about throughout this book, it may be beneficial to seek professional assistance.

Seeking professional help can be rough for many students. Going to see a mental health professional means acknowledging that your life is not as satisfactory as you would like it to be and that something needs to be done. Often, the prospect of seeking help raises a number of doubts and questions. Am I "crazy?" Am I incapable of helping myself? What if others knew that I need help? Will I be able to afford it? Will it help me?

You may resist the idea of seeking professional help. Many people believe that psychologists and counselors only work with "crazy" people. Yet, counselors work with people who have a wide range of concerns, from roommate or relationship problems, to depression, anxiety, academic concerns, and with many other types of problems in-between. It is also important to know that you don't have to be able to pinpoint what's wrong before seeking assistance. It's common for students to seek help when they feel down or nervous and can't explain why, or when unusually troubled by even minor frustrations.

Think of it this way: There are three possibilities. One may have issues, problems and dilemmas and yet cope effectively with the support of their network of family, friends, and community. Or, one may face problems and dilemmas and seek the services of a professional to help them develop better ways of coping. Finally, one may be experiencing distress regarding issues, problems, and dilemmas—not coping well—and yet not seek professional help. The bottom line: in our view everyone deals with issues, problems, and dilemmas. They are a fact of life.

DISPELLING FEARS AND MYTHS ABOUT COUNSELING

"My concerns are too strange or embarrassing to talk about with a counselor." This is an understandable concern, but trained mental health professionals deal with a range of problems, many of which may seem embarrassing to the student but are quite common to the counselor. What may seem weird to an individual often is reported by a lot of people when asked about problems. On the other hand, don't consider your problems too trivial or unimportant; if they are causing distress then they are indeed important enough to address with someone who can help you develop an effective plan of coping.

"People who receive counseling or therapy are needy, crazy, sick, or weird." Unfortunately, this is a common but false belief. There are individuals in counseling who have mental health concerns that require attention. However, there are many people who consider counseling because they feel stuck in any number of areas in their life: academically, socially, personally, and so on. Most of us have times that feel more difficult than others. Seeking counseling during these times is usually considered a sign of health and strength and indicates the ability to effectively cope with challenges. It is common sense knowledge that "talking to someone," whether a friend, colleague, or family member, is helpful in times of stress. Professional help is an extension of this and often professionals are better at it than our friends and family! A professional offers the additional benefit of bringing objectivity and expertise to the table.

"Dealing with my problems may make them worse and I can't afford this while I'm in school." While it is true that sometimes the process of counseling can be challenging, the benefits to uncovering and learning about oneself usually outweighs the effects of not dealing with the concerns you may be experiencing. Furthermore, there are highly effective approaches for dealing with problematic anxiety. Making headway in dealing with one's anxieties can often pay almost immediate dividends in one's ability to function more effectively in school.

"I don't know how to start and I'm too nervous about how to go through the beginning steps of the process." It is common to feel uneasy about how to begin and counselors understand this uneasiness, and will guide you slowly and supportively through the process.

WHICH TYPE OF PROVIDER IS BEST FOR YOU?

If you've never consulted a mental health professional before, you may not know where to begin. This section will offer some suggestions for finding a mental health professional, along with questions and issues to consider as you decide whether a particular individual suits your style and needs.

Your college counseling center is an excellent resource. Most college counseling centers offer trained counselors who can provide students with the support they need to work through and understand difficult issues in their lives. Many colleges have counseling centers that offer free or low-cost services to any student who wishes to discuss concerns in his or her life. In addition to problems with anxiety, some of the topics that students frequently bring to the counseling center include relationships with family members and friends, academic difficulties, drug and/or alcohol use, eating and body issues, loneliness, grief, loss, stress, life transitions, and issues of personal growth—among others. One of the advantages of seeking assistance in the college counseling center is that the staff have a wealth of experience in working with college students. The counselors know the "culture" of the school and are tuned in to the unique pressures faced by students at that college or university. In addition, the services are easy to access and convenient. Many students, because of limited financial resources or restrictive health insurance plans, cannot easily seek services off-campus. Furthermore, without ready access to a car, seeking services off-campus may be very difficult.

The college counseling center may not be for everyone. While high quality services are provided by college counseling centers, there may be reasons to seek professional assistance off-campus in the community. It is important to note that services provided by college counseling centers are private and confidential, yet there may be some limits to confidentiality regarding certain types of issues or policies specific to certain campuses. You should carefully check the privacy policies of your college or university counseling center to ensure that you are comfortable with them. Some college counseling centers limit the number of sessions of service that can be provided. In addition, many college counseling centers only offer services during the academic year and not over the summer months. This can be a significant issue if you are nearing the end of the school year and feel you need to see someone for more than a few weeks.

If you are having problems such as obsessions or compulsions, panic attacks, severe social anxiety, or phobias, you may benefit from a professional that specializes in the treatment of anxiety. If you are experiencing a less severe form of anxiety, then you may find that your college or university counseling center is an excellent choice.

WHAT TO EXPECT

Good counselors, regardless of the setting within which they work, feel strongly about working in a collaborative manner with the student; thus, each decision about the counseling process will be discussed as sensitively and as openly as possible. The initial visit will typically consist of an evaluation of your problems and issues. In this first visit, you will meet with a staff member, who may or may not be the person who provides your counseling. The staff member will ask questions to get to know you and ask information about your reason(s) for coming to the counseling center, clinic, or practice. He or she will take time in these first meetings to talk about what counseling will consist of and will share a plan for your care. If, after this initial evaluation, it is agreed that the service would be beneficial, you can begin to make regular appointments. It may be the case that a referral to another agency makes the most sense. In that case, you will be provided with referrals to the appropriate professionals in the area.

FINDING A MENTAL HEALTH PROFESSIONAL

If you choose not to begin with the college counseling center, finding a mental health provider can require some legwork. If it seems like more time and energy than you can muster, given the demands of school and the emotional difficulty you may be experiencing, consider enlisting help from your primary care doctor, family, or friends.

Here are some ways to find mental health providers:

- Seek a referral or recommendation from your family doctor
- Ask trusted friends, family, or clergy.
- Check phone book listings under such categories as community service numbers, counselors, physicians, psychologists, or social services organizations.
- Ask your health insurance provider for a list of providers that are covered by your insurance company.
- Contact a local or national mental health organization. If you think you are suffering from an anxiety disorder, the Anxiety Disorders Association of America can be a great resource.

THE MANY MENTAL HEALTH PROFESSIONALS

You may not realize just how many types of mental health providers are available until you start looking for one. What follows is a list of possible types of providers. We will use the term "psychotherapy" in this section. It's just another term for counseling but may include more action strategies in the process of working together on a person's difficulties with the provider.

A *psychologist* is a professional, usually with a doctoral degree in psychology, who specializes in psychological assessment and therapy. Practicing psychologists may be either clinical or counseling psychologists. There are a few differences between these two categories. Clinical psychologists may tend to have more experience in psychological testing, diagnostic assessment, and in working with more severe mental illness. Counseling psychologists may have more training and experience with issues related to vocation and career concerns. Psychologists should be licensed in the state within which they practice. Psychologists cannot prescribe medication.

Clinical social workers are health professionals who assist clients with information, referral, and direct help in dealing with local, state, or federal government agencies. As a result, they often serve as case managers to help people "navigate" the mental health system. Some clinical social workers may also provide psychotherapy. Clinical social workers generally hold a master's degree and should be licensed within their state. They cannot prescribe medication.

The *professional counselor* generally holds a master's degree in counseling, which they received within a psychology or other human service program. They should hold a license within their state of practice. They cannot prescribe medication.

Marriage and family therapists have specific training (and typically hold master's degrees) in working with relationship and family problems. They also may provide individual counseling. They should be licensed in their state of practice and cannot prescribe medication.

Pastoral counselors are counselors working within traditional faith communities to incorporate psychotherapy with prayer and spirituality to effectively help some people with mental disorders. Some people prefer to seek help for mental health problems from their pastor, rabbi, or priest, rather than from therapists who are not affiliated with a religious community. These individuals can be especially helpful with difficulties that also involve issues of faith and spirituality. Keep in mind, though, that pastoral counselors may be less familiar than other mental health professionals (though not always) with treatment approaches that have been supported by scientific research, and instead may provide services consistent with their faith community. They cannot prescribe medication.

A *psychiatrist* is a professional with an M.D. degree who has completed both medical school and training in psychiatry and is a specialist in diagnosing and treating mental illness. Nowadays, few psychiatrists provide psychological counseling or psychotherapy, instead focusing exclusively on medication management of mental health problems.

Psychiatric nurses typically have an R.N. plus a master's degree in a mental health specialty. This specialized training may be referred to as a C.N.S. (clinical nursing specialist) and/or N.P. (nurse practitioner). These individuals should be licensed and can under some circumstances (for example, with M.D. supervision), prescribe medication.

While your *primary care doctor* is not likely to provide counseling, they can provide medication and facilitate a referral to a psychiatrist or to a professional who provides psychotherapy, if needed. Seeing your physician can be a good option if you have easy access to your family doctor and if your doctor is comfortable prescribing medication for difficulties such as anxiety. In addition, a doctor is in the best position to evaluate your physical functioning and whether there may be any medical conditions related to your experience of anxiety.

A word about *unlicensed therapists*. It is very important to ensure that your mental health care provider holds a license appropriate to their profession. Virtually anyone can claim to be a counselor but licensure helps to ensure that the professional has completed an appropriate course of study at a recognized college or university, and has passed a state licensure exam that helps to indicate that the professional is knowledgeable of professional standards of practice. If you have any questions or concerns about a professional, you can call the appropriate state licensing board (phone numbers are typically in the yellow pages of your community) to verify their licensure and determine whether they have had any complaints made against them.

MAKING A DECISION ABOUT PROVIDERS

Should you see a family practice doctor? A psychiatrist? Psychologist? Social worker? Does it matter? Several considerations can help guide your decision:

- The severity and nature of your symptoms. If your anxiety symptoms are severe, you may benefit from a psychologist, therapist, or psychiatrist with specialized expertise in treating anxiety.
- If you are struggling primarily with relationship or family problems, you may instead want to consult a marriage and family therapist.
- Whether medication may be needed for your problem (only psychiatrists and some psychiatric nurses prescribe medication).
- The provider's level of competence and expertise (mental health professionals with doctoral degrees typically have more training, although specific experience with the treatment of anxiety may be most important consideration).
- Your health insurance coverage (today's insurance plans may offer limited coverage and stipulate which providers can provide care that is covered by the plan). Check with your health insurance carrier and consult your policy regarding the specifics of your mental health coverage.

If your symptoms are severe and you might need medication to control them, you may want to consult a psychiatrist, who can prescribe medications. Although your family doctor can also prescribe medications, a psychiatrist or psychiatric nurse may be more familiar with the wide range of psychiatric medications, how to use these medications in combination, and how to manage their side effects. If you are hesitant or unsure about whether medication is appropriate, you might want to start with a psychologist or therapist, and ask whether they believe a "combined" approach would be best for you. If so, they can assist you with an appropriate referral to a psychiatrist or family physician.

Or you may want to see both a counselor and a psychologist to talk about your problems and a psychiatrist to manage your medications.

On the other hand, you may not have a choice. Your health insurance may dictate who you can visit. Your insurance company can tell you what types of mental health providers it provides coverage for and what your benefit limits are, such as how many visits you're allowed. Some insurance plans, for instance, authorize more visits to a nurse, social worker, or psychologist than to a psychiatrist, whose fees are usually higher. It's a good idea to check with your insurance carrier about your mental health coverage.

A word about specialty care for anxiety disorders—there are well-established psychological treatment approaches for the anxiety disorders that were described throughout this book. They involve specific *cognitive-behavioral treatments*. Many of the suggestions that we have addressed for dealing with anxiety are consistent with these approaches. While many mental health professionals are skilled in the use of these treatments for anxiety, it may be important for you to seek help from a mental health professional who specializes in treating anxiety disorders, as this person will be more familiar with the specific cognitive-behavioral strategies that are most effective with your particular anxiety condition. Again, the Anxiety Disorders Association of America can be a great resource for specialty providers in your area.

Respect Your Personal Preferences

You should feel comfortable with the professionals involved in your care. Before scheduling your first appointment, think about whether you have preferences or needs regarding:

- The gender of the professional
- Their age and level of experience
- Their religion or faith persuasion
- Their cultural background

Your comfort level is very important since you may be establishing a long-term relationship. Even the individual's "personality" or appearance may matter to you. It is important that you exercise your preferences at this stage of the process. It is increasingly common for clinics, organizations, or associations to post pictures and biographies of their counselors and other mental health professionals online.

Be a Good Consumer and Ask Questions

Once you've found a few mental health providers who seem like they may suit you, it's time to call and ask a few more questions. In some cases, a receptionist may be able to answer the bulk of your questions. However, some mental health providers are in private practice, and don't have a receptionist. In that case, you may be able to ask some questions on the phone, or the professional may ask you to come in for an initial session.

Here are some questions to address, either on the phone or at your first appointment:

- Education, training, licensure, and years in practice. Licensing requirements can vary widely by state. You can double-check credentials by contacting your state's licensing boards.
- Office hours, fees (don't hesitate to ask about costs!), length of sessions, and the insurance providers with whom they work.
- Their treatment approach and philosophy, to make sure it suits your style and needs. Be sure to ask about their approach to treating the specific problems with anxiety that you are experiencing.
- Specialization. Mental health providers often specialize in treating certain disorders or age groups. Some, for instance, work only with adolescents. Others specialize in eating disorders or substance abuse. Again, if you are struggling with one of the anxiety disorders, specialization may be important. Don't hesitate to ask lots of questions of a potential provider. Finding the right match is crucial to establishing rapport and making sure you're getting the best treatment.

Once You have Begun, Reflect on Your Relationship With Your Provider

If you don't feel comfortable after the first visit, talk about your concerns at your next session or consider finding a new mental health provider. As time goes by, periodically reevaluate how you feel and whether your needs are being met. Don't feel compelled to stay with a provider if you're not comfortable with their approach or their manner of interaction

Although the process of choosing a mental health provider and the treatment itself can be challenging, it can also be one of the most rewarding choices you make in your life.

MENTAL HEALTH TERMINOLOGY

Here are some terms that you may encounter as you seek and/or participate in mental health care:

Couples Counseling and Family Therapy

These two similar approaches to therapy involve discussions and problem-solving sessions facilitated by a therapist, sometimes with the couple or entire family group, and sometimes with individuals. These therapies can help couples and family members improve their understanding of, and the way they respond to, one another. This type of therapy can resolve patterns of behavior that might lead to more severe mental illness. Family therapy can help educate the individuals about the nature of mental disorders and teach them skills to cope better with the effects of having a family member with a mental illness, such as how to deal with feelings of anger or guilt.

Deductible

The amount an individual must pay for health care expenses before insurance (or a self-insured company) begins to pay its contract share. Often insurance plans are based on yearly deductible amounts.

Emergency and Crisis Services

A group of services that is available 24 hours a day, 7 days a week, to help during a mental health emergency. Examples include telephone crisis hotlines, suicide hotlines, crisis counseling, crisis residential treatment services, crisis outreach teams, and crisis respite care.

Fee for Service

A type of health care plan under which health care providers are paid for individual medical services rendered.

Gatekeeper

Primary care physicians or local agency responsible for coordinating and managing the health care needs of members. Generally, in order for specialty services such as mental health and hospital care to be covered, the gatekeeper must first approve the referral.

Group Therapy

This form of therapy involves groups of usually 4 to 12 people who have similar problems and who meet regularly with a therapist. The therapist uses the emotional interactions of the group's members to help them alleviate distress and possibly modify their behavior.

Health Maintenance Organization (HMO)

A type of managed care plan that acts as both insurer and provider of a comprehensive set of health care services to an enrolled population. Services are usually furnished through a network of providers. While many plans allow you to see an "out-of-network" provider, these services are typically not paid for at the same level as a provider that belongs to their network.

Individual counseling/Psychotherapy

Counseling in a therapeutic relationship that is tailored for a client and administered one-on-one.

Inpatient treatment

Mental health treatment provided in a hospital setting 24 hours a day. Inpatient hospitalization provides: 1) short-term treatment in cases where a person is in crisis and possibly a danger to him/herself or others, and 2) diagnosis and treatment when the patient cannot be evaluated or treated appropriately in an outpatient setting. Several specialized inpatient treatment programs exist for severe anxiety disorders. They typically provide intensive psychotherapy using cognitive-behavioral techniques which is provided individually and in groups. Information about such programs can be obtained through the Anxiety Disorders Association of America.

Intake/Screening

This refers to services designed to briefly assess the type and degree of a client's mental health condition to determine whether services are needed and to link him/her to the most appropriate and available service. Services may include interviews, psychological testing, physical examinations including speech/hearing, and laboratory studies. At the conclusion of the intake or screening session, the mental health professional may reach a diagnosis of your problem and generate a treatment plan.

Intensive outpatient/Day treatment

Day treatment includes special education, counseling, parent training, vocational training, skill building, crisis intervention, and recreational therapy. It lasts at least four hours a day. Day treatment programs work in conjunction with mental health, recreation, and education organizations and may even be provided by them. They offer a higher level of care than individual or group treatment

without necessitating admission to a hospital. There are some specialized day treatment programs for anxiety around the country, and information can be obtained through the Anxiety Disorders Association of America.

Medically Necessary

Health insurers often specify that, in order to be covered, a treatment or drug must be medically necessary for the consumer. Anything that falls outside of the realm of medical necessity is usually not covered. The plan will likely look at your diagnosis and the degree to which your symptoms are interfering with your functioning to determine whether or not the term "medically necessary" is applicable.

Network

The system of participating providers and institutions in a managed care plan.

Preferred Provider Organization (PPO)

A health plan in which consumers may use any health care provider on a fee-for-service basis. Consumers will be charged more for visiting providers outside of the PPO network than for visiting providers in the network.

Primary Care Physician (PCP)

Physicians with the following specialties: group practice, family practice, internal medicine, obstetrics/gynecology, and pediatrics. The PCP is usually responsible for monitoring an individual's overall medical care and referring the individual to more specialized physicians for additional care.

Prior Authorization

The approval a provider must obtain from an insurer or other entity before furnishing certain health services, particularly inpatient hospital care, in order for the service to be covered under the plan.

Telephone Hotline

A dedicated telephone line that is advertised and may be operated as a crisis hotline for emergency counseling or as a referral resource for callers with mental health problems.

SUMMARY

The bottom line is that anxiety is treatable, there are many professionals who can help, and that being a wise consumer will benefit you when seeking professional help. While it does take time and effort, it can be an important step toward feeling better. Whether or not you seek professional help, there are many self-help resources available that can assist you in your quest to reduce your anxiety and its effect on your life. Many of these resources are listed at the end of the book.

Resources

NATIONAL ORGANIZATIONS

The Anxiety Disorders Association of America
11900 Parklawn Drive, Suite 100
Rockville, MD 20852
Tel: (301) 231–9350
Web Page: www.adaa.org

Freedom from Fear
308 Seaview Avenue
Staten Island, NY 10305
Tel: (718) 351–1717
Web Page: www.freedomfromfear.org

Obsessive-Compulsive Foundation, Inc.
676 State Street
New Haven, CT 06511
Tel: (203) 401–2070
Web Page: www.ocfoundation.org

BOOKS

Students' Guide for Coping with a Variety of Issues

> *Beating the College Blues* by Paul Grayson and Philip Meilman.

General Self-help for Anxiety

> *The Anxiety & Phobia Workbook, Fourth Edition (Paperback)* by Edmund
> J. Bourne.

Reactions to Traumatic Events

Life After Trauma: A Workbook for Healing by Dena Rosenbloom and Mary Beth Williams.
The PTSD Workbook: Simple, Effective Techniques for Overcoming Traumatic Stress Symptoms by Mary Beth Williams & Soili Poijula.

Shyness and Social Anxiety

The Shyness & Social Anxiety Workbook: Proven Techniques for Overcoming Your Fears by Martin Antony and Richard Swinson.
No More Butterflies: Overcoming Shyness, Stage Fright, Interview Anxiety, and the Fear of Public Speaking by Peter Desberg.

Relaxation and Meditation

The Relaxation & Stress Reduction Workbook (Paperback) by Martha Davis, Matthew McKay, and Elizabeth Robbins Eshelman.
Insight Meditation: A Step-By-Step Course on How to Meditate (Spiralbound) by Sharon Salzberg and Joseph Goldstein.
Guided Mindfulness Meditation (Guided Mindfulness) [AUDIOBOOK] [UNABRIDGED] (Audio CD) by Jon Kabat-Zinn.

Dating

Dating for Dummies by Joy Browne.
The Complete Idiot's Guide to Dating by Judith Kuriansky.
Unofficial Guide to Dating Again by Tina Tessina.

Social and Communication Skills

Messages: The Communication Skills Book by Mathew McKay, Martha Davis, and Patrick Fanning.

INTERNET RESOURCES

Although the authors attempted to provide up-to-date information when the book went to press in 2007, note that web changes come and go and addresses for internet resources change frequently. In order to access more up-to-date information we suggest conducting a search using the key words mentioned here.

A Great Site Dedicated to Anxiety and the College Student

http://www.gotanxiety.org

College Students and Depression

http://www.nimh.nih.gov/publicat/students.cfm

Suicide Prevention in College Students

http://www.sprc.org/featured_resources/customized/college_student.asp

Eating Disorders

http://www.edap.org/p.asp?WebPage_ID = 655

Resources on the Topic of Sexuality

The following resources are provided to help you become better informed, but the authors do not endorse content.

Outlines two recent surveys and their results about the sexual victimization of women on US college campuses

www.ojp.usdoj.gov/nij/pubs-sum/181867.htm

Informative website about sexual violence with statistics and general information

www.nsvrc.org

Information and link to statistics about sexual assault. Advice on how to help a friend who has been assaulted

www.RAINN.org

Information about sexual orientation and homosexuality from the American Psychological Association

www.apa.org/topics/orientation.html

Resources on the Use of Tobacco, Alcohol, and Other Drugs

Resources pertaining to alcohol abuse in college students

http://www.drugfreeinfo.org/acollege.html

A resource for quitting smoking

http://www.cdc.gov/TOBACCO/how2quit.htm

Tobacco use and College Students

   http://www.ttac.org/college/facts/costs.html

Resource on General Health Issues, Nutrition, and Other Topics

A Q & A site with a wealth of information about health, nutrition, and many other topics of interest to college students

   http://www.goaskalice.columbia.edu

Notes

CHAPTER 1

1. "Gyre" means circle or spiral.

2. "Middle States University" is a fictitious university used throughout the text.

3. National Institute of Mental Health, "The Numbers Count: Mental Disorders in America," retrieved on October 29, 2006 from: http://www.nimh.nih.gov/publicat/numbers.cfm.

4. Twenge, J.M., "The Age of Anxiety? Birth Cohort Change in Anxiety and Neuroticism," *Journal of Personality and Social Psychology*, 79 (2000, December), 1007–1021.

5. Twenge, 2000.

6. Speilberger, C.D., and Rickman, R.L., "Assessment of State and Trait Anxiety," in N. Sartorius, V. Andreoli, G. Cassano, L. Eisenberg, P. Kielkolt, P. Pancheri, and G. Racagni (Eds.), *Anxiety: Psychobiological and Clinical Perspectives* (New York: Hemisphere Publishing, 1990), 69–83.

7. Kearney, L., and Baron A., "Highlights of the Research Consortium 2002 Non-Clinical Sample Study. A Research Report of The Research Consortium of Counseling and Psychological Services in Higher Education," retrieved August, 22, 2004 from: http://www.utexas.edu/student/cmhc/research/rescon.html.

8. Benton, S.A., Robertson, J.M., Wen-Chih, T., Newton, F.B., and Benton, S.L., "Changes in Counseling Center Client Problems Across 13 Years," *Professional Psychology: Research and Practice*, 343:1 (2003), 66–72.

9. Twenge, 2000.

10. Stewart, D., and Cairns, S., "Objective Versus Subjective Evaluation of Student Distress at Intake: Considerations for Counseling Centers," *Journal of College Student Development*, 43 (2002), 386–394.

11. Benton et al., 2003.

12. Sax, L.J., "Health Trends among College Freshmen," *Journal of American College Health*, 45:6 (1997, May), 252–262.

13. Erikson, E., *Childhood and Society* (2nd Edition, Revised) (New York: W.W. Norton & Co, 1963).

14. Chickering, A.W., and Reisser, L., *Education and Identity* (2nd Edition) (San Francisco: Jossey-Bass, 1993).

15. Ross, S.E., Niebling, B.C., and Heckert, T.M., "Sources of Stress among College Students," *College Student Journal*, 33:2 (1999, June), 312–317.

16. D'Zurilla, T.J., and Sheedy, C.F., "Relation between Social Problem-Solving Ability and Subsequent Level of Psychological Stress in College Students," *Journal of Personality and Social Psychology*, 61:5 (1991), 841–846.

17. Towbes, L.C., and Cohen, L.H., "Chronic Stress in the Lives of College Students: Scale Development and Prospective Prediction of Distress," *Journal of Youth and Adolescence*, 25 (1996), 199–217.

18. Barlow, D.H., *Anxiety and its Disorders* (2nd Edition) (New York: Guilford, 2002).

19. Beck, A.T., *Depression: Causes and Treatment* (Philadelphia: University of Pennsylvania Press, 1967).

20. Beck, A.T., Rush, A.J., Shaw, B., and Emery, G., *Cognitive Therapy of Depression: A Treatment Manual* (New York: Guilford, 1979).

21. Beck, A.T., Emery, G., and Greenberg, R.L., *Anxiety Disorders and Phobias: A Cognitive Perspective* (New York: Basic Books, 1985).

22. Barlow, 2002.

CHAPTER 2

1. Lazarus, R.S., and Folkman, S., *Stress, Appraisal, and Coping* (New York: Springer, 1984).

2. Cannon, W.B., *Bodily Changes in Pain, Hunger, Fear and Rage* (2nd Edition) (New York: Appleton-Century-Crofts, 1929).

3. Kagan, J., and Snidman, N., *The Long Shadow of Temperament* (Cambridge, MA: Belknap Press, 2004).

4. LeDoux, J.E., *The Emotional Brain: The Mysterious Underpinnings of Emotional Life* (New York: Simon and Schuster, 1996).

5. Skinner, B.F., *The Behavior of Organisms* (New York: Appleton Century Crofts, 1938).

6. Mowrer, O.H., *Learning Theory and the Personality Dynamics* (New York: Arnold Press, 1950).

7. Yerkes, R.M., and Dodson, J.D., "The Relations of Strength of Stimulus to Rapidity of Habit Formation," *Journal of Comparative Neurology and Psychology*, 18 (1908), 459–482.

8. National Institute of Mental Health, "The Numbers Count: Mental Disorders in America," retrieved on October 29, 2006 from: http://www.nimh.nih.gov/publicat/numbers.cfm.

9. Robins L.N., and Regier, D.A. (Eds.), *Psychiatric Disorders in America: The Epidemiologic Catchment Area Study* (New York: The Free Press, 1991).

10. Bourdon, K.H., Boyd, J.H., Rae, D.S., et al., "Gender Differences in Phobias: Results of the ECA Community Survey," *Journal of Anxiety Disorders*, 2 (1988): 227–241.

11. Barlow, D.H., *Anxiety and its Disorders* (2nd Edition) (New York: Guilford, 2002).

12. Kessler, R.C., Chiu, W.T., Demler, O., and Walters, E.E., "Prevalence, Severity, and Comorbidity of Twelve-Month DSM-IV Disorders in the National Comorbidity Survey Replication (NCS-R)," *Archives of General Psychiatry*, 62:6 (2005, June), 617–627.

13. Van Ameringen, M., Mancini, C., and Farvolden, P., "The Impact of Anxiety Disorders on Educational Achievement," *Journal of Anxiety Disorders*, 17 (2003), 561–571.

14. Kushner, M.G., Sher, K.J., and Beitman, B.D., "The Relation between Alcohol Problems and the Anxiety Disorders," *American Journal of Psychiatry*, 147:6 (1990), 685–695.

15. Kessler et al., 2006.

16. Noshirvani, H.F., Kasvikis, Y., Marks, I.M., Tsakiris, F., and Monteiro, W.F., "Gender-Divergent Aetiological Factors in Obsessive-Compulsive Disorder," *British Journal of Psychiatry*, 158 (1991), 260–263.

17. Barlow, 2002.

CHAPTER 3

1. Chickering, A.W., and Reisser, L., *Education and Identity* (2nd Edition) (San Francisco, CA: Jossey-Bass, 1993).

2. Paul, E.L, Brier, S., Phan, L. Vereen, L., and Garret, M. "Friendsickness in the Transition to College: Precollege Predictors and College Adjustment Correlates," *Journal of Counseling and Development*, 79:1 (2001), 77–90.

3. Schneider, K., "International Students Coping with Culture Shock," University of WI Counseling Services, retrieved on September 26, 2006 from http://www.uwec.edu/Counsel/pubs/shock.htm.

4. Grotevant, H.D., "Toward a Process Model of Identity Formation," *Journal of Adolescent Research*, 2 (1987), 203–222.

5. Marcia, J.E., "Development and Validation of Ego Identity Status," *Journal of Personality and Social Psychology*, 3 (1966), 551–558.

CHAPTER 4

1. Sanderson, R. (Oregon State University), "2003 Your First College Year Survey Results (Student Affairs Research Report 03–03)," retrieved on October 29, 2006 from: http://hdl.handle.net/1957/1377.

2. Paul, E.L, Brier, S., Phan, L., Vereen, L., and Garret, M., "Friendsickness in the Transition to College: Precollege Predictors and College Adjustment Correlates," *Journal of Counseling and Development*, 79:1 (2001), 77–90.

3. Levy, P., "Madison Tries New Tricks to Keep Peace for Halloween," *Star Tribune*, October 27, 2006, p. A.

CHAPTER 5

1. Berscheid, E., and Walster, E., "Physical Attractiveness," in L. Berkowitz (Ed.) *Advances in Experimental Social Psychology* (Vol. 7) (New York: Academic Press, 1974).

2. Cash, T.F., and Smith, E., "Physical Attractiveness and Personality among American College Students," *Journal of Psychology*, 111 (1982), 183–191.

3. Aufreiter, N., Elzinga, D., and Gordon, J., "Better Branding," *The McKinsey Quarterly*, 4 (2003), 28–40.

4. Myers, P., and Biocca, F., "The Elastic Body Image: The Effect of Television Advertising and Programming on Body Image Distortions in Young Women," *Journal of Communication*, 42:3 (1992), 108–133.

5. Wiseman, C., Gray, J., Mosimann, J., and Ahrens, A., "Cultural Expectations of Thinness in Women: An Update," *International Journal of Eating Disorders*, 11 (1992), 85–89.

6. Cusumano, D., and Thompson, J. K., "Body Image and Body Shape Ideals in Magazines: Exposure, Awareness, and Internalization," *Sex Roles*, 37 (1997), 701–721.

7. Cameron, E., and Ferraro, R., "Body Satisfaction in College Women after Brief Exposure to Magazine Images," *Perceptual and Motor Skills*, 98 (2004), 1093–1099.

8. Jones, D.C., "Social Comparison and Body Image: Attractiveness Comparisons to Models and Peers among Adolescent Girls and Boys," *Sex Roles*, 45 (2001), 645–664.

9. Turner, S., and Hamilton, H., "The Influence of Fashion Magazines on the Body Image Satisfaction of College Women: An Exploratory Analysis," *Adolescence*, 32 (1997), 603–615.

10. Cameron, E., and Ferraro, R., 2004.

11. King, N., Touyz, S., and Charles, M., "The Effect of Body Dissatisfaction on Women's Perceptions of Female Celebrities," *Journal of Eating Disorders*, 27 (2000), 341–347.

12. Waters, E.B., and Goodman, J., *Empowering Older Adults* (San Francisco, CA: Jossey-Bass Inc., 1990).

CHAPTER 6

1. Kearney, L., and Baron A., "Highlights of the Research Consortium 2002 Non-Clinical Sample Study. A Research Report of the Research Consortium of Counseling and Psychological Services in Higher Education," retrieved on August 22, 2004 from: http://www.utexas.edu/student/cmhc/research/rescon.html.

2. Pritchard, M.E., and Wilson, G.S., "Using Emotional and Social Factors to Predict Student Success," *Journal of College Student Development*, 44 (2003), 18–28.

3. Robbins, S.B., Lauver, K., Le, H., Davis, D., Langley, R., and Carlstrom, A., "Do Psychosocial and Study Skill Factors Predict College Outcomes? A Meta-Analysis," *Psychological Bulletin*, 130:2 (2004), 261–288.

4. Cohen, S., and Willis, T.A., "Stress, Social Support, and the Buffering Hypothesis," *Psychological Bulletin*, 98 (1985), 310–357.

5. Coffman, D.L., and Gilligan, T.D., "Social Support, Stress, and Self-Efficacy: Effects on Students' Satisfaction," *Journal of College Student Retention*, 4:1 (2003), 53–66.

6. Emmons, R.A., and Colby, P.M., "Emotional Conflict and Well-Being: Relation to Perceived Availability, Daily Utilization, and Observer Reports of Social Support," *Journal of Personality and Social Psychology*, 68:5 (1995), 947–959.

7. Jacobs, S.R., and Dodd, D.K., "Student Burnout as a Function of Personality, Social Support, and Workload," *Journal of College Student Development*, 44:3 (2003), 291–303.

8. Robbins, ibid.

9. Lepore, S.J., Evans, G.W., and Schneider, M.L., "Dynamic Role of Social Support in the Link Between Chronic Stress and Psychological Distress," *Journal of Personality and Social Psychology*, 61:6 (1991), 899–909.

10. Edsell, R.D., "Anxiety as a Function of Environmental Noise and Social Interaction," *The Journal of Psychology*, 92 (1976), 219–226.

11. Joiner, T.E., "Contagion of Suicidal Symptoms as a Function of Assortative Relating and Shared Relationship Stress in College Roommates," *Journal of Adolescence*, 26 (2003), 495–504.

12. Strahan, E.Y., "The Effects of Social Anxiety and Social Skills on Academic Performance," *Personality and Individual Differences*, 34 (2003), 347–366.

CHAPTER 7

1. Kessler, R.C., McGonagle, K.A., Zhao, S., Nelson, C.B., Hughes, M., Eshelman, S., Wittchen, H., and Kendler, K.S., "Lifetime and 12-Month Prevalence Of DSM-III-R Psychiatric Disorders in the United States," *Archives of General Psychiatry*, 51 (1994), 8–19.

2. LeSure-Lester, E.G., and King, N., "Racial-Ethnic Differences in Social Anxiety Among College Students," *Journal of College Student Retention: Research, Theory, and Practice*, 6 (2004–2005), 359–367.

3. Kushner, M.G., Sher, K.J., and Beitman, B.D., "The Relation between Alcohol Problems and Anxiety Disorders," *American Journal of Psychiatry*, 147 (1990), 685–695.

4. Carducci, B.J., and Zimbardo, P.G., "Are You Shy?" *Psychology Today*, 6 (1995), 34–82.

5. Antony, M.M., and Swinson, R.P., *The Shyness and Social Anxiety Workbook: Proven Techniques for Overcoming Your Fears* (Oakland, CA: New Harbinger Publications, Inc., 2000).

CHAPTER 8

1. Zeidner, M. *Test Anxiety: The State of the Art* (New York: Plenum Press, 1998).

2. Sarason, I.G., "Anxiety, Self-preoccupation, and Attention," *Anxiety Research*, 1 (1988), 3–7.

3. Mann, W., and Lash, J., *Test and Performance Anxieties*, University of Cincinnati; Psychological Services Center and the Student Affairs and Services, retrieved on September 20, 2006 from: http://www.uc.edu/cc/Test.html.

4. Sarason, I.G., and Sarason, B.R., "Test Anxiety," in Leitenberg H. (Ed.), *Handbook of Social and Evaluative Anxiety* (New York: Plenum Press, 1990), 475–496.

5. University of Illinois Counseling Center. *Self-help brochures: Test Anxiety*, retrieved on September 20, 2006 from: http://www.couns.uiuc.edu/brochures/testanx.htm,.

6. University of Illinois Counseling Center, 2006.

7. Ibid.

8. Ibid.

CHAPTER 9

1. Covey, S.R., *The 7 Habits of Highly Effective People: Powerful Lessons in Personal Change* (New York, NY: Fireside Press, 1990).

2. Kearney, L., and Baron A., "Highlights of the Research Consortium 2002 Non-Clinical Sample Study. A Research Report of The Research Consortium of Counseling and Psychological Services in Higher Education," retrieved on August 22, 2004 from: http://www.utexas.edu/student/cmhc/research/rescon.html.

3. U.S. Bureau of Labor Statistics. (2005), retrieved on July 18, 2006 from: http://www.bls.gov/oco/oco2003.htm.

4. Newman, J.L., Fuqua, D.R., and Seaworth, T.B., "The Role of Anxiety in Career Indecision: Implications for Diagnosis and Treatment," *The Career Development Quarterly*, 37 (1989), 221–230.

5. Corbishley, M.A., and Yost, E.B., "Assessment and Treatment of Dysfunctional Cognitions in Career Counseling," *Career Planning and Adult Development Journal*, 5 (1989), 20–26.

6. Morgan, T., and Ness, D., "Career Decision-Making Difficulties of First-Year Students," *The Canadian Journal of Career Development*, 2 (2003), retrieved on August 22, 2004 from: www.contactpoint.ca/cjcd/v2-n1/article4.pdf.

7. Weinstein, F.M., Healy, C.C., and Ender, P.B., "Career Choice Anxiety, Coping, and Perceived Control," *Career Development Quarterly*, 50 (2002), 339–349.

8. Lounsbury, J.W., Tatum, H.E., Chambers, W., Owens, K., and Gibson, L.W., "An Investigation of Career Decidedness in Relation to 'Big Five' Personality Constructs and Life Satisfaction," *College Student Journal*, 33 (1999), 646–652.

9. Dennis, J.M., Phinney, J.S., and Chuateco, L.I., "The Role of Motivation, Parental Support, and Peer Support in the Academic Success of Ethnic Minority First-Generation College Students," *Journal of College Student Development*, 46:3 (2005), 223–236.

10. Ross, S.E., Niebling, B.C., and Heckert, T.M., "Sources of Stress among College Students," *College Student Journal*, 33 (1999), 312–317.

11. Misra, R., and McKean, M., "College Students' Academic Stress and its Relation to their Anxiety, Time Management, and Leisure Satisfaction," *American Journal of Health Studies*, 16:1 (2000), 41–52.

12. Cote, J.E., and Levine, C., "Student Motivation, Learning Environments, and Human Capital Acquisition: Toward an Integrated Paradigm of Student Development," *Journal of College Student Development*, 83:3 (1997), 229–243.

13. McKee, B., "The New College Mixer," *The New York Times* (September 1, 2005).

14. Finney, J.E., and Kelly, P.J., "Affordability," *Change*, 36:4 (2004), 54–59.

15. Paulsen, M.B., "Recent Research on the Economics of Attending College: Returns on Investment and Responsiveness to Price," *Research in Higher Education*, 39:4 (1998), 471–489.

16. St. John, E.P., Paulsen, M.B., and Carter, D.F., "Diversity, College Costs, and Postsecondary Opportunity: An Examination of the Financial Nexus between College Choice and Persistence for African Americans and Whites," *The Journal of Higher Education*, 76:5 (2005), 545–569.

17. Reynolds, L.M., and Weagley, R.O., "Academic Persistence in Higher Education," *Consumer Interests Annual*, 49 (2003), 1–8.

18. St. John, E.P., Cabrera, A.F., Nora, A. and Asker, E.H., "Economic Influences on Persistence Reconsidered: How Can Finance Research Inform the Re-Conceptualization of Persistence Models?" in Braxton J. (Ed.), *Rethinking the Departure Puzzle: New Theory and Research on College Student Retention* (Nashville, TN: Vanderbilt University Press, 2000), 29–47.

19. Andrews, B., and Wilding, J., "The Relation of Depression and Anxiety to Life-Stress and Achievement in Students," *British Journal of Psychology*, 95 (2004), 509–521.

20. Finney and Kelly, 2004.

21. McKee, 2005.

22. Ibid.

CHAPTER 10

1. Ross, S.E., Niebling, B.C., and Heckert, T.M., "Sources of Stress among College Students," *College Student Journal*, 33 (1999), 312–317.

2. Misra, R., and McKean, M., "College Students' Academic Stress and its Relation to their Anxiety, Time Management, and Leisure Satisfaction," *American Journal of Health Studies*, 16:1 (2000), 41–52.

3. Sushko, J., *Time and Meeting Management*, Business Training Group, Unpublished Workshop Manual, (Minnetonka, MN: 2005).

4. George Mason University Counseling Center, "Time Management," retrieved on July 1, 2006 from: http://counseling.gmu.edu/timemana.htm.

5. Covey, S.R., *The 7 Habits of Highly Effective People* (New York: Simon and Schuster, 1989).

6. Covey, 1989.

7. Sirois, F.M., Melia-Gordon, M.L., and Pychyl, T.A., "I'll Look After My Health, Later," An Investigation of Procrastination and Health. *Personality and Individual Differences*, 35:5 (2003), 1167–1184.

CHAPTER 11

1. Barnett, A., *Air Safety: End Of The Golden Age?* Blackett Memorial Lecture. OR Society, UK, November, 2000.

CHAPTER 12

1. Benson, H., and Klopper, M., *The Relaxation Response* (New York: William Morrow, 1975).

2. Jacobson, E. *Progressive Relaxation*. (Chicago, IL: University of Chicago Press, 1929).

3. Walsh, R., and Shapiro, S.L., "The Meeting of Meditative Disciplines and Western Psychology: A Mutually Enriching Dialogue," *American Psychologist*, 61 (2006), 227–239.

4. Kabat-Zinn, J., *Full Catastrophe Living: Using the Wisdom of Your Body and Mind to Face Stress, Pain, and Illness* (New York: Delacorte Press, 1990).

5. Racette, S.B., Deusinger, S.S., Strube, M.J., Highstein, G.R., and Deusinger, R.H., "Weight Changes, Exercise, and Dietary Patterns During Freshman and Sophomore Years of College," *Journal of the American College of Health*, 53 (2005), 245–251.

6. National Institutes of Health, *Facts about Insomnia*, (1995). Pub No. 95–3801, retrieved on October 29, 2006 from http://www.nhlbi.nih.gov/health/public/sleep/insomnia.txt.

7. Jacobs, G.D., Pace-Schott, E.F., Stickgold, R., and Otto, M.W., "Cognitive Behavior Therapy and Pharmacotherapy for Insomnia," *Archives of Internal Medicine*, 164 (2004), 1888–1896.

CHAPTER 13

1. Gallagher, R.P., Sysko, H.M., and Ahang, B., *National Survey of Counseling Center Directors 2001*, International Association of Counseling Service (Alexandria, VA; 2001).

2. Kitzrow, M.A., "The Mental Health Needs of Today's College Students: Challenges and Recommendations," *NASPA Journal*, 41:1 (2003, Fall), 167–181.

3. National Institute of Mental Health, "What Do These Students Have in Common?" retrieved on October 29, 2006 from http://www.campusblues.com.

4. National Institute of Mental Health, D/ART Campaign, *Depression: What Every Woman Should Know*, (1995). Pub No. 95–3871, retrieved on October 29, 2006 from http://www.nimh.nih.gov/publicat/depwomenknows.cfm.

5. Butcher, J.N., Mineka, S., and Hooley, J.M., *Abnormal Psychology* (13th Edition) (Boston: Allyn & Bacon, 2006).

6. National Institute of Mental Health, 2006.

7. American Psychiatric Association, *College Mental Health Statistics*, retrieved on October 29, 2006 from http://www.healthyminds.org/collegestats.cfm.

8. Wisconsin United for Mental Health, *College Stress Can Lead to Depression*, retrieved on October 29, 2006 from http://www.wimentalhealth.org/topics/collegedepression.htm.

9. National Mental Health Association, *Tips on Dealing with Depression in College*, retrieved on October 29, 2006 from http://www.nmha.org/infoctr/factsheets/Depressionin College.cfm.

10. U.S. Department of Health and Human Services, "The Surgeon General's Call to Action to Prevent Suicide," retrieved on February 25, 2007 from http://www.surgeon-general.gov/library/calltoaction/fact1.htm

11. Butcher et al., 2006.

12. Mental Health Sanctuary, *How to Help a Suicidal Person*, retrieved on October 29, 2006 from http://www.mhsanctuary.com/suicide/sui2.htm, 2006.

13. American College Heath Association, *ACHA—National College Health Assessment: Reference Group Data Report Fall 2005* (Baltimore: American College Health Association, 2006).

14. Butcher et al., 2006.

15. Centers for Disease Control and Prevention, "Youth Risk Behavior Surveillance: National College Health Risk Behavior Survey—United States, 1995," *Surveillance Summaries*, 46 (Surveillance Summary 6), 1–54.

16. U.S. Department of Justice: Bureau of Justice Statistics, *Research Report: The Sexual Victimization of College Women (December, 2000)*.

17. Wechsler, H., Lee, J.E., Kuo, M, Seibring, M, Nelson, T.F., and Lee, H., "Trends in College Binge Drinking During a Period of Increased Prevention Efforts: Findings from 4 Harvard School of Public Health College Alcohol Study Surveys, 1993–2001," *Journal of American College Health*, 50 (2002), 203–217.

18. Ibid.

19. Ibid.

20. Wechsler, H., Lee, J.E., Kuo, M., Seibring, M., and Lee, H., "College Binge Drinking in the 1990s: A Continuing Problem—Results of the Harvard School of Public Health 1999 College Alcohol Study," *Journal of American College Health*, 48 (2000), 199–210.

21. Wechsler et al., 2002, 199–210.

22. Meilman, P.W., Leichliter, J.S., and Presley, C.A., "Greeks and Athletes: Who Drinks More?" *Journal of American College Health*, 47 (1999), 187–190.

23. Wechsler et al., 2002, 199–210.

24. Ibid.

25. Kapner, D.A., "Infofacts Resources: Secondary Effects of Heavy Drinking on Campus, retrieved on October 29, 2006 from http://www.higheredcenter.org/pubs/factsheets/secondary-effects.html.

26. National Institutes of Health, National Institute on Alcohol Abuse and Alcoholism, Task Force of the National Advisory Council on Alcohol Abuse and Alcoholism, *A Call To Action: Changing the Culture of Drinking at U.S. Colleges* (Washington, D.C: National Institute on Alcohol Abuse & Alcoholism (NIAAA), Bethesda, M.D., 2002). For more information on the report, visit www.collegedrinkingprevention.gov.

27. Borsari, B.E., and Carey, K.B., "Understanding Fraternity Drinking: Five Recurring Themes in the Literature, 1980–1998," *Journal of American College Health*, 48 (1999), 30.

28. Wechsler et al., 2000.

29. Ibid., 2002.

30. National Eating Disorders Association, "Eating Disorders Information Index," retrieved on October 29, 2006 from http://www.nationaleatingdisorders.org.

31. Ibid.

32. George Mason University Counseling Center, *Eating Disorders: Myths and Campus Resources*, retrieved on October 29, 2006 from http://www.gmu.edu/departments/csdc/eat.html.

Index

Page numbers in italics represent illustrations

ABOUT THE AUTHOR

CHRISTOPHER VYE is Associate Professor in the Graduate School of Professional Psychology at the University of Saint Thomas. He is an experienced researcher and therapist in the area of anxiety. He is co-founder of Anxiety Treatment Resources, a specialty clinic for the treatment of anxiety located in Bloomington, Minnesota.

KATHLENE SCHOLLJEGERDES is Director of Career Services at Bethel University.

I. DAVID WELCH is Dean and Professor in Graduate School of Professional Psychology at the University of Saint Thomas.